D0049143

THE
BETRAYAL
OF
CANADA

THE
BETRAYAL
OF
CANADA

MEL
HURTIG

First published in 1991 by
Stoddart Publishing Co. Limited
34 Lesmill Road
Toronto, Canada
M3B 2T6

Canadian Cataloguing in Publication Data

Hurtig, Mel
The betrayal of Canada

ISBN 0-7737-2542-3

1. Canada - Economic conditions - 1991-   .*
2. Canada - Economic policy - 1991-   .*
3. Investments, Foreign - Canada.   4. Canada - Social
policy.   I. Title.

HC115.H87 1991   330.971'0647   C91-094808-9

The author and publisher are grateful to the following for permission to quote from copyright mate-
rial: Dr. Marc Baltzan; David R. Beatty, speech, Conference Board of Canada, "Adjusting to Free
Trade," 10 March 1988; Monique Bégin; Neil Brooks, *Pro-Canadian Network Dossier*; *Calgary
Herald*; Duncan Cameron, *Canadian Forum*; Canadian Press; Jean Chrétien, *Straight from the
Heart*, Key Porter Books, 1985; Thomas Courchene; Arthur Donner; *The Edmonton Journal*; *The
Financial Post*; James Gillies, *Inside Guide*; *The Globe and Mail*; Bob Hepburn; Hal Jackman; Eric
Kierans, "Light Bulbs May Be Cheaper," address, World Trade Centre, Halifax, N.S., 10 June
1988, and articles from *Policy Options*; William Loewen; John McCallum; Don McGillivray;
Maclean's; Senator Heath Macquarrie; *New England Journal of Medicine*; Peter Newman; Sylvia
Ostry, "Canadian Competitiveness: Future at Risk," Amdahl Canada Ltd., Senior Executive
Institute, Toronto, 9 May 1991; Douglas Peters, address, Rubber Association of Canada, 1 March
1991; Southam News; Lester Thurow; *The Toronto Star*; *The Wall Street Journal*; Bruce Wilkinson.
Every effort has been made to credit all sources correctly. The author and publisher will be
grateful for any information that will allow for the correction of any omissions or errors.

Cover Design: Brant Cowie/ArtPlus Limited
Indexing by Heather Ebbs

Printed and bound in Canada

To
Tommy Douglas
Walter Gordon
George Grant
and
Eric Kierans

four wise and courageous Canadians

Contents

List of Charts

Preface

CANADA IS DISINTEGRATING. THE WORK AND THE DREAMS OF generations of Canadians are being destroyed. The tragedy of Canada is that this is happening after we had done so very well. Compared with all other nations, we were probably the most fortunate people on earth. Our real standard of living, combined with the quality of life we have had, was un-equalled. Our great potential for the future was the envy of the world.

The tragedy of Canada is that having been blessed with so much good fortune, we have allowed inept political leader-ship and manipulative, greedy, and selfish corporate leaders to destroy the labours and accomplishments of generations — the work and dreams of many millions of Canadians from every political background and from every part of Canada. Blessed with bountiful resources, an enormous area forming the second-largest nation in the world, with a comparatively well-educated people from many diverse backgrounds . . . and having inherited a natural beauty of magnificent moun-tains, gigantic forests, abundant fresh water, and vast reserves of mineral and petroleum wealth, we created a truly remark-able nation with a very high standard of living, a compassion-ate social philosophy, a balanced mix of public and private enterprise, and a much-admired reputation as a country of good people and a land of great freedom and opportunity.

True, we did some things very badly. Our treatment of the aboriginal people is a national and, more and more, interna-tional disgrace. Far too many Canadian men, women, and especially children live in real, debilitating poverty. Our tax system, our laws relating to corporate concentration, and our laws governing the election and conduct of our politi-cians, are all desperately in need of radical reform, as we shall see in what follows. These laws are at the heart of the disastrous situation in which we now find ourselves.

Every Canadian who travels abroad knows how fortunate we are to live in Canada, and polls taken around the world reinforce the view that Canadians are a most fortunate people. Most Canadians travel to the United States and most like the United States, but they would not want to live there or to become Americans. Year after year, the public opinion polls confirm that an overwhelming majority of Canadians do not want Canada to become part of their southern neighbour. But, thanks to Brian Mulroney and his friends, very soon they will have no choice.

Brian Mulroney and his friends lied to Canadians. It is one thing not to tell the truth through ignorance, but it is quite another to mislead through fervent belief in an ideology. The very worst combination is ignorance, ideology, and betrayal. This is exactly what we have had from the political and corporate leadership of Canada since the federal election of 1984.

The Betrayal of Canada is an examination of the devastating impact of the one promise Brian Mulroney has kept — that under his leadership Canada would be changed beyond recognition.

We still have a chance to turn Canada around, but very little time left to do it in. I hope that readers of this book will decide to become actively involved in this urgent process.

T HE FIRST PART OF THIS BOOK CONTAINS NUMEROUS STATISTICS, while the second part dwells less on numbers and more on the important political, social, and economic changes that will have to be made if Canada is to survive. Chapter 39, on the next federal election, may well be the most important chapter of all. Other chapters, on such subjects as foreign ownership, taxation, corporate concentration, social policies, our undemocratic democracy, and centralization versus decentralization, provide new information and perspectives that rebut a great deal of broadly accepted conventional "wisdom."

Readers who have an aversion to tables of figures will find the fifty-four charts of value. Some of them are truly startling. The notes at the back of the book contain some very important material for researchers and others interested in the economics of our deindustrializing and disappearing country.

I AM VERY GRATEFUL TO MY WIFE KAY HURTIG AND TO RHONDA Bouchard, Lisa Shaw, Bill Loewen, Carlotta Lemieux, Jack Stoddart, Stuart Smith, Arthur Donner, Bruce Wilkinson, Peter C. Newman, David Perry, Douglas Peters, Neil Brooks, Thomas Courchene, James Gillies, Lorraine Eden, Alan Cairns, Bob Oldham, John Orr, Deborah Coyne, David Schneiderman, and Wayne Easter for their permissions, advice, comments, criticism, and assistance. I am also especially grateful to the many first-class people at Statistics Canada who have been so very helpful.

MEL HURTIG
Edmonton, August 1991

We have only been in power for two months, but I can tell you this: give us twenty years, and it is coming, and you will not recognize this country.

BRIAN MULRONEY, *House of Commons, 7 November 1984*

Part I

TENANTS IN OUR OWN LAND

1

The Free Trade Agreement

A Real Beauty for You

> Canadians rejected free trade with the United States in
> 1911. They would do so again in 1983.
>
> BRIAN MULRONEY, *Maclean's, 13 June 1983*

> There's a real beauty for you. . . . There's a real honey.
> Free trade with the United States is like sleeping with an
> elephant. It's terrific until the elephant twitches, and if
> the elephant rolls over you are a dead man.
>
> BRIAN MULRONEY, *speech at Thunder Bay, Ontario, 1983*

ONE CAN ONLY SPECULATE AS TO WHAT ASPECT OF
sleeping with an elephant Brian Mulroney thought to be so
"terrific." Of greater importance is the contrast between
the above two quotations attacking the concept of free
trade with the United States and what actually happened
as soon as Brian Mulroney became prime minister in
September 1984.

In 1983, Michael Wilson, Joe Clark, and Brian Mulroney
all vigorously attacked the idea of free trade with the United
States. But by the fall of 1984, plans were already well
underway for negotiations with the U.S., and by the time of
the October 1988 "free trade election," Brian Mulroney considered an agreement with the U.S. as "absolutely essential
to sustain economic growth and prosperity for Canada."

The Conservatives were very worried about this switch in policy and how it could be explained; they were also concerned about how the change in policy would be perceived. How could the prime minister possibly explain such a dramatic one hundred and eighty degree policy reversal, especially since he hadn't even mentioned it during the federal election campaign? For months he tried very hard not to, stressing "freer trade" or "more open trading arrangements" but never free trade.

A confidential memo leaked from the Prime Minister's Office in September 1985 showed just how honest and forthright Brian Mulroney intended to be with the people who had elected him to the nation's highest post: "The strategy should rely less on educating the general public than on getting across the message that the trade initiative is a good idea. In other words, a selling job. It is likely that the higher the profile the issue attains, the lower the degree of public approval will be. Benign neglect from a majority of Canadians may be the realistic outcome of a well-executed communications program." So not only had Brian Mulroney completely altered his position on free trade which had helped him become leader of the Progressive Conservative Party of Canada, but now, as prime minister, he proposed to implement a policy he had attacked and ridiculed, and he proposed to do so with "a selling job" and a program designed to encourage "benign neglect."

Everyone knows that Canadians have become deeply cynical about their political leaders. The devious, unprincipled, cynical manipulations of Brian Mulroney are the main reason for this. Internal government documents make it clear that the Conservative government fully understood how profoundly a Canada–U.S. Free Trade Agreement would change Canada, economically, politically, socially, and culturally, and how much sovereignty Canadians would have to give up. Yet the strategy was not to consult, not to educate, not to encourage debate, not to examine the issues and alternatives, but rather to implement a well-executed communications program to foster benign neglect and to do a selling job on the people of Canada. Brian Mulroney intended to change the fundamental character of Canada and hoped that nobody would notice or object.

By early 1985, opposition to the government's plans was beginning to coalesce. By mid-year, it was clear that a major "selling job" would be necessary. The Free Trade Agreement was aggressively sold to Canadians as a panacea for all things that afflict Canada, real or imaginary — and "sold" is indeed the operative word. Never before in the history of our country has so much effort and so much money been spent in a massive multimedia propaganda campaign designed to influence public opinion and the result of a federal election. The federal government, along with several provincial governments, joined with big business (from both inside and outside Canada) in an unparalleled spending splurge in an effort to convince Canadians that the proposed Free Trade Agreement was not only necessary but was a guaranteed cure-all for our economic problems.

Most of the many tens of millions of dollars spent on this campaign came either from taxpayers' money or from undisclosed sources. Much came from foreign-controlled corporations. Unfortunately, we shall never know exactly how much was spent and where most of the funds came from. While politicians, constituencies, and political parties are bound by election laws, there are no such laws governing the kind of enormous "third-party" campaign that was conducted by big business in 1987 and 1988. For such third parties there are no disclosure rules, no limits on the amounts spent, few restrictions on advertising, and no mandatory reporting of funds spent or of the sources of those funds.

Moreover, in a remarkable yet poorly reported decision that has escaped the attention of most Canadians, Revenue Canada ruled that such spending may be deducted by business as a legitimate expense, despite the fact that much of this spending during the 1988 federal election was clearly political in nature and was expressly designed to elect Brian Mulroney's Conservative government. From now on, federal elections can be bought by big business, even if the money comes from outside Canada.

The implications of this government tax decision are horrendous. Whatever may have been the inadequacies of the democratic process in Canada in the past (and they have been many), the prospects for the future are even more disturbing, for big corporations now have *carte blanche* to manipulate elections through the paid media, or otherwise, without restraint. Having spent tens of millions of dollars assuring Brian Mulroney a majority government in 1988 (with 43 per cent of the vote) the appetite of our corporate elite has been whetted. They have tasted political blood and they love it. If the tens of millions of dollars spent on the 1988 election was unprecedented, just wait until the next federal election in 1993 (especially if the NDP looks strong or if the Liberals find the courage to take a firm stand for Canada).

Meanwhile, the very same Revenue Canada has refused the same rights to numerous public-interest organizations that opposed the trade deal across the country. Donations made to these organizations are not tax deductible, because the organizations are unable to provide tax receipts. Since most organizations opposing the Free Trade Agreement are dependent on donations from individuals and rarely receive donations from large corporations, the political scales are dramatically tipped. Big business now calls the shots in federal elections, not only through its funding of two of the three national political parties, but also through its direct political intervention from outside the regulated, formal political process.

Before and during the 1988 "free trade" federal election, in television and magazine ads, in newspaper ads, glossy pamphlets and slick brochures, and four-page, nationally distributed newspaper supplements, Canadians were promised that the trade agreement would bring new jobs, increased investment, greater economic activity, better business conditions, lower consumer prices, lower inflation, expanded consumer choices, more exports, and a better standard of living. There would be prosperity for all. At the same time, we were promised that there would be no erosion of the social structure and social values that Canadians had developed over generations through a social contract built up by Liberals and Conservatives and the CCF and NDP, with values and benefits that greatly distinguish Canadian society from that of the United States. Both big business and the Conservative government solemnly promised Canadians that our social programs would in fact be strengthened, not weakened. Meanwhile, those of us who warned about the potential for serious economic consequences, damage to the Canadian social fabric, the likely erosion of east-west relations and national unity, and the consequences of abandoning huge areas of national sovereignty were denounced as "liars" or "scaremongers."

Throughout much of 1987 and 1988, the public opinion polls showed that most Canadians were apprehensive and sceptical about the Mulroney government's plans and were concerned about the kind of deal Ottawa would be able to strike with Washington. The massive pro-deal government and business campaign was brilliantly manipulative, massively financed, and perfectly timed. Enough Canadians were temporarily convinced to allow Mulroney's re-election in November 1988. Today, the polls reveal an entirely different story. Increasingly, Canadians are against the agreement. The latest national poll shows 57 per cent against and only 31 per cent in favour; 56 per cent of Canadians say they have been hurt by the deal and only 7 per cent say they have been helped.

Many of the chapters that follow examine the economic, social, and political consequences of the Free Trade Agreement for Canada. Both the Canada West Foundation and the Royal Bank of Canada produced widely reported documents early in 1991 which purported to be reliable analyses, but the statistics employed were very incomplete and failed to include abundant documentation that was inconsistent with their pro-free-trade ideology. Some may wonder about their motivation in omitting important information. Perhaps it might have something to do with the fact that much of the foundation's funding comes from corporations and governments that supported the Free Trade Agreement, as well as the fact that the Royal Bank of Canada has long been the most powerful and influential continentalist[1] corporation in Canada.

Similarly, some of the business press in Canada has been either negligent or reluctant in its analysis of the devastating impact of this agreement. Many of the most important figures given on the following pages have never been reported in Canada's business press or, for that matter, in most daily newspapers or on television or radio. Many of the key graphs and charts in this book are the result of new research and have never been published before. However, it is also true that some of the most important statistics have in fact been in the public domain for quite some time — yet they still have not been published in Canadian newspapers or magazines. Some of them are so astonishing, even shocking, that readers may shake their heads in disbelief. Similarly, the graphs will destroy many well-entrenched Canadian myths. All of the statistics come from official government documents and publications or from the Organization for Economic Co-operation and Development (OECD) in Paris. Most are from Statistics Canada, the Department of Finance, the Bank of Canada, the Petroleum Monitoring Agency, the U.S. Department of Commerce, and other government sources.

Canada, today, is in grave economic and political trouble. The source of most of this trouble will be found in the following chapters. Those who value our country and believe its survival is important should do whatever they can to share this information with their friends, relatives, and fellow citizens. If Canada is to survive, the Mulroney government must be soundly defeated in the next federal election, and it must be replaced by a government that has the strength and the wisdom to abrogate the terrible, truncating trade agreement and return Canada to the fundamentals that most Canadians have long respected and supported: fairness, compassion, democratic reform, egalitarianism, and economic policies that have a human dimension. Some of these policies are discussed in the second part of the book.

Brian Mulroney and his government have betrayed Canada and have even betrayed the historical principles of their own party. It is ironic to hear this prime minister frequently and fondly quoting the words and memory of the great Conservative, Sir John A. Macdonald. Canada's first prime minister would be lurching out of his grave if he had any idea of what Brian Mulroney is doing to Canada.

In a speech in the House of Commons on 3 November 1873, John A. said, "If Canada is never sold in the future by a greater traitor than myself, Canada will be a fortunate country." Read these pages and decide for yourself whether seven years of Mulroney government have made Canada a fortunate country.

2

The Fatal Flaw

Stupidity or Conspiracy?

> The adverse impact of the valuation of the Canadian dollar
> has twenty times the impact of free trade.
>
> GORDON RITCHIE *(former deputy chief negotiator for the Canada–U.S.*
> *Free Trade Agreement), Financial Post, 25 March 1991*

THE FREE TRADE AGREEMENT (FTA) WAS SOLD TO
Canadians as just that — a trade agreement. In reality it was
much more: a comprehensive agreement for the economic
integration of Canada and the United States.

Canada entered the negotiations with oft-repeated warnings from the Mulroney government that we had to have an
agreement. Whatever faults Americans may have, they are
not stupid. If Canada had to have an agreement, Canadians
would have to pay. And pay we did. The Americans obtained
almost everything they wanted, including vital concessions
which most Canadians knew nothing about, or which they
had little reason to believe would be part of an agreement
that most thought to be essentially about tariffs.

In an interview with the Montreal *Gazette* on 26 November
1987, the prime minister reassured Canadians about our
capacity to negotiate a comprehensive bilateral agreement
with the United States: "When you bargain, the key to bargaining is that you never give away anything until you sit
down at the table." But instead of adopting this policy, the

government made numerous major unilateral concessions in advance of the negotiations. The infamous Bill C-22 weakened Canada's generic drug laws at the request of the White House, which was acting in response to a powerful lobby from U.S. pharmaceutical manufacturers. Both the Foreign Investment Review Agency and the National Energy Program were dismantled. New film distribution legislation was weakened and then abandoned. And in an unprecedented and appalling abdication of sovereignty, the Mulroney government let Washington determine that Canadian softwood lumber stumpage fees were supposedly too low. The softwood lumber agreement will go down in history as one of the most shameful examples of the abandonment of national self-determination in the history of our country.[1] All of this was done in advance of the formal negotiations. Even the chairman of the board of one of Canada's major banks, Cedric Ritchie of the Bank of Nova Scotia, suggested that Canada had "given up most of its bargaining chips" without obtaining "adequate progress towards our principal goal of secure access to the U.S. market."

When the final agreement was belatedly released for public scrutiny on 11 December 1987, there were numerous surprises. Canada's negotiators had caved in in many vital areas. Rules restricting U.S. ownership were radically relaxed. Canada's ability to control its own energy supplies and energy prices was dramatically diminished. Mandatory sharing of Canada's resources was an astonishing, unprecedented concession; even if we ran short of key energy supplies or other resources, we still had to continue selling to the United States at exactly the same prices charged in Canada.

All the while, the Canadian people were being sold an agreement that was ostensibly designed to get rid of tariffs; consumer prices would drop, we were told, and exports would be easier, with "guaranteed access" to the U.S. market. In reality, tariffs were only a relatively small part of a very comprehensive list of vital areas under discussion, many of them unknown to Parliament, the press, and the Canadian public. Canada gave away the shop, the farm, the house, and the factory to get what was sold as "guaranteed access." It is now crystal clear that we did not achieve even that. Canadian exporters are still being harassed. In the first two years of the agreement, our trade balance with the United States is down, not up. U.S. law, not international law, remains the basis of most Canada–U.S. trade disputes.

Even if Canada had made an infinitely better deal with the United States, there would still have been a crucial, fatal flaw in the logic underlying the agreement. It seems incomprehensible that the supposedly capable economists, business leaders, and government officials who masterminded Canada's bargaining position and negotiated the agreement were oblivious of the potentially disastrous impact of a large increase in the value of the Canadian dollar *vis-à-vis* the U.S. dollar.

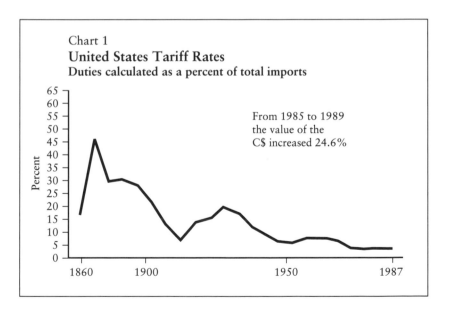

Chart 1
United States Tariff Rates
Duties calculated as a percent of total imports

From 1985 to 1989
the value of the
C$ increased 24.6%

Chart 1 tells the story. As can be seen, exports to the United States have faced steadily decreasing tariffs. Through the General Agreement on Tariffs and Trade (GATT), the international trade body representing almost one hundred trading nations,[2] world tariffs have been progressively reduced. Canada has played a prominent role in this process over a forty-year period. The chart shows that the effective tariff rate on exports to the United States had fallen rapidly by the time the Mulroney government was elected in 1984. After the 1979 GATT Tokyo Round reductions were implemented, U.S. tariffs on industrial products were only 4 per cent on dutiable industrial goods. Eighty per cent of Canadian exports to the U.S. entered duty-free and 96 per cent of Canadian exports entered at duties of 5 per cent or less. Clearly, tariffs were not an impediment to most Canadian exports to the U.S. For years Canada had maintained large merchandise trade surpluses with its southern neighbour.[3]

Incredibly, while our negotiators gave away many vital concessions that severely reduced our ability to plan our own future and manage our own economy (all so that we would, supposedly, gain "guaranteed access to the U.S. market" and be able to abolish the small remaining tariffs), we allowed the value of the Canadian dollar to appreciate almost 25 per cent from the time free trade became an issue in Canada to the time it went into effect in 1989. Astonishing! We give away control of our country to abolish tariffs of 2 or 3 per cent and then, at the same time, we adopt a strategy that puts a 25 per cent penalty on all Canadian exports to the United States. The high value of the Canadian dollar both hinders exports and encourages imports. (The severe impact of the currency appreciation will be seen in the trade and employment charts in later chapters.)

How could Canada have been so stupid as to enter into a "level playing field" agreement and then send our team out onto the field with the heavy iron balls and thick chains of high interest rates and an artificially high dollar? There has been much speculation about what really happened here, not to mention abundant incredulity. Are the loquacious gurus of free trade — the Richard Lipseys, the Wendy Dobsons, the Donald Macdonalds, and John Crispos — really that obtuse?[4] Or is there some other explanation? Are John Crosbie, Pat Carney, Simon Reisman, and our departments of Finance and External Affairs simply inept, or is there something we don't know?

There has been much rumour and speculation about whether there was a secret deal to guarantee a higher Canadian dollar. Certainly, we know that key U.S. politicians and trade officials were vociferous in their demands for an increase in the value of our dollar. U.S. trade negotiator Peter Murphy repeatedly stressed the U.S. Congress's concern about the advantages Canada had from a 70 to 75 cent dollar, and American politicians and U.S. manufacturers consistently attacked so-called trade distortions and demanded a "target zone" for the Canadian dollar. Even former Conservative cabinet minister Sinclair Stevens claims that we capitulated to U.S. pressure that made it clear there would be no deal unless we agreed to a substantial increase in the value of the Canadian dollar. Others have speculated that when Canada lobbied (along with Italy) for entry into what was then the G5 Western industrialized nations, part of the entry fee was a promise to stabilize our currency at a considerably higher level.

We shall probably never know what happened, with any certainty. But it remains utterly beyond comprehension that any smaller country, seeking to reach a comprehensive door-opening trade agreement with a much larger and far more powerful industrialized giant, would voluntarily agree to drive up the value of its own currency, to the substantial detriment of the very exporters and workers who were supposed to benefit from the agreement. If indeed there has been such a secret agreement, it would be impossible to reverse it without U.S. retaliatory actions under the "nullification and impairment" provisions of the FTA, or without Canada's abrogation of the agreement.[5]

The Canadian Exporters Association (CEA) has estimated that every one-cent rise in the value of the Canadian dollar decreases our exports by $1.3 billion. Since early 1986, before the start of the FTA talks, the Canadian dollar has risen some 16 cents. Given the CEA estimate, this means an annual loss of almost $21 billion in exports; and, of course, that means huge job losses, as we shall see shortly. The high Canadian dollar means that American exporters have gained a large direct advantage in the Canadian market which corresponds to the disadvantage Canadian exporters now face in the United States.

Without the behind-closed-doors blackmail scenario, it is impossible to explain how even the obsequious Mulroney government could have been so incredibly inept. It is difficult to know which scenario is more depressing to contemplate — allowing ourselves to be bullied into an inevitably horrendous deal, or discovering that our own Department of Finance and Bank of Canada have acquiesced voluntarily.

Stupidity or conspiracy? Perhaps both? What is important is the terrible economic effect.

3

Employment and Unemployment

The Devastating Impact of the FTA *on Jobs in Canada*

> *[Free Trade] will create more jobs, especially for our young people, and put more money in the pockets of our workers. The Economic Council of Canada predicts that free trade will provide 250,000 additional jobs.*
>
> BRIAN MULRONEY, *election speech, October 1988*

> *Question: Could you, as one of Canada's leading economists, tell us where the new jobs will be coming from — what is your opinion of all the optimistic job creation studies? Answer: I don't believe that those kinds of estimates, which are conditional on a series of assumptions . . . are worth very much, Mel. I don't think they are worth a lot. Don't quote me on that, but I've said it over and over and over.*
>
> *Exchange between MEL HURTIG and economist SYLVIA OSTRY*
>
> *at a seminar, Val-Morin, Quebec, 16 January 1987*

CANADIANS WERE PROMISED THAT THE TRADE agreement would bring hundreds of thousands of new jobs and great prosperity. Right-wing continentalist think tanks and government agencies tripped over one another on the way to press conferences to release studies that promised economic growth and abundant new job creation. One Ottawa study predicted

370,000 new jobs. Leading the pack were the C. D. Howe Institute, the Economic Council of Canada, the Canadian Manufacturers' Association, the departments of Finance and External Affairs, and, of course, the prime minister. Canadians were promised over and over again that huge numbers of new jobs would be created, that unemployment would drop, and that the Canadian people would prosper.

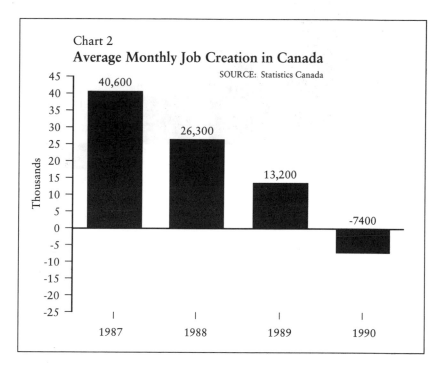

Chart 2
Average Monthly Job Creation in Canada
SOURCE: Statistics Canada

Chart 2 presents a very different picture. It requires little comment. As can be seen, the first two years of free trade, 1989 and 1990, showed a precipitous decline in new jobs for Canadians. Chart 3 presents a similarly depressing record, this time on an annual basis for the two years preceding the FTA and for the first two years of the agreement. Note that some 803,000 new jobs were created in Canada during the two years before the FTA, while only 73,000 new jobs were created in 1989 and 1990. By any measure, this is a staggering comparison. Chart 4 shows the job losses in Canada for the last twelve months as the graphs for this book were being prepared.

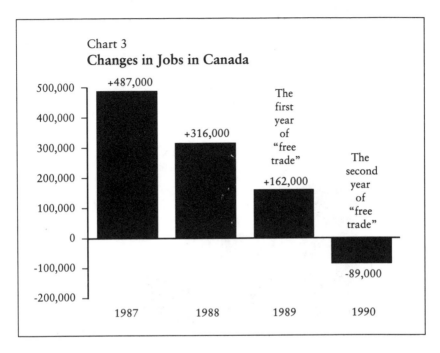

Chart 3
Changes in Jobs in Canada

These figures, and those that follow, are sickening. The huge decline in full-time jobs and the huge increases in the number of unemployed are clear indications of damaging government policies. From January 1989, the first month of the FTA, to the end of June 1991, the increase in the number of unemployed Canadians exceeded 452,000. The unemployment rate is now more than 10 per cent for the first time in five years, and even the Department of Finance predicts a rate of 10 per cent for 1991. The Bank of Montreal predicts that it will rise to 10.7 per cent in 1991 and 11.2 per cent in 1992. Mike McCracken, president of Infometrica Ltd., suggests that "we could average 11 per cent this year and 13 per cent next year"; Peter Cook, *Globe and Mail* business columnist, says that unemployment will stay above 10 per cent until 1993 at the earliest.

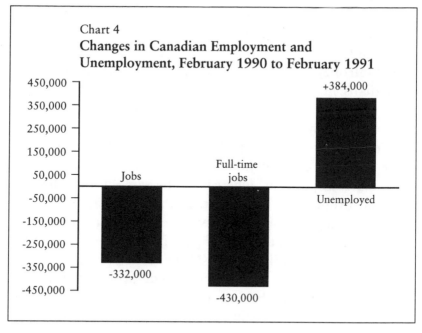

Chart 4

Changes in Canadian Employment and Unemployment, February 1990 to February 1991

+384,000

Jobs

Full-time jobs

Unemployed

-332,000

-430,000

High as unemployment is, compared with the years before the FTA and compared with other OECD nations, the official rate is understated. If workers who want to work full-time but can only find part-time employment are included, the "underemployment rate" is already close to 13 per cent. In April 1991, some 535,000 Canadians were working part-time because they were unable to find full-time jobs.

Obviously, the lost income is substantial. And the full picture is far worse. Jobs in the goods-creating sector of the Canadian economy had been increasing steadily since mid-1986 until the end of 1988, but beginning in January 1989, they dropped all the way back to the level of 1984. Service-sector jobs have made up some of the job losses, but mainly in employment that offers lower wages, fewer full-time jobs, poorer benefits, and overall substantially less income than is normally received in the goods sector. In the first two months of 1991, 151,000 more jobs were lost in Canada. By the end of June, there were 1,453,000 Canadians unemployed. If the underemployed had been included, the total number would have been closer to 2 million.

It is interesting to make some international comparisons. The Mulroney government has had a penchant for telling Canadians how well they have performed compared with other nations. Yet while the average projected unemployment rate for the twenty-four OECD countries in 1991 is only 7.1 per cent, the unemployment rate in Canada will likely be some 10.6 per cent. In June 1991, Canada's unemployment rate was 10.5 per cent, whereas in the same month the U.S. rate had dropped to 7 per cent. In the first year of the FTA, Canada's unemployment rate was 1.3 per cent higher than the OECD average. In the second year it was 2 per cent higher. In the third year it will be almost 4 per cent higher.

If, as so many devotees of free trade are predicting, the recession will be well behind us by the second half of 1991, how is it that they are still predicting appallingly high rates of unemployment? The answer is simple. Of course the recession will end eventually,[1] but at the same time there will be high unemployment, poorer quality jobs, vastly underutilized capacity, and a lower standard of living overall. It is safe to say that at least twice as many job layoffs in the current recession will be permanent compared with the recession of 1981-82. Some 60 to 70 per cent of the jobs recently lost in secondary industry in Ontario and Quebec will be jobs lost forever. In the 1982 recession, only one-quarter of the job losses were permanent.

Aside from the personal and family agony and humiliation, aside from the billions of dollars in income lost to the economy, there is another heavy cost. For the first time in Canadian history, more than 2 million Canadians are receiving welfare under the Canada Assistance Plan, and more than 600,000 Canadians now rely on food banks. At the same time, federal spending on job creation and job training has been cut. The "safety net" and the "trampoline" to allow workers to bounce back, which were recommended in the Mulroney-commissioned Grandpré Report, are nowhere to be found. Meanwhile, unemployment benefits have been reduced, and transfer payments from Ottawa to the provinces have been sharply curtailed, with the inevitable increasing pressure on the provinces and municipalities to cut back services. For the unemployed and underemployed in Canada, the prospects are bleak. For millions of Canadians, the lavish promises of the Mulroney government are now looked upon with scorn. Is it any wonder that Brian Mulroney is the least popular prime minister in the history of polling in Canada and that his party ranks with him?[2]

One cannot leave the question of job losses without noting the performance of those corporations which — both publicly and very much behind the scenes — pushed, pleaded, and made promises for the agreement. An analysis of the *Financial Post*'s mid-year 1990 report on Canada's top 500 corporations shows that the top 200 decreased employment in Canada by almost 215,000 jobs. These are essentially the same giant corporations that make up the powerful Business Council on National Issues lobby and that were the foremost advocates, if not the principal instigators, of the FTA. The 1991 issue of the *Post*'s top 500 shows another decrease of 73,400 jobs for these same corporations.

4

The Deindustrialization of Canada

On the Road to a Warehouse Economy

*Since the Free Trade Agreement came into effect . . . our
industrial base has been seriously eroded. . . . In nearly
every sector, factories are curtailing their operations, being
abandoned, moving south of the border, or being convert-
ed to mainly distribution and storage functions. . . . The
most immediate effect of free trade has been the accelerated
de-industrialization of Canada; we've gone straight from
smokestacks to warehouses. . . . Canada is establishing an
unheard-of precedent. We are about to become the only
country in recorded history to reverse the traditional evolution from underdevelopment to a manufacturing economy.*

PETER C. NEWMAN, *Maclean's, 23 October 1989*

*Once ratified and implemented, it will encourage a process
of industrial adaptation, resource allocation, and investment in infrastructure that will not easily be reversed.*

ECONOMIC COUNCIL OF CANADA, *Venturing Forth, 1988*

IN VENTURING FORTH,[1] THE ECONOMIC COUNCIL
of Canada predicted that "the most likely outcome [of the FTA]
. . . will be a net gain of 251,000 jobs." The council also predicted greater productivity increases, greater investment, lower
consumer prices, and a lower unemployment rate. It was

wrong on all five counts (though, unfortunately, it was correct in stating that the process "will not easily be reversed").

In the first two years of the FTA, Canada lost 264,000 manufacturing jobs, and since June 1989 a total of 281,000 manufacturing jobs have disappeared. Manufacturing jobs as a percentage of Canada's total employment are down 20 per cent from a decade earlier. Our manufacturing capacity utilization rate was 86.4 per cent the year before the FTA commenced. As this is being written, it is down to 70.5 per cent. The "soft landing" has turned into crash and burn. In a list of the top thirteen industrial powers, Canada stands dead last in industrial production performance (Chart 5).

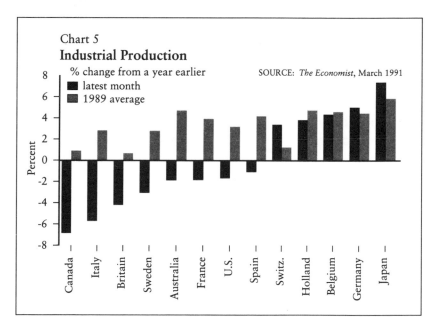

Chart 5
Industrial Production
% change from a year earlier   SOURCE: *The Economist*, March 1991
■ latest month
■ 1989 average

Chart 6 shows the dramatic comparisons for the two years before the FTA (job growth in manufacturing) and the first two years of the FTA (huge combined job losses). I have said many times that instead of calling it the "Free Trade Agreement," we should call it the "Deindustrialization of Canada Agreement," for this indeed is what it is. Even

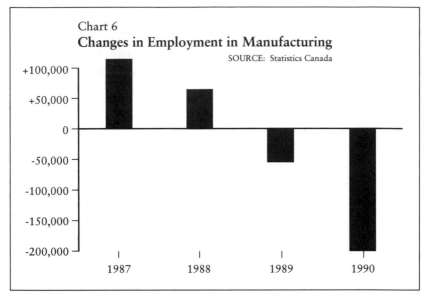

Chart 6
Changes in Employment in Manufacturing
SOURCE: Statistics Canada

before the FTA, while in OECD nations manufacturing accounted, on average, for some 23.5 per cent of gross domestic product (GDP) in 1988, in branch-plant Canada it was only 19 per cent. By 1991 this had declined to only 16 per cent. In terms of manufacturing as a share of GDP, Canada is now nowhere near the top twenty nations.

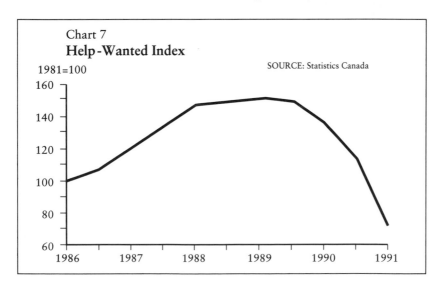

Chart 7
Help-Wanted Index
1981=100
SOURCE: Statistics Canada

Chart 7 tells of things yet to come. Note what has happened to the "help-wanted index" since the FTA went into effect. Compare the trend for the two years before the FTA with the trend in 1989 and 1990. In June 1991, the "help-wanted index" was less than half what it was in early 1989.

Numbers, charts, and graphs can tell a great deal, but the heartbreak and agony of unemployed men and women — of impoverished families and undernourished and poorly clothed children — tell a great deal more. The economic costs of jobs lost and increasing unemployment are devastating, and the tragedy for one and a half million unemployed Canadians is a legacy of despair and bitterness.

5

The Bottom Line

The Performance of Canada's Economy

> *A number of studies have shown that Canada's gross national product could expand by 3 per cent to 8 per cent as a result of the agreement.*
>
> ROYAL BANK OF CANADA, *Summer 1989*

> *Canada will suffer the worst economic performance of all industrial countries this year. . . . Only two of 20 other countries — Britain and Sweden — will also see their economies shrink, though less than Canada's.*
>
> SOUTHAM NEWS, *May 1991*

> *I don't believe the economy is in a recession or approaching the point of a recession.*
>
> BRIAN MULRONEY, *Quebec City, August 1990*

CHART 8 SAYS MORE ABOUT THE FTA THAN A THOU-sand speeches by Brian Mulroney, Michael Wilson, John Crosbie, or Thomas d'Aquino, and more, too, than the Royal Bank's biased propaganda.

The bottom line of a country's economic performance is the growth or decline of gross domestic product (GDP) after inflation is removed. The GDP is the total value of the goods and services produced in the economy by both residents and non-residents. The chart shows the growth rate in the

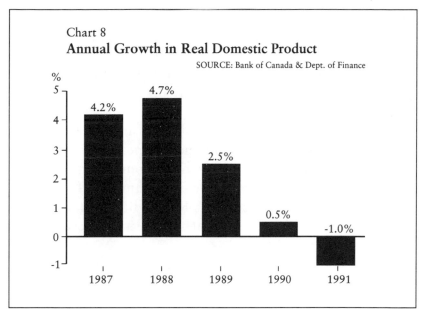

Chart 8
Annual Growth in Real Domestic Product
SOURCE: Bank of Canada & Dept. of Finance

Canadian economy for 1987 and 1988, the two years before the FTA went into effect, and compares this with the first two years of free trade and a projection for 1991. Once again, as in previous graphs and in many of those that follow, the trend line goes straight downhill towards the right. Even the Department of Finance is predicting a decline of 1 per cent in real GDP for 1991 and a decline of 1.7 per cent in final domestic demand. From March 1990 to March 1991, GDP in Canada declined by 3.2 per cent. One brokerage house described the last quarter of 1990 and the first quarter of 1991 as "probably the worst half-year for the Canadian economy since the Second World War." Incidentally, before implementation of the FTA, from 1980 to 1988 inclusive, Canada's average annual real GDP increase was more than 3.5 per cent.

The OECD predicts that, of its twenty-four industrialized members, twenty-one will produce a better economic performance than Canada in 1991. One hardly needs point out what a sharp contrast this is to the repeated bragging of

Brian Mulroney and Michael Wilson about how well Canada does compared to other nations. In the two years before the FTA, Canada's GDP grew by a combined total of 8.9 per cent. In the first *three* years of the FTA, the combined total will be less than 2.5 per cent (or an average of well under 1 per cent per year).

All this is very different from the lavish forecasts of the C.D. Howe Institute, the Economic Council of Canada, the Department of Finance, the Business Council on National Issues, the Canadian Alliance for Trade and Job Opportunities, and the "non-partisan" Royal Bank of Canada. Canadians would be wise to treat their future forecasts with the scepticism they deserve.[1]

6

Heading South

What the "Trade" Deal Was Really All About

> When the year is over, I think we will be able to get a pretty good indication of what some of the effects of the free trade agreement have been with respect to investment.
> JOHN CROSBIE, *September 1989*

> I can only tell that trade is expanding, investment intentions are expanding and employment has grown in Canada. . . .
> I don't have hard figures to base that on, but I have anecdotal accounts from people you run into at airports.
> DEREK BURNEY, *Canadian ambassador to the U.S.,*
> *Financial Times, 11 December 1989*

> No longer is (the issue) how high we have to pay to attract and retain people, but how much less to pay to get a competitive advantage.
> MICHAEL McINERNEY *of Northern*
> *Telecom, Globe and Mail, March 1989*

CHART 9 IS ONE OF THE MOST IMPORTANT IN THIS book. Since 1985, I have been saying that a free trade agreement with the United States would be more about where new investment would locate than about any other aspect of the agreement.

Canadians were repeatedly told that the FTA would produce bountiful amounts of new investment, leading to increased

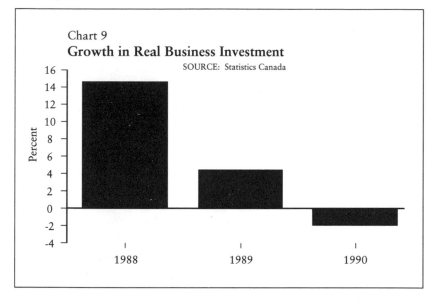

Chart 9
Growth in Real Business Investment
SOURCE: Statistics Canada

economic activity. While Chart 8 detailed the "increased economic activity," Chart 9 illustrates the "bountiful new investment." The decline in business investment in Canada began
shortly after the FTA went into effect, and investment has
dropped drastically ever since. The last annual report of the
governor of the Bank of Canada has a graph of business fixed
investment in Canada showing year-over-year percentage
changes; for the years since the FTA legislation, this graph
heads straight downhill at an angle resembling the near-verti-
cal north face of Mount Robson.

Below are the annual percentage changes in the growth
rate in real business non-residential investment in Canada in
the two years before the FTA and the two years after:

1987   +9.3 per cent
1988   +15.2 per cent

1989   +5.0 per cent
1990   –2.25 per cent

The estimated figure for 1991 is a further decline of 6 to 10 per cent.

By every investment comparison — business fixed capital in 1986 dollars or business investment in machinery and equipment — the FTA has been a disaster for Canada. Some of the business media have hyperventilated over increases in foreign direct investment in 1990, but just how vacuous these glowing reports are will be appreciated better after reading the chapters on foreign ownership and Investment Canada. The bottom line is that the total of all investment in Canada (domestic and foreign combined) is but a pale shadow of what business investment was before the FTA. By the end of 1991, this pale shadow will be invisible.

It is fascinating to note the comments of Simon Reisman, the man who negotiated the FTA for Canada, in relation to investment. In July 1990, as more and more plants were closed and as more and more jobs were lost to the low-wage southern United States[1] and Mexico, Mr. Reisman attended a conference organized by the U.S. subsidiary, Continental Canada (no doubt an excellent forum for one of Canada's leading continentalists), where he explained that the true measure of the impact of the FTA on Canada's economy was not the number of jobs lost but the investment climate created by the treaty — ironic words when one looks at both the actual investment figures and the job losses that I have shown on the previous pages.

And what about the future? Vancouver entrepreneur Jimmy Pattison minces no words: "We're taking everything we've got and pushing into the United States. . . . I keep telling our people to forget the border — it doesn't exist anymore." Or, if you prefer, listen to the words of another well-known Canadian patriot, Adam Zimmerman, chairman of Noranda Forest Inc.: "If you are in a business that can move, why bother with the hassle of staying in Canada?" Eric Kierans sums it up well: "As our great corporations prepare to move south, they are indifferent to what they leave behind them." And the *Globe and Mail* quotes a recent bank credit analysis report: "Canada's manufacturing sector is being hollowed out. . . . It's standing room only at seminars on setting up shop in the United States!" Almost every day there are new reports of factories closing and jobs being moved to the United States or Mexico. The list of corporations relocating in the Mexican *maquiladoras* now looks like a *Who's Who* of Canadian and multinational business.

Among the strongest proponents of the FTA have been Canada's biggest banks. Cedric Ritchie, chairman and chief executive of the Bank of Nova Scotia, is very articulate now about the impact of the agreement (a shining contrast to most of his continentalist banking colleagues). In a recent interview, Ritchie said, "There is no doubt that Canadian firms are adjusting to the Free Trade Agreement. The problem is that too many are adjusting by leaving Canada."

For years, those of us opposed to a comprehensive bilateral agreement[2] warned of the consequences, but there is little satisfaction in listing plant closing by plant closing, job transfer by job transfer. In this respect, the press has done a good job. There are dozens of well-documented stories of Canadian employees being threatened if they refuse to accept lower wages or poorer benefits, of plants closed down in the middle of the night with machinery loaded onto trucks and shipped to Mexico, and of both Canadian and multinational corporations transferring their production south of the border.

Rather than dwelling on such matters, it is more important to go back to the basic reasons for our opposition to the agreement and the consequences as demonstrated so clearly in Charts 2 to 9 and in most of those that follow. There were many reasons for our opposition to the FTA, both in theory and then even more so when we belatedly had the opportunity to see the final agreement. Never did we ever imagine that Canada would give away so much for so little in return.

My own overriding concern was about where new investment would take place. (I shall come back to this in a moment.) Second, I was extremely worried about the basic theory of free trade. The theory assumes that in a bilateral arrangement, benefits will accrue if both countries are enjoying almost full employment. Yet Canada has had a consistently high number of unemployed compared with OECD averages. Since 1970, Canada's unemployment rate has been higher than the OECD average every single year, mostly because Canada is a branch-plant country. (This will be examined later, in the chapters on foreign investment and its impact on the Canadian economy.)

Thirdly, and this is very important, how can the basic economic theories of free trade possibly have any relevance when two-thirds to three-quarters of the two-way trade in many industries is conducted between parent companies and their subsidiaries or affiliates? Such trade has nothing whatsoever to do with free trade. It is essentially manipulated trade, where head office calls the shots and where prices and purchases are largely determined in the United States, as are profit levels and hence the place where taxes are to be paid. Since the United States has no comprehensive, universal medical-care system, and since overall it has grossly inferior social programs compared with those of Canada, then obviously its taxes will be lower than those in Canada; and, of course, the transnational or multinational corporation makes sure that profits materialize wherever taxes are lower.

More than half of Canada's manufacturing sector is made up of branch plants. That the majority of Canadian economists so hastily and enthusiastically jumped on the free trade bandwagon, without properly considering the fact that real free trade is impossible when so much of the trade is between related firms, speaks volumes about the quality of the economics being taught at Canadian universities. The blind, doctrinaire adherence to age-old Adam Smith economics is about as relevant in a branch-plant society as Madonna's presence in a nunnery.

Simply put, free trade can never work to Canada's advantage as long as so much of Canada is owned and controlled in the United States. The greatly relaxed investment provisions of the FTA exacerbate an already impossible situation. While it is true that many branch plants in Canada are closing shop and moving production to underutilized facilities in the United States, it is also true that new takeovers are intended to cement market control and diminish competition. (The chapter on U.S. investment in Canada deals with the resulting decreased employment and other economic ramifications.)

Fourthly, many Canadians were worried about Canada's ability to get a decent deal with the United States. We went down to Washington on bended knee. Cedric Ritchie put it well in August 1990: "Canada weakened its negotiating position with the U.S. by declaring repeatedly that a free trade agreement was essential for our economic future. This made failure politically unacceptable and.may have reduced our bargaining power." Exactly — except for the "may have."

There were many other good reasons why so many Canadians were apprehensive; but none of us, in our worst nightmares, ever dreamed that the Canadian government would sign as horrendously bad a deal as it did. When the text of the agreement was finally made public, those of us who had closely followed the negotiations were stunned by how many vital concessions Canada had made. The Americans got what they wanted, principally Canada's natural resources and the unimpeded right to buy up much of the rest of the country. Canadians got guaranteed access to integration with the United States.

As I mentioned above, my number-one concern was about where new investment would take place. The following story, along with Chart 9, pretty well sums it up. Shortly after the FTA went into effect, I spoke at a Service Club dinner in a small Ontario city. The person who drove me from my hotel in Toronto and back was a senior executive with a Canadian manufacturing firm that owned plants in four Canadian provinces. He said that soon after the agreement was signed, his company purchased a large factory in the southern United States. In Canada they paid an average of $16.00 an hour, plus benefits. In the U.S. they paid $6.50 an hour, with no benefits: no medicare, no pension plan, inferior unemployment protection, and no pregnancy leave for women; as well, working hours were longer, safety practices were almost nonexistent, and there was no air-conditioning in the factory. He said that if you saw how dreadful the conditions were in the washrooms, you simply wouldn't believe it. He then said, "Guess where all our new investment will be taking place. And guess where we'll be closing plants in the future."

Eric Kierans has put it as well as anyone:

> Think about the agreement in this way. Suppose your senior management comes to you with the following problem. . . . The FTA is in force. There is one economy. There are not two nations trading with each other. As Simon Reisman and the economists say, "lofty issues such as sovereignty and independence, national and cultural integrity . . . do not lend themselves to the analysis of hard facts." So, forget about Canada, forget about the United States, we are both in one playpen, one commercial sandbox, one market.

> Your management knows that it is in a new ballgame and wants your advice on an investment program for the next five years. Specifically, should the company expand its operations in Bramalea, Ontario, or build new facilities in Camden, New Jersey? Remember, you no longer have to think Canadian, i.e. East-West.

> 1) New Jersey — When you walk out your front door, there is a market of 100 million and more within a radius of 100-150 miles. Camden is the core of your market; Bramalea, the perimeter. Should you recommend locating in the heart of your market or on the outer rim, Bramalea, 500 miles north?

> 2) New Jersey — The climate is much less severe. Your building costs, annual heating costs will be much cheaper than in

Ontario. Your pro forma analysis makes clear that both over-head and operating costs will be cheaper in Camden.

3) New Jersey — Money is much more plentiful, cheaper and the banks are more risk-supportive than in Canada. Community banks are interested in their community. They go to you; they don't wait for you to go to them.

4) New Jersey — Transportation costs for the raw materials in to your plant and the finished products out are unbelievably cheaper. Would you prefer to ship 90% of your sales 500 miles to Camden from Bramalea or 10% of your sales 500 miles from Camden to Bramalea?

5) Taxes — Don't forget to take into consideration the cheaper tax rates on your company's profits. I doubt that many of you will advise the building of your plant 500 miles away from the core of your market. All in all, you will be about 20% more effi-cient, not smarter, in Camden than in Bramalea. (Speech, World Trade Centre, Halifax, N.S., 10 June 1988)

Here is David R. Beatty, president of Weston Foods, on the subject of what will happen to U.S. plants in Canada:

There is excess capacity in the U.S.; these are large-scale facili-ties in many segments; momentum will be to supply from the U.S. home base; you don't put the plant at the end of a spoke of the wheel but at the hub; you don't choose Winnipeg, you choose Raleigh, North Carolina. There will be a clear tilt towards U.S.-based manufacturing. The tilt is against the Canadian plant. The clear tilt, over the next decade, will be towards American sourcing. (Speech, Conference Board of Canada, 10 March 1988)

In all of the many debates I had between 1985 and 1988 with Richard Lipsey, Donald Macdonald, Wendy Dobson, Carl Beigie, John Crispo, and John Godfrey, among others, I never once heard a logical answer to the question as to why new investment would ever take place in Canada. Of course, there would be investment for takeovers of Canadian businesses to eliminate competition; but overall, as we have seen, domestic investment would inevitably decline sharply. Our harsher climate, our longer distances, our higher transportation costs, our higher taxes to pay for our vastly superior social programs, our smaller industrial base and smaller population, and the large U.S. ownership of our manufacturing sector would all mitigate against investment taking place in Canada.

This time, Simon Reisman is dead right. The true measure of the impact of the FTA on Canada's economy is indeed the investment climate created by the agreement. And if you want a good understanding of what the future holds for Canada, look again at Chart 9.

7

Prophets and Profits

Adam Smith Gone Haywire

> *Canadian companies have just gone through their most*
> *savage profits squeeze in more than 40 years, and now*
> *must face tough competition under free trade and a*
> *global economy while having little money to invest in*
> *their own competitiveness. . . . This wipeout has impli-*
> *cations beyond just the current poor returns to share-*
> *holders. Economists predict it could be years before*
> *investment in new plant and equipment begins rising*
> *again — even though upgraded technology and produc-*
> *tivity are needed now as the global economy becomes*
> *more competitive.*   FINANCIAL POST, *5 August 1991*

IT IS FASCINATING AND AT THE SAME TIME DISCOUR-
aging to watch how big business in Canada is now reacting
to the dismal economic results of the first three years of the
FTA. Chart 10 gives a pretty good indication of why there are
now so many second thoughts among some of the business
leaders who, at every possible Chamber of Commerce or
Board of Trade meeting, leapt so eagerly to the platform to
endorse an agreement of which most of them knew little or
nothing. The theory sounded great. What could possibly be
better than "guaranteed access to the giant U.S. market,"
along with substantially weakened powers for the federal
and provincial governments? The exchange rate was rarely

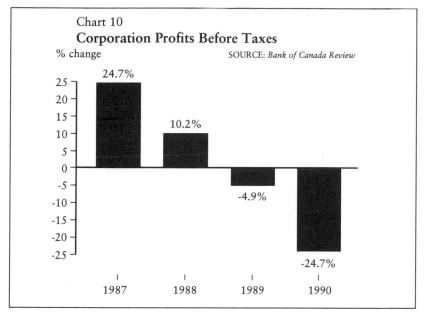

Chart 10
Corporation Profits Before Taxes
% change   SOURCE: *Bank of Canada Review*

24.7%

10.2%

-4.9%

-24.7%

1987   1988   1989   1990

mentioned; and when it was, we were promised that in a free market any problems would automatically resolve themselves. High interest rates and an inflated value for the Canadian dollar were apparently of no concern.

Looking back at the blind, bandwagon endorsement of the FTA by the Canadian business community, one can only be dismayed by how vacuous and naive much of their ideological rhetoric was. The average Canadian business person's enthusiasm for free trade was based almost entirely on a fuzzy concept of Adam Smith economics and skilful big business and government propaganda. Not one in a hundred business persons actually read the agreement. It was clear, from countless speeches, interviews, and articles from across Canada, that even many of the business "experts" who were called upon by the media for comment had little idea of the actual contents of the final signed documents.

But this murky myopia in itself does not tell the whole story. Can we, for example, expect that the branch-plant executives of U.S. corporations in Canada would have approached the debate about the FTA with any degree of freedom or objectivity? Yet many of these executives were in the forefront of the debate from 1985 right through 1988. Also, because of the huge amount of U.S. ownership in Canada, could we really expect, for example, that the owner of a Canadian oilfield service company would stand up and contradict the president of Imperial Oil (77 per cent owned in the U.S., 70 per cent by Exxon), or that he would contradict the president of Mobil Oil or Chevron or any other U.S.-controlled company? Not many business people go around speaking out against policies that are being forcefully proposed by their biggest customers, even if those policies are not in the Canadian interest. This vitally important aspect of the democratic consequences of a branch-plant society has, for reasons I find difficult to understand, been virtually ignored by Canadian political scientists and sociologists. The president of a large Canadian-owned auto parts manufacturer explained another major reason why so many Canadian business people failed to speak out against the agreement: "I would love to talk to the press," he said. "This deal is going to kill us. But if I say that, my board and our stockholders will murder me first. Our stock will drop like a rock."

The profit figures shown in Chart 10 are creating three reactions. Many businesses are simply moving to the United States or Mexico. Others are doing exactly what we predicted, explaining that they cannot afford the taxes required to pay for "our costly social programs": "We must lower wages and benefits. We must harmonize our taxes and other economic policies with the U.S." And so on. I shall return to this topic later, when discussing taxation and social spending in Canada. The point here is that, once again, we can see that the rhetoric before the FTA and the reality after it are far apart. The third reaction by business to the dismal profit figures is a growing and increasingly widespread understanding of how disastrous the FTA is for Canada and how inept the

Mulroney government is in its economic strategies — or absence thereof — and in its protection of Canada's interests.

As profits decline[1] and bankruptcies soar, the business community now represents a significant proportion of the growing discontent in all regions of Canada. The big business prophets who led the corporate charge towards free trade no longer convince the majority of the small and medium-size businesses across the country. The statistics tell the story for themselves. Not only are corporate profits down considerably, but business bankruptcies are at all-time record levels:

Before FTA		*After* FTA	
1987	7,371	1989	8,314
1988	7,721	1990	11,180

In the first six months of 1991 another 6947 Canadian businesses went under. The business prophets of free trade are much quieter these days.

8

The Phantom Consumer Savings

Paying More and Buying Less

> *Suppose you are building and furnishing a new home.*
> *Duty-free trade could save you up to $8,000 over present*
> *costs. . . . Extra money in your pocket will recycle through*
> *the economy. It will create thousands of new jobs. . . . All*
> *regions of Canada will benefit.*
> GOVERNMENT OF CANADA *pamphlet on the benefits of the* FTA, *1987*

> *Prices for a wide range of consumer goods will begin to*
> *decline, expanding the purchasing power of Canadian*
> *households.* DEPARTMENT OF FINANCE, *January 1988*

> *It will cut costs for our consumers on a wide range of*
> *imported goods and raise the living standards of all*
> *Canadians.* BRIAN MULRONEY, *election speech, October 1988*

D URING THE FREE TRADE DEBATE, THERE WERE
lavish promises on almost a daily basis about lower prices,
big consumer savings, reduced inflation, and the abundant
good life that would be certain to come with the trade agreement. Here are the Canadian inflation rates (consumer price
index) for the two years before the FTA and the two years
after:

Before FTA		After FTA	
1987	4.4%	1989	5.0%
1988	4.0%	1990	4.8%

Once again, this is not exactly what we were promised; and the consensus of economists forecasting inflation for 1991 was that it would jump to well over 6 per cent. For the previous seven years it had averaged only 4.4 per cent.

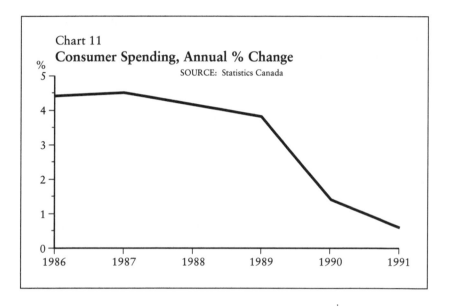

Chart 11
Consumer Spending, Annual % Change
SOURCE: Statistics Canada

Chart 11 takes another look at consumer "benefits." Note what happened to consumer spending once the FTA kicked in early in 1989. People who are unemployed do not spend very much. People with lowered standards of living tend to be careful spenders. People with little extra money do not buy a lot. People who are worried about their future are cautious.

Remember how Brian Mulroney, Pat Carney, John Crosbie, and Harvie Andre promised that a typical family furnishing a new house would save $8000 because of the FTA?

Well, let's just have a look at how housing starts in Canada have been affected:

Before FTA		After FTA	
1987	245,986	1989	215,382
1988	222,562	1990	181,630

People who can't afford to buy houses may not realize that they were supposed to save $8000 on the furnishings. On the other hand, those people who did buy and furnish houses in 1989, 1990, or 1991 can explain just how hollow the profuse promises were.

The same economic geniuses who brought us the FTA also brought us high interest rates and the GST. A high school student entering first-year economics could have predicted the impact on the cost of living. We now know that the Mulroney government either seriously miscalculated the impact on consumer prices or intentionally misled us. Take your choice.

Vastly increased cross-border shopping and declining retail sales in Canada are two of the results. From 1987 to 1990, automobile trips from Canada to the United States doubled from 3 million to some 6 million, and cross-border spending jumped from $800 million to some $2 billion. Retail sales in Canada are a disaster. Thousands of retail employees have lost their jobs. The ripple effect into the wholesale industry and domestic manufacturing has had a devastating impact on the entire Canadian economy.

9

Trick or Trade?

Canada's Merchandise Trade Balances

> *The economic benefits from the free trade agreement will start to be realized shortly after the implementation of the agreement on Jan. 1, 1989.* DEPARTMENT OF FINANCE, *January 1988*
>
> *No other nation has this degree of security of access to the huge U.S. market, nor is likely to get it.*
> THE CANADIAN ALLIANCE FOR TRADE AND JOB OPPORTUNITIES,
> *lauding the* FTA *in cross-Canada newspaper supplements*
> *during the 1988 federal election campaign*

W E NOW KNOW THAT CANADA DID NOT GAIN anything close to secure access to the U.S. market. We also know that no one bothered to explain to the Alliance and friends that the U.S. might have similar plans to involve Mexico in free trade discussions.

As previously mentioned, the bilateral agreement with the United States was sold to Canadians as an agreement about trade. We also now know that it was very much more comprehensive and included many important areas which, according to long-standing rules and definitions of the General Agreement on Tariffs and Trade (GATT), are not normally associated with a trade agreement. Nevertheless, let us take a look at how Canada has fared in its merchandise trade since the agreement went into effect.

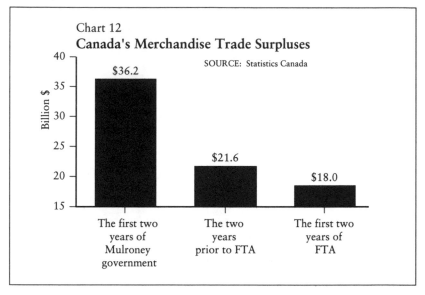

Chart 12
Canada's Merchandise Trade Surpluses

SOURCE: Statistics Canada

Chart 12 shows Canada's merchandise trade surpluses since 1984. It is a portrait of policy failure. Contrary to reports published by the Royal Bank of Canada and the Canada West Foundation, and contrary to recent statements by Michael Wilson, our country has clearly been a big loser. In the first two years of free trade, our merchandise trade surplus declined by 20 per cent compared with the previous two-year period; and compared with the merchandise surplus for the first two years of the Mulroney government, the decline was a whopping 50 per cent.

Chart 13 looks only at Canada-U.S. trade; here, the first two years of the FTA brought a 7 per cent decline in Canada's merchandise trade surplus from the previous two years, and a decline of 25 per cent from the surplus of the first two years of Mulroney government. Incidentally, it is important to understand that Canada *must* have large merchandise surpluses to help pay for the enormous costs of foreign investment in the country (more about this shortly). Consequently, the declining merchandise surpluses under the FTA are ominous. In 1984, when Brian Mulroney became prime minister,

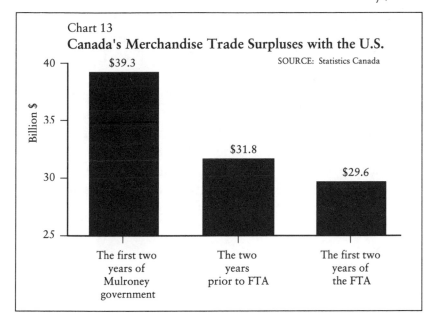

Chart 13
Canada's Merchandise Trade Surpluses with the U.S.
SOURCE: Statistics Canada

Canada's share of total world exports was 5.1 per cent. By 1990, it was down to 3.8 per cent.

Sombre as this trend may be, it is really much worse when "ownership-based" trade balances or "product presence" is considered. A far more important measurement of real national balances would include not only imports and exports but also local sales by U.S. companies located in Canada and by Canadian companies located in the United States. This "product presence" merchandise trade balance measurement would substantially erode or completely wipe out our supposed trade surpluses with the United States.

Two-way trade between Canada and the U.S. should also be measured in terms of jobs created and jobs lost. Our large trade surplus in crude products that produce comparatively few jobs — and our large deficit in labour-intensive finished products — substantially reduce our apparent trade benefits. This is, of course, a very different picture from the down-on-our-knees trade-dependent perspective presented to Canadians throughout the free trade debate. The importance of trade as a net job producer in Canada has been greatly exaggerated and is a far cry from the 25 per cent or one-third of all Canadian jobs so frequently cited by Peter Lougheed and other free trade advocates.

At all events, simply by looking at the figures for our merchandise trade balances it is clear that Canada has been the loser since the FTA went into effect. Most Canadians thought it was supposed to be the other way around. Wasn't the FTA supposed to *increase* our trade balances? Or were we just supposed to rationalize our industries and lose not only trade surpluses but jobs as well?

10

Forgetting about the Mortgage Payments

The Real Bottom Line of Trade

> For a nation to judge its changing international economic
> situation by looking only at the trade flows in its merchan-
> dise account, instead of at its entire current account, is as
> foolish as it would be for a family, in determining its
> changing financial situation, to consider only its purchases
> and sales of merchandise, while ignoring such things as its
> mortgage payments and all other payments and receipts for
> services.   BRUCE WILKINSON, economist, 16 July 1991

MOST PEOPLE THINK OF TRADE BETWEEN NATIONS
in terms of merchandise trade: automobiles, appliances, oil,
computers, wheat, forest products, and so on. But that is like
looking at the balance in your bank account only in terms of
the cheques you deposit and not the cheques you write. It
would be great if you could get away with it. The real comprehensive bottom line of trade is the current account balance, which is the all-inclusive balance of merchandise trade
plus "invisibles" (various forms of money and service transactions flowing in and out of the country). It is like the balance in your bank account. If you have a deficit in your bank
account, you have to find funds to eliminate it. Similarly,
when a country has a current account deficit, it must also

find a solution; but it has only two options: either to borrow money from abroad or to sell off part of the country to non-residents. In either case, balancing the current account will automatically become more difficult the following year.

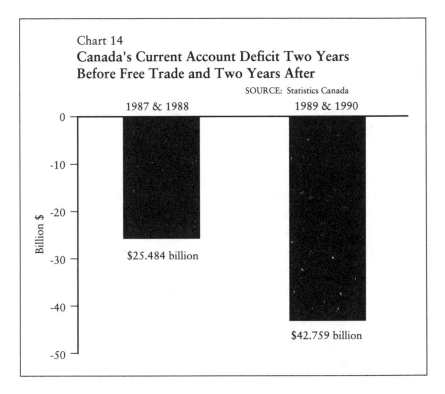

Chart 14
Canada's Current Account Deficit Two Years Before Free Trade and Two Years After

SOURCE: Statistics Canada

1987 & 1988   1989 & 1990

$25.484 billion

$42.759 billion

Chart 14 shows the huge deterioration in Canada's current account, a sharply increased deficit in the first two years of free trade of more than 67 per cent compared with the two years before the agreement went into effect. This represents a very serious decline. Chart 15, which looks at Canada's current account balance with the United States, also shows an ominous decline. Persistent current account deficits inevitably lead to even more serious problems in the future.[1] While the current account is the real bottom line of trade, the real bottom line of large current account deficits is a lower standard of living.

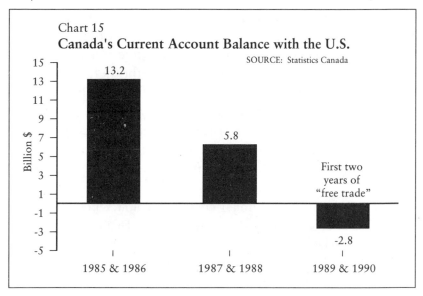

Chart 15
Canada's Current Account Balance with the U.S.

SOURCE: Statistics Canada

Billion $

13.2

5.8

First two
years of
"free trade"

-2.8

1985 & 1986   1987 & 1988   1989 & 1990

Canada had current account surpluses, not deficits, in the year Brian Mulroney became prime minister and in the two previous years. By contrast, our total current account deficit for the first two years of free trade has been Canada's worst-ever two-year performance, by far. The year Brian Mulroney became prime minister, Canada had a $6.7 billion current account surplus with the United States; but in the first two years of free trade, we had our first consecutive current account deficits with the U.S. since the recession years of 1981 and 1982.

The $42.759 billion current account deficit for the past two years translates into more than 1 million jobs. Another major problem is that the large current account deficits mean more reliance on foreign capital and more control of Canada by non-Canadians. But as we shall see in the following chapters, the dominant contributor to our current account deficits is the heavy cost of servicing foreign investment, foreign ownership, and foreign control in Canada.

The process is like a rapidly quickening, rapidly deepening whirlpool. Canada has been sucked into the swirling waters, and our current political and business leadership seems determined to adopt every conceivable policy that will drown the country. For each of the past five years, Canada's current account deficits have exceeded the deficits for any previous years in the nation's history. The ramifications of large current account deficits are clearly spelled out by Dr. Douglas Peters, senior vice-president and chief economist of the Toronto-Dominion Bank, consistently the most astute and articulate of all bank economists in Canada:

> [The] increased international current account represents the increase in debt that Canadians owe abroad. That debt will one day have to be paid in real goods and services, which will reduce Canadians' real standard of living. Those debts are not the same as ones incurred to finance the federal fiscal deficit, because the federal fiscal deficit comprises debt owed largely by Canadians to Canadians. The difference is that, when Canadians repay debts owed abroad, they must reduce their standard of living; whereas repaying the fiscal deficit only shifts income among Canadians. (Paper presented to Standing Committee on Finance, House of Commons, 26 March 1991)

11

Open for Business and Up for Sale

Foreign Ownership, Foreign Investment, and Foreign Control

Free Trade with the United States would be like sleeping with an elephant. If it rolls over, you're a dead man. And I'll tell you when it's going to roll over. It's going to roll over in a time of economic depression and they're going to crank up those plants in Georgia and North Carolina and Ohio, and they're going to be shutting them down up here.

BRIAN MULRONEY, PC *leadership campaign, 1983*

As American investment takes over more of the Canadian economy, the transactions between parents and branch plants may grow, but this is not trade. . . . When one is exchanging with oneself or with someone not at arm's length, one cannot call it trade.

ERIC KIERANS, *House of Commons Committee on External Affairs and International Trade, 3 December 1987*

W E HAVE ALREADY SEEN WHY FREE TRADE THEORY goes out of "the window of opportunity" when trade is largely between parent companies and their subsidiaries or affiliates. Yet as soon as Brian Mulroney became prime minister, he headed straight south to Wall Street to explain to the Americans that his government was going to be much more accommodating to American investment. In a speech to some seven hundred American corporate leaders at the Economic Club in New York in December 1984, our prime minister said that Canada's policies relating to investment had been excessively restrictive and prohibitive but that he intended to change all that forthwith. He received a very warm response, indeed "wave after wave" of applause.

In 1984, before the prime minister declared Canada "open for business," foreign-controlled corporations already received 43.3 per cent of all non-financial industry corporate profits and 53.2 per cent of the profits of the top 500 non-financial corporations in Canada.

Chart 16
Foreign Profits in Canadian Industry: 1985

MINERAL FUELS	68%
TOTAL MINING	68%
FOOD PROCESSING & PACKAGING	53%
TOBACCO PRODUCTS	100%
RUBBER PRODUCTS	84%
TEXTILE MILLS	45%
PAPER & ALLIED INDUSTRIES	39%
PRIMARY METALS	46%
MACHINERY	63%
TRANSPORTATION EQUIPMENT	94%
ELECTRICAL PRODUCTS	67%
NON-METALLIC MINERAL PRODUCTS	71%
PETROLEUM & COAL PRODUCTS	47%
CHEMICALS & CHEMICAL PRODUCTS	87%

In 1987 the official figures for foreign ownership in Canada for 1985 were finally published. Chart 16 (which is based on statistics in the Corporations and Labour Unions Returns Act Report for 1985) lists the share of profits that foreign corporations took in various Canadian industries that year. If these figures are of a country that was "closed to business" and hostile to foreign investment, as Mr. Mulroney suggested, one wonders what goals the new prime minister had in mind when he abolished the Foreign Investment Review Agency and replaced it with the toothless and prone Investment Canada.

For as long as I can remember, most of the business press in Canada has been continentalist (with the notable exception of the *Toronto Star* and Southam's Don McGillivray), and one consistent message has been that Canadians need not be concerned with the levels of foreign ownership and control in the country. Well, Canadians should best judge for themselves. The latest official figures for the foreign-controlled share of corporate profits are for 1987, and in that year 50 per cent of all manufacturing profits went to foreign-controlled corporations. Of the top 500 corporations in Canada, 49 per cent were foreign-controlled. And, of course, these 1987 figures now understate the degree of foreign control. Since Brian Mulroney became prime minister, the levels of foreign ownership have increased every single year.

Habitually, whenever foreign takeovers threatened in Europe, the Europeans spoke of the dangers of "the Canadian disease." Canada has consistently had rates of foreign ownership and control that would simply not be tolerated in other developed nations — or, increasingly, in any of the developing nations. Certainly, the Americans would never accept rates of foreign ownership and control that are even remotely similar to those of Canada.

Chart 17 shows some comparative levels of foreign ownership in 1989. Bear in mind that 1990 saw a record growth in foreign direct investment in Canada, almost all of it for the takeover of businesses in this country. Unfortunately, it will be some time in 1993 (after the next federal election) before we shall learn from our government in Ottawa exactly what the level of foreign ownership, control, and profits was in 1990. However, we do know that when the figures are at length published, they will show large increases in each industrial category.

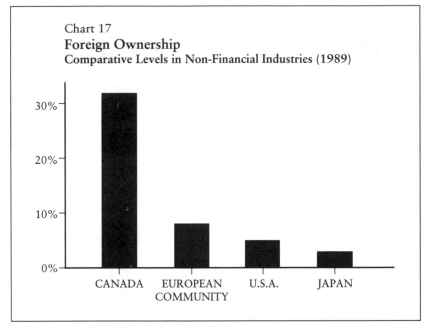

Chart 17
Foreign Ownership
Comparative Levels in Non-Financial Industries (1989)

In 1965, George Grant published his influential book *Lament for a Nation*, which was subtitled "The Defeat of Canadian Nationalism." Grant eloquently and sadly proclaimed that U.S. dominance had reached the point where it prevented Canadians from building the more independent, ordered society they had so long aspired to. For Grant, it was already too late. Canada had ceased to be a nation capable of controlling its own future. Chart 18 shows Canada's foreign indebtedness compared with gross domestic product (GDP) in the year Grant wrote his *Lament*, and it also shows the level at the end of the first year of the FTA. At the end of 1990, Canada's net international investment position (the amount we owe non-residents over and above what they owe us) was more than $259 billion.[1] When George Grant wrote his book in 1965, it was less than $22 billion.

A look at the summer 1991 issue of the *Financial Post 500* provides an insight into how much Canadian ownership and control has deteriorated since Brian Mulroney became prime

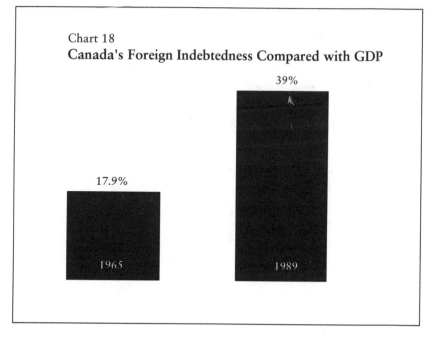

Chart 18
Canada's Foreign Indebtedness Compared with GDP

39%

17.9%

1965   1989

minister. Of the largest 500 companies in Canada, 54 per cent (268) are 100 per cent foreign-owned. Another 88 are partially foreign-owned.

12

Investment Canada

The Ultimate Hypocrisy

> *For a decade, Canadian legislation in the form of the*
> *Foreign Investment Review Agency (FIRA) had been sub-*
> *jected to vicious and unparalleled attacks by the American*
> *press, by American corporate associations and by*
> *Washington itself.*
>   *We believed it when they called us xenophobic and*
> *chauvinistic. A simple desire to control one's own economy*
> *(is this not what a state is for?) was equated to nationalism*
> *(which is true) and nationalism was equated to xenophobia*
> *(which is false). Despite the fact that Canada ranks far*
> *ahead of other industrialized nations in the proportion of*
> *its resource and manufacturing sectors that are foreign-*
> *controlled, charges of economic chauvinism and protec-*
> *tionism continue unabated.*   ERIC KIERANS, *Policy Options, 1986*

SINCE INVESTMENT CANADA BEGAN OPERATIONS IN
1985, it has approved the takeover of thousands of companies. The agency is both a farce and a national disgrace.
Perhaps a better definition would be the term commonly
used for those who oversee street solicitors (and I don't mean
lawyers). The agency's "investment counsellors" solicit new
foreign investment in Canada in forty-eight cities in twenty-
three different countries, including nineteen cities in the

United States. As the new finance minister, Donald Mazankowski, said in his debut speech to Wall Street: "We have transformed a Foreign Investment Review Agency, that was often hostile to investment from abroad, into an investment promotion agency."

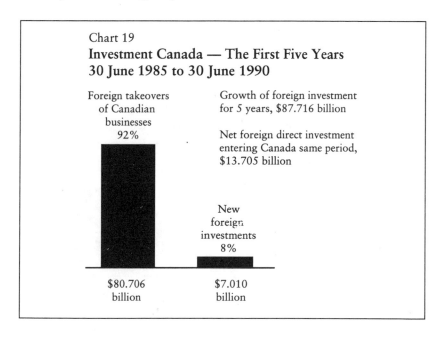

Chart 19
Investment Canada — The First Five Years
30 June 1985 to 30 June 1990

Foreign takeovers of Canadian businesses 92%

Growth of foreign investment for 5 years, $87.716 billion

Net foreign direct investment entering Canada same period, $13.705 billion

New foreign investments 8%

$80.706 billion

$7.010 billion

Now, let us look closely at Chart 19. In the first five years of Investment Canada, the agency reported almost $88 billion in foreign investment activity. A startling 92 per cent was for the takeover of businesses in Canada, while only 8 per cent was in the form of new foreign business investment. Clearly, Canada is not "open for business": it is up for sale. There were 3374 companies in Canada taken over during this five-year period and, incredibly, not one single takeover was rejected.

Note that during these five years, a total of less than $14 billion in net direct investment capital actually came into Canada to finance this massive new foreign presence in the Canadian economy. Contrary to long-established myth, the

vast majority of the money used by non-Canadians to buy up
our country comes from Canada itself, not from foreign
countries. The next three charts are so startling that some
readers may find them difficult to believe. Unfortunately, they
are accurate and are based entirely on official government figures. (The best source for balance of payments information is
Statistics Canada Catalogue 67-001, issued quarterly.)

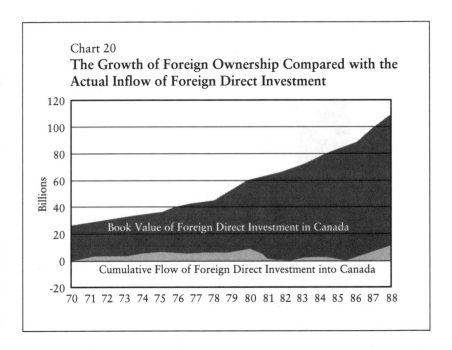

Chart 20
**The Growth of Foreign Ownership Compared with the
Actual Inflow of Foreign Direct Investment**

Chart 20 shows the *cumulative* (not the annual) net flow of
foreign direct investment[1] into Canada from 1970 to 1988
and the growth in the book value of foreign direct investment
during the same period. The relatively flat thin line at the bottom, beginning just above the 0 in the lower left, represents
the cumulative net *total* of foreign direct investment entering
Canada from all countries (gross inflows, less outflows of foreign direct investment). In contrast, the book value of foreign
ownership heads straight uphill towards $120 billion. Using
only a tiny amount of their own imported money, foreign cor-

porations have bought up many of the key sectors of the Canadian economy.

From the end of World War II to the end of 1987, the cumulative net inflow of foreign direct investment into Canada was only $17 billion, but the book value of foreign direct investment in Canada was over $100.27 billion. It is important to understand that the book value figures employed to measure foreign ownership in Canada vastly understate the true magnitude of the foreign presence in the Canadian economy. Foreign ownership has been a factor in the economy for decades. In many cases, the book value figures represent only a small fraction of the current market value. Moreover, while foreign takeovers are recorded at the book value, the actual acquisitions are often at multiples of the book value price.

As well, it must be noted that foreign-controlled investment is significantly higher than foreign direct investment. For example, at the end of 1986, foreign direct investment in Canada was $92.4 billion, but foreign-controlled investment was more than $135.5 billion. (Figures beyond 1986 are not yet available.) In short, Canada has a much greater foreign presence in its economy than the perspective that is often presented. (It is interesting to note that most of the business press in Canada studiously ignores the subject of market value and foreign-controlled investment but concentrates on the lowest possible measurement — book value — when comparing U.S. investment in Canada with Canadian investment in the United States.)

By the end of March 1991, Investment Canada had allowed 3869 acquisitions without rejecting a single takeover.[2] Of the total foreign activity amounting to more than $100.518 billion, takeovers amounted to 92.7 per cent and new business investment only 7.3 per cent. Clearly, rather than protecting the national interest, Investment Canada has been peddling the country.[3]

13

Free Trade and American Ownership of Canada

The Impossible Combination

> *A free trade agreement which includes investment will not
> be acceptable to the United States.*
> BRUCE SMART, *U.S. Department of Commerce, April 1987*

> *The investment issues are not on the table; they might
> never be on the table.* JOE CLARK, *House of Commons, May 1987*

> *This agreement will provide enormous benefits for the
> United States. It will remove all Canadian tariffs, secure
> improved access to Canada's market for our manufactur-
> ing, agriculture, high technology and financial sectors, and
> improve our security through additional access to
> Canadian energy supplies. We have also gained important
> investment opportunities in Canada.*
> *I congratulate Prime Minister Mulroney.*
> RONALD REAGAN *after the signing of the* FTA

CHART 21 IS STARTLING. HERE WE SEE THE REMARK-
able figures for U.S. direct investment in Canada from the
end of World War II to the end of 1990. I have yet to show
these figures to a single person who has not found them
astonishing, because they so directly fly in the face of the

Chart 21
Summary of U.S. Direct Investment in Canada since World War II (1946-1990 Inclusive)

	$billion
Net flow of U.S. direct investment into Canada	6.631
Dividend payments from Canada to the U.S.	69.460
Growth in the book value of U.S. direct investment in Canada	76.710

taken-for-granted, long-standing conventional wisdom in Canada about how "dependent" we are on U.S. investment. Even more remarkable are the figures in the table below, which shows U.S. investment in Canada during the Mulroney years.

	Net flow of direct investment from the U.S. to Canada ($ billion)	Dividend payments from Canada to the U.S. ($ billion)	Increase in the book value of U.S. investment in Canada ($ billion)
1984	0.801	3.528	4.909
1985	–2.841	4.345	2.658
1986	–1.464	5.294	1.012
1987	1.770	3.996	4.599
1988	0.148	7.760	1.146
1989	1.239	4.972	3.095
1990	1.480	5.651	3.290
	1.133	35.546	20.709

Summary

Net amount of investment inflow to Canada from the U.S.	$ 1.133 billion
Total profits sent to the U.S., plus the growth in the book value of U.S. ownership of Canada	$56.255 billion

(Source: Statistics Canada Catalogue 67-202)

For generations, Canadians have been force-fed the myth of Canadian dependency on U.S. investment. Federal and provincial politicians, continentalist economists, chambers of commerce, and boards of trade, as well as the many foreign-dominated industry organizations such as the Canadian Petroleum Association and the Canadian Manufacturers' Association, all have impressed on us the idea that we are heavily reliant on U.S. investment capital to sustain our standard of living and to create new opportunities for the future.

Large foreign corporations operating in Canada are major contributors to continentalist think tanks and research institutes (such as the C.D. Howe Institute) which publish a steady stream of right-wing studies that are about as objective as the people who finance them. Unfortunately, most of the press in Canada report these publications extensively, rarely questioning their validity or the motivations behind them. It is reasonable to say that the myth of Canada's heavy dependency on foreign capital has originated, at least in part, from the very foreign corporations that are in control of so many of the vital sectors of the Canadian economy and, thanks to Brian Mulroney, are now rapidly expanding that control. At the same time, anyone who believes that the U.S. State Department and various other U.S. government agencies are not actively involved in perpetuating this myth is hopelessly naive.

In Chart 21 we can see that the net inflow of American direct investment into Canada during the past forty-five years has been under $7 billion. But during the same period, the dividend payments (profits) flowing from Canada to the United States amounted to almost $70 billion! In other words, for every $1 billion of net inflow of U.S. direct investment into Canada, we sent back to the U.S. more than $10 billion in dividends. At the same time, the growth in the book value of U.S. ownership of Canada was almost $77 billion up to the end of 1990. The real market value of U.S. control in Canada is probably closer to some $130 billion.

To summarize, only $6.6 billion came in, a huge $69.5 billion went out, and well over $100 billion more of Canada became controlled by Americans.

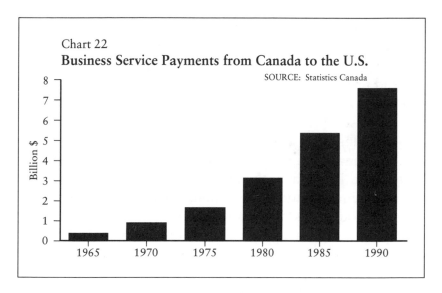

Chart 22
Business Service Payments from Canada to the U.S.

SOURCE: Statistics Canada

As devastating as these figures are, the situation is in fact even worse. American companies in Canada buy a very large percentage of their goods and services from the United States, mostly from their parent companies or their affiliates. In business services alone (see Chart 22) Canada has an increasing deficit with the United States. For example, in the decade 1971-80 inclusive, Canada's business services deficit with the U.S. was $10.883 billion. In the following decade, 1981-90, the deficit increased by more than 155 per cent to $27.791 billion.[1] (Note that none of the figures in this chapter include the billions of dollars in interest payments that leave Canada each year.) In 1988, of all business services payments to the United States, some 70 per cent were made by U.S.-controlled companies. Overall, foreign-controlled firms in Canada purchase some 80 per cent of their foreign business services from their parent companies or affiliates.

Among the many business services that end up producing jobs in the United States instead of in Canada are automotive industry R & D and tooling, consulting and management services, accounting and data processing, advertising, transportation-related services, airline transactions, broker and agent commissions, insurance, promotional and financial services, equipment rentals, communications, and refining and processing.

Dismal as this picture is, it is but the tip of the iceberg when transfer pricing is considered. Transfer pricing is probably the single most important undiscussed economic problem in Canada. Since total taxes are lower in the United States than in Canada, the head offices of U.S. corporations charge their operations in Canada whatever they possibly can for goods and services so that profits show up in the U.S. rather than in Canada. Such charges obviously make mockery of theories of free trade and market economics. Wherever possible, the costs of parts and components and of advertising services, accounting services, management services, and so on — all determined by head office in the United States — are set in such a way as to minimize profits in Canada. The economic impact on Canada is enormous and, of course, is unknown to the public and, for the most part, unknown to the government, too. Some three-quarters of Canada-U.S. trade in manufactured goods is in the form of non-arm's-length commercial transactions between parent corporations and their subsidiaries or affiliates.

About ten years ago an official of Revenue Canada, testifying before a House of Commons committee, suggested that if Revenue Canada were given a few more staff, it could easily return to the government some $4 billion in "monkey-business" transfer pricing. Since then, there has been a dramatic expansion in the value of two-way commercial intercourse between parent companies and subsidiaries in the United States and Canada. I believe that much of the federal government's annual, burdensome deficit could be wiped out if Revenue Canada and the federal government properly addressed the question of parent-subsidiary transfer pricing.[2] Lorraine Eden, an expert on transfer pricing from Carleton University, has commented:

> In Canada, over half of our imports and exports involve transfer pricing. Autos trade may be as high as 90 per cent. . . . Overinvoicing imports, head office fees and interest costs are ways firms can shift profits abroad and reduce Canadian taxes. Fancy methods such as double dipping, the Dutch treat, butterflies, and the rhythm method keep the tax authorities busy trying to plug loopholes.[3]

That more than half of Canada's imports and exports likely involve transfer pricing has immense ramifications. In 1990, Canada's total imports and exports were almost $334 billion, so only a modest 10 per cent transfer-pricing manipulation would amount to almost $17 billion.

Beyond the issue of the transfer pricing of goods and services, there is other parent-subsidiary manipulation that sucks profits out of Canada before those profits are subject to Canadian taxes. An example is the conduct of Canada Safeway Ltd. and its U.S. parent, as reported in the *Calgary Herald* (2 April 1991):

> Canada Safeway Ltd. says its profits dropped 23 per cent in 1990 from the previous year because of a large dividend payment to its U.S. parent company. . . .
>
> The company [Canada Safeway] reported its interest expenses rose to $52.5 million last year from $16.9 million in 1989. The increase resulted from the assumption of $484 million in debt which partially funded the dividend of $538.7 million paid to parent company Safeway Inc., of Oakland, California . . . .
>
> The dividend . . . is to provide long-term tax benefits to the parent company.

So Canada Safeway, on sales of $4.3 billion, declares a substantially decreased net profit amounting to 1.7 per cent of sales. The 1990 annual report of Canada Safeway states: "The debt restructuring and the related dividend is providing long-term tax benefits to the parent." There is nothing shy about Safeway! And guess who it is that gets to make up the government's lost tax revenue in Canada. It's you, the person holding this book, and other members of the Canadian public. Anyone who believes that Safeway is an exceptional case is naive. Profits leave Canada untaxed every day, and it is the average Canadian who pays to "provide long-term tax benefits to the parent company" in Oakland and the like. "The like" dominates the industrial structure of Canada.

Of course, these billions of dollars of lost tax revenue automatically raise taxes for all Canadians. Nor is the lost revenue recirculated in the Canadian economy. The enormous cumulative effects of the tiny real inflow of foreign direct investment, the hemorrhaging outflow, the expanding foreign control, the billions in lost revenue, the artificial pricing, and the lost business opportunities for Canadians are a suffocating combination. Brian Mulroney's Free Trade Agreement (Chapter 16, articles 1601-11) locks us forever into an escalating American takeover of our country, with its debilitating consequences.

Over and beyond the severe economic consequences, there are other crucial elements to this pervasive process that are becoming more and more pronounced in Canada every year. First, massive U.S. ownership of Canada[4] obviously brings with it a heavy degree of mandatory economic integration, whether we like it or not. A generation ago, if a Canadian finance minister stood up in the House of Commons and suggested that it was obvious that our basic monetary policies of necessity had to be closely tied to those in the United States, he would have been hooted out of the Commons in derision. In recent years, our finance ministers (including Jean Chrétien in 1979) have made it clear that Canada's interest rate policies are largely determined by monetary policy in Washington.

Beyond this, one of the most important impacts of the FTA is that now big business in Canada is saying that we have no choice: we must also follow U.S. taxation and spending policies. Heavy U.S. ownership of Canada makes independent monetary policy out of the question. The FTA means economic integration with the U.S., and it takes us well down the road of harmonized fiscal policies, too. Harmonized fiscal policies mean the end of Canada's social programs and the end of the Canada which the vast majority of Canadians want to preserve.

The most important aspects of the growing American ownership and control of our country go beyond balance of payments and other economic questions. If we continue to sell off ownership and control of our manufacturing industries, natural resources, retail and wholesale companies, forests and farms, hotels and resorts, high-tech and advertising firms, transportation and communications companies, and our other assets, what exactly will be left for our children? Brian Mulroney's Canada of the future seems little more than a place where our children will have the splendid opportunity of growing up as tenants in a country that should have been their own. How will we explain to them that, unlike people anywhere else, we have sold their birthright and the land and resources that should have been theirs?

14

The Biggest Myth of All

Foreign Investment and Jobs for Canadians

> *Doubleday told its Canadian employees that warehousing, marketing and editorial jobs were being moved to the U.S.*
> FINANCIAL TIMES, *3 June 1991*

> *Carbide shifts jobs south. . . . U.S.-owned Union Carbide Canada Ltd. is partially withdrawing from Canada and will close its Toronto head office and Edmonton plastics plant in coming weeks. There will be a president of Canadian operations but he will reside in Connecticut at Union Carbide's head office, [a] Union Carbide spokesman said.*
> FINANCIAL POST, *4 June 1991*

> *Uniroyal Goodrich Tire Co. will close one or perhaps both of its Canadian tire manufacturing plants, throwing up to 2,000 people out of work, the [Akron, Ohio-based] company said yesterday.*
> GLOBE AND MAIL, *5 June 1991*

NOTE THE DATES ON THE ABOVE QUOTATIONS. They were selected from newspapers just as this chapter was being written. Since then, there have been dozens more examples of the same process at work. Since the beginning of the FTA, scores of plants across Canada have closed forever. As noted in earlier chapters, this was hardly what we were promised. The Mulroney government and the Business

Council on National Issues (BCNI) had their own agenda. But unfortunately, many other Canadians bought the theory of free trade hook, line, and sinker. Had they known more about the built-in economic consequences of a branch-plant economy, perhaps they would have been far less credulous.

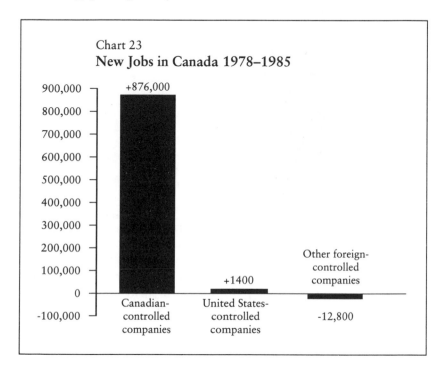

Chart 23
New Jobs in Canada 1978–1985

Chart 23 shows who it was that has created all the new jobs in Canada in recent years. While foreign corporations in Canada were taking about one-third of all profits in this country — and doing so during a period when they managed to double their profits here — they actually reduced their employment in Canada. Meanwhile, Canadian-controlled firms were creating almost 900,000 jobs. Chart 24 is even more dramatic. In some respects, it is the most telling illustration in this book. Moreover, if the left-hand bar on the graph were drawn to scale compared to the right-hand bar, it would extend for pages. What a remarkable comparison!

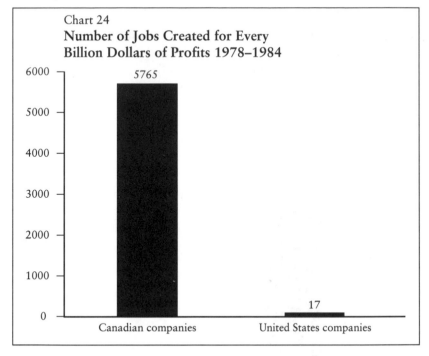

Chart 24
**Number of Jobs Created for Every
Billion Dollars of Profits 1978–1984**

Canadians have always been told what a great benefit for-eign investment has been. Even some of those who recognize the huge costs involved reluctantly still defend foreign invest-ment because, they say, "at least it creates jobs." But usually, when American companies come into Canada to take over Canadian firms, they soon begin to transfer research and development back to the United States, as well as much of their advertising and design. Many even do their payroll back in the U.S., and much or most of their data processing. When times get tough and cutbacks are in order, more jobs end up back at head office or in a plant in the U.S. that is operating at less than capacity.[1] Canadians get to do some assembling; but, more and more, Canada becomes simply a distributing centre for goods that are researched, designed, and produced in other countries — where the jobs are. Foreign ownership and foreign control, most of which is American, do not pro-vide Canadians with jobs, as our politicians and many foreign corporations are so prone to tell us; on the contrary, they rob Canadians of jobs. Foreign ownership is one of the major reasons why Canada's unemployment rates are so consistently high compared with OECD averages.[2]

The high unemployment that comes with heavy foreign ownership and foreign control means high unemployment insurance costs, high welfare payments, lower tax revenue for government, and an economy that functions at levels well below any realistic capacities and expectations. It also means that Canada's ability to compete in an increasingly competitive world is severely restrained. The higher costs of unemployment and welfare and the lower tax revenue combine to increase the national debt. The increasing national debt and our self-defeating high interest rate policies curtail our ability to provide government services, including the universal social programs which Canadians have developed and have become accustomed to. The increasing costs of servicing the debt destroy the opportunity to use public funds to help private or public corporations develop new, innovative, and competitive industries.

Once again, we are caught in a rapidly quickening, rapidly deepening economic whirlpool. Brian Mulroney and his doctrinaire Conservative, continentalist policies are turning Canada into a warehouse economy. As the FTA matures, even the warehouses will be in Buffalo, Minneapolis, and Seattle, on the other side of the border. (Witness, for example, the recent speculation that the Bay might be forced to locate its warehouses in the United States.)

Job creation in Canada is not a goal of foreign corporations. But it is their goal to maximize profits outside Canada.[3] The propensity of foreign firms to purchase their parts and components and their services, as well as machinery and equipment, from outside Canada severely damages the development of the Canadian economy. In most cases, the subsidiaries or branch plants simply have no choice — head office gives the orders. The excuse is sometimes made that "we've gone wherever we can in Canada looking for suppliers," but the record clearly speaks for itself. In industry after industry, foreign corporations purchase three, four, or five times more from outside Canada than Canadian firms do on a comparative basis, and their purchases are mostly from their parent company or an affiliate.

The effects of this are all too obvious. Many long-established Canadian industries that should be able to purchase their capital goods domestically are dependent on imported machinery and equipment. At the same time, Canadian companies are frequently simply out of luck when trying to sell to foreign-controlled corporations based in Canada, even if their prices are competitive and their products equal or superior to those of the U.S. suppliers.

The negative impact of foreign ownership was discussed in the 1972 Gray Report. Other studies and recent developments have added to the picture of economic truncation that accompanies excessive foreign ownership and foreign control. The list is long and dismaying:

- Most foreign subsidiaries do not even attempt to compete for export opportunities.
- Jobs are transferred out of Canada to head office or other affiliated locations.
- Parts and components and services are purchased from the parent company or from affiliates outside Canada at non-arm's-length, manipulated prices.
- R & D performance of branch plants is dismal.
- Most key decisions about plant openings and closings, wages, conditions of work, investments, etc., are made outside Canada.
- Management development in Canada is truncated. A report from the *Financial Times* of September 1989 is an example:

No one can say that Michael Sanderson wasn't prepared to fight to the end. For months, the chairman and president of Merrill

Lynch Canada Inc. wrestled with his New York bosses over the fate of his operation. The U.S. owners wanted more Canadian decisions made on Wall Street; Sanderson wanted them made on Bay Street. . . . But defeat was inevitable. Last month head office told Sanderson to fire 25 corporate-finance professionals, arguing that much of the work could be handled in New York.

The more foreign ownership and foreign control increase in Canada, the more there will inevitably be:

- fewer jobs for Canadians;[4]
- poorer jobs for Canadians;
- less diversification of exports;
- fewer jobs for engineers, researchers, advertising agencies, data processors, and many other professions;
- more and more money flowing out of Canada to pay dividends and business service payments;
- more and more imports of goods and services that should have been sourced in Canada;
- increasing failure to develop new competitive products in Canada; and
- more and more decisions made outside Canada about wages, investment, purchases, dividends, financial arrangements, charitable donations, firing and hiring, advertising strategies, and numerous other decisions that typify the way a branch-plant economy operates.[5]

There is an easy way to sum up the economic impact of heavy ownership in Canada. It is no accident that Canada has consistently high, chronic levels of unemployment compared with OECD averages and, as we shall see, such a steadily weakening ability to be competitive. But the harmful effects are not only economic, for heavy foreign ownership brings with it profound political and cultural consequences.

Excessive foreign ownership and control severely distorts the formation of Canadian public policy, since the interests of transnational corporations will often be very different from the interests of the community. Once dependent, the community, the province, or the country becomes vulnerable: "Don't toughen pollution standards, or we'll move our investment elsewhere" . . . "Don't demand less clear cutting, or we'll close the mill" . . . "Give us the money for infrastructure development, or we won't invest" . . . "Build the new railways or highways and bridges for us, or we'll go to New Guinea."

A serious and relatively recent development is the increasing role of senior executives of foreign corporations in the public debate about key issues that affect the future of Canada. Since the free trade debate, Canadians have been regular recipients of wisdom and advice from the CEOs of foreign transnationals in Canada. Perhaps a classic example was the recent comments of James O'Connor, the new president of Ford Motor Co. of Canada Ltd. — the first American to hold the post since 1929. "Ford boss supports trade deal" read the headline in the *Globe and Mail* (May 1991). The trade deal in question was the trilateral Canada-United States-Mexico deal that is now being negotiated. Every auto-parts manufacturer in Canada knows that a deal with Mexico will mean thousands of lost jobs in Canada and numerous plant closings and industry bankruptcies. But few, if any, dared contradict Mr. O'Connor. Apparently you don't contradict your customer, even if you think you are being pushed down the end of the plank.

Another example of colonial-minded supplication is the presence of Japanese assembly plants in the Canadian economy, lured by big incentives and promises from government but creating comparatively few jobs and employing minimal domestic auto-parts production.

A rarely mentioned and little understood aspect of the heavy concentration of foreign ownership and control in Canada is the inability of employees to speak out against increasing foreign ownership or against the foreign companies' activities that are harmful to Canada (for instance, transfer pricing) or against the increasing public policy role of the transnational corporations in Canada. If you work for Safeway or IBM or Imperial Oil, you are not likely to stand up at a public meeting or write a letter to the editor or to your member of Parliament, suggesting that Canada already has too much foreign ownership and too much foreign control. Nor will your spouse be likely to speak out.

As I noted earlier, this muzzling influence goes well beyond the actual employees of foreign corporations. For instance, if your company supplies goods and services to Safeway, you are not likely to make public your concerns about head office burdening Safeway Canada with a large debt so that profits show up in the United States rather than in Canada. If you do business with IBM, there is little chance that you will complain in public about how few researchers are employed in Canada. And if you are an Imperial Oil employee, the chances are zero that you would speak out about suspicions that Imperial has maximized and minimized its estimates of Canadian oil and natural gas reserves to suit Exxon's corporate strategy. It is disappointing that Canadian political scientists and sociologists have ignored this vitally important and very pervasive aspect of public discussion and public policy formulation in Canada. As foreign ownership grows, not only are employees silenced, but the employees of firms doing business with the foreign firms are also unable to speak out.

Not to be underestimated is the effect of heavy foreign ownership on the media in Canada. In 1990, of the ten top advertisers in Canada, five were under foreign ownership and control, and a sixth was probably under foreign control. Only two of the ten biggest advertising agencies in Canada are Canadian-owned. To their credit, most newspaper editors throughout the country ignore the potential problems of criticizing foreign ownership and control. But few people would be likely to argue that many of our newspaper and magazine publishers and owners are totally insensitive to the prospect of losing advertising revenue as a result of such criticism.

At the extreme lies the continentalist, compradorian *Financial Post*. As its key shareholder Conrad Black puts it, "If the lure of the U.S. proved irresistible, this would not be a tragic fate."[6] Canadians in search of new public policies that would benefit Canada do not have far to go. All they need do is read the *Financial Post*'s editorial page and the page opposite it — and then establish national policies that are diametrically the opposite of those recommended.

15

The Petroleum Industry

How Americans Put the Oil and Gas in the Ground

> *If it weren't for U.S. enterprise and capital, it's a pretty*
> *good bet that Canada would still be a nation of trappers*
> *and dirt farmers.*
> Editorial in the U.S. financial journal BARRON'S, 19 November 1974

> *American money will every year more and more develop*
> *Canadian industries. A working commercial agreement of*
> *far-reaching importance will be made between the United*
> *States and Canada.* CHEIRO'S WORLD PREDICTIONS, 1927

CHART 25 GIVES A PAIR OF FIGURES THAT YOU
would hunt for in vain in Canadian business publications.
Those of us who were raised in western Canada have heard
a never-ending chorus of solemn pronouncements about foreign investment in our petroleum industry: "Where would
we be without the Americans?" Or . . . "If it hadn't been for
U.S. capital, we'd never have had an oil and gas industry."
Ernest Manning, Peter Lougheed, and Don Getty have done
more than their fair share in perpetuating this long-standing
and widely accepted myth, but nobody did a better public
relations job than Exxon-controlled Imperial Oil and the
Canadian Petroleum Association (which is about as Canadian

Chart 25

**Foreign Investment in the Petroleum Industry
for the Decade of the 1980s (1980–1989 inclusive)**

Outflow from Canada of long-term investment, interest payments, dividends, and business service payments from foreign-controlled corporations	- $22,941,000,000
During the same period of time the assets of foreign-controlled petroleum corporations in Canada grew by	+ $22,994,000,000

SOURCE: Petroleum Monitoring Agency

as Mount Rushmore). The forty-year propaganda campaign has succeeded. Almost all Albertans accept it as gospel (as do most Canadians): the Americans put the oil and gas in the ground.

The figures in Chart 25 present a fascinating juxtaposition, showing a $23 billion growth in the assets of foreign petroleum corporations in Canada for the decade of the 1980s, while, at the same time, the petroleum industry sent $23 billion out of the country.[1] I cannot think of another developed country in the world that would tolerate the kind of figures illustrated in the last few charts.

The myth of Canada's dependency on foreign capital — perpetuated by our own myopic and inept politicians, and by foreign corporations from both inside and outside of Canada — is probably the single most damaging fabrication in the history of our country. Foreign ownership and control clearly costs, rather than benefits, Canada and Canadians. The costs are punitive, pervasive, and destructive. Until Canadians understand this, we shall never be able to regain control of our own public policy and our own country.

16

Canadian Investment in the United States

The Exaggerated Presence

*Over the past decade . . . there has been a remarkable shift
in bilateral investment flows. Investment by Canadian
firms in U.S. operations has accelerated and the stake of
Canadian multinational enterprises in the U.S. economy
has risen rapidly relative to the value of U.S. holdings in
Canada.* ADAM H. ZIMMERMAN *and* STEPHEN C. EYRE,
foreword to Alan M. Rugman's Outward Bound: Canadian
Direct Investment in the United States, *June 1987*

*Canada and the United States can only strengthen their rel-
ative positions by the free movement of direct investments.
. . . The closer balance of outward and inward direct
investment may also help Canadians to resolve some of
their lingering concerns about foreign ownership.*
ALAN M. RUGMAN, Outward Bound: Canadian Direct
Investment in the United States, *June 1987*

BEFORE AND DURING THE FREE TRADE DEBATE,
many "informed" observers from the business community —
respected economists, columnists, and editorial writers — predicted that Canada would soon have as much foreign investment in the United States as there is U.S. investment in Canada.

Such speculation was ill-founded and in some ways irrelevant. Not only is U.S. investment in Canada substantially greater than Canadian investment in the United States, but the true market value differential is far greater still, and Canadian control in the United States is but a tiny fraction of U.S. control in Canada.

Beyond this, it is remarkable that the business press and economists in Canada have somehow managed to ignore the fact that a great deal of so-called Canadian investment in the United States is not Canadian at all. During the free trade debate, the right-wing continentalist press frequently cited figures for increasing Canadian investment abroad, mostly in the United States. However, in 1987, some 24.5 per cent of all so-called Canadian direct investment abroad was made not by Canadians but by foreign corporations that were investing from Canada for all kinds of reasons, including tax considerations, the ability to utilize undisclosed funds, and other corporate motives. By 1990, possibly some 30 per cent of the so-called Canadian investment abroad was really American, British, European, or Asian. Because of budgetary constraints, Statistics Canada has recently decided that it will no longer keep track of non-resident equity in Canadian direct investment abroad.

A perfect example of how our press and public opinion are manipulated on the issue of foreign investment, foreign ownership, and foreign control was the publication *Outward Bound: Canadian Direct Investment in the United States*, written by University of Toronto economist Alan M. Rugman and published during the free trade debate, in June 1987. This publication was a product of the Canadian-American Committee, which it says "was established in 1957 to study and discuss the broad range of economic factors affecting the relationship between Canada and the United States. . . . The work of the Committee is financed by funds contributed from private sources in the two countries." (The Canadian-American Committee is sponsored by the C. D. Howe Institute in Canada and by the National Planning Association in the United States. Note the "private sources.")

If the study was not expressly commissioned to exert a strategic influence on the free trade debate, particularly the provisions that would relax the barriers to increased U.S. ownership and control of Canada, it certainly helped do the job. On page after page, the methodology, the concepts, and the conclusions are open to debate. Yet, with the exception of the *Toronto Star*, the business press accepted the document as gospel. Lead editorials supported the view that relaxed investment provisions should be incorporated in the trade agreement. From a strategic point of view, the document was a brilliant success.

I have already discussed the C. D. Howe Institute and its right-wing continentalist bias. The National Planning Association is a private American organization based in Washington, D.C., that is partially funded by the U.S. government. A look down the list of members of the Canadian-American Committee produces yet another reflection of the membership of the Business Council on National Issues, the Alliance for Trade and Job Opportunities, the C. D. Howe Institute, and other continentalist organizations. Procter & Gamble, Texaco, Honeywell, Metropolitan Life, Citibank, Westinghouse, Morgan Bank, Boise Cascade, Weyerhaeuser, Nabisco, Mellon Bank, Exxon, Xerox, General Motors, and Fiberglas, among others, frequently link up with their own subsidiaries in Canada, which are also members. Canada is represented by continentalist Canadian corporations and organizations such as Canadian Hunter Exploration Ltd., Imperial Oil, the Canadian Bankers' Association, the Conference Board of Canada, several Bronfman-controlled corporations and, of course, the Royal Bank of Canada. A few academics and trade unionists are thrown in for window dressing.

The public in Canada has no idea where the funding for such studies comes from. There is no question that substantial funds come from the U.S. government and its agencies, either directly or, more likely, indirectly. There is also no question that large U.S. transnational corporations have a

strong vested interest in the affairs and publications of organizations such as the Canadian-American Committee. Yet,
incredibly, most of the press in Canada treats its publications
and pronouncements as if they were unbiased, informed,
down-from-the-mountain revelations.

For the press in Canada to accept such publications, virtually
without question, from organizations that refuse even to open
their funding to public scrutiny is in itself a strong indictment
of the quality of many of Canada's business journalists and
business editors. The fact that Canadian economists and politicians seem mesmerized by such publications says a great deal
about what is wrong with Canada. Much has been said about
increasing foreign investment and foreign ownership in the
United States — and much of it is simply nonsense. The U.S.
would never tolerate levels of foreign ownership and control of
the kind that exist in Canada. Despite the massive increases in
foreign direct investment that poured into the United States in
the 1980s, there is simply no comparison between Canadian
and American levels of foreign domination. No single important U.S. industry has majority foreign ownership and control,
let alone Canadian ownership and control. In Canada, dozens
of industries are owned and controlled by Americans and other
non-residents. In the United States the chemical industry is only
31 per cent foreign-controlled; stone-clay and glass is 26 per
cent foreign-controlled; primary metals, 20 per cent; mining
and petroleum, 19 per cent; printing and publishing, 14 per
cent; electronic equipment and food products, 11 per cent; and
from there the numbers decrease rapidly in single digits. Only
about 6 per cent of foreign direct investment in the United
States is really Canadian. This compares with the 64 per cent
U.S. share of foreign direct investment in Canada.

The Canadian politicians, editorial writers, business columnists, and economists who made such specious comments
comparing Canadian direct investment in the United States
with U.S. ownership and control of Canada have badly misled Canadians.

17

Paying for Foreign Investment

The $4-Million-an-Hour Hemorrhage

> With the U.S. so powerful and her investments becoming
> greater in Canada, we will have a great difficulty. . . . U.S.
> foreign policy, at bottom, is to bring Canada into as many
> situations affecting themselves as possible with a view to
> leading ultimately to the annexation of our country.
>
> MACKENZIE KING, Diary entry, 1943

CHART 26 SHOWS THE RAPIDLY INCREASING COSTS
of servicing (paying for) foreign investment in Canada.
Translated into an hourly rate, in 1990 we paid out — every
single hour of every day, seven days a week, twenty-four
hours a day, Monday through Sunday, through the fifty-two
weeks of the year — an average of $3,758,333 an hour.
That's more than $62,600 per minute which left Canada to
pay the heavy cost of foreign investment in this country. By
the time you read this, the figure will be well over
$4,000,000 an hour, and increasing every minute.

Note the prominent, cross-Canada attention given the
Canadian Chamber of Commerce's "national debt clock"
which, at the time this was being written, showed that the
national debt was increasing at the rate of $58,000 every
minute. The same concerned conservatives who take every
possible opportunity to publicize the federal debt totally

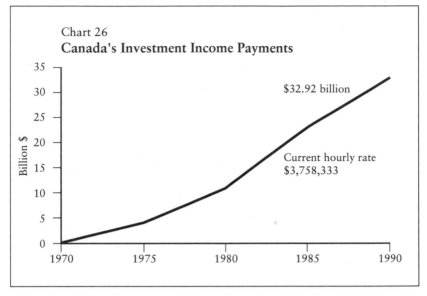

Chart 26
Canada's Investment Income Payments

$32.92 billion

Current hourly rate
$3,758,333

ignore the heavy costs of financing foreign investment, foreign ownership, and foreign control; such criticism would contradict the "open for business — up for sale" policies which many of them insisted had to be part of the FTA.

This huge outflow does not include business service payments, transfer-pricing considerations, or the other heavy costs associated with foreign investment in this country. Canada is now the world's second-largest debtor nation, behind only the United States, but in terms of both GDP and per capita comparisons, our international indebtedness is some four times that of the United States. It is hard to fathom why our elected representatives seem unable to comprehend that our enormous and rapidly increasing external debt will be at least as great a burden in the future as our federal government debt, to which they give so much attention.

At the end of 1990, Canada's total external liabilities stood at $465 billion. The Economic Council of Canada, in its November 1989 annual report, said: "Commitments that are being incurred for ongoing payments to foreigners will reduce the income and consumption opportunities for future

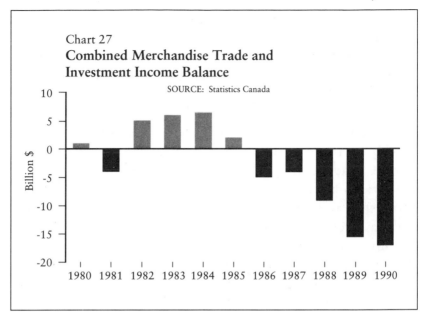

Chart 27
**Combined Merchandise Trade and
Investment Income Balance**

SOURCE: Statistics Canada

generations" (a strange warning from an organization that has consistently encouraged foreign investment in Canada).

The enormous, increasing flow of money out of Canada, mostly to the United States, creates our current account deficit and produces the results seen in Chart 27. Note the trend beginning in 1984, when Brian Mulroney became prime minister. This chart adds our perennial merchandise trade surpluses, of which Canadians are so proud, to the increasing annual net costs of servicing foreign investment in Canada. Once again, the trend is ominous. Yet few Canadians are aware of this problem, and our press and politicians have largely ignored it. The consequences are simple: the trends we see here and in Chart 26 mean a lower standard of living for Canadians and much poorer prospects for the future; they also mean that Canada must endure high interest rates, even though the domestic economy requires low interest rates.

A continuation of this trend will inevitably mean control of all future Canadian economic policies by the U.S. government in Washington, D.C., and by the International Monetary Fund, which will simply tell Canadians what can and cannot be done. Like it or not, we will have no choice but to obey. Loss of economic control means loss of political control. Will this mean that Canada will join the United States as one or more states in the Union? I think not. More likely we will become the Puerto Rico of the north.

In both trade practices and foreign investment regulations, Canada is the world's ultimate naive Boy Scout. Other countries employ a variety of means to regulate foreign ownership and control of their economy. The United States still has sectoral restrictions. Japan, Germany, and France all have numerous overt and covert barriers to foreign investment. The screening of foreign investment is common around the world. Key areas of the economy, such as resources, financial services, and transportation and communications, are often prohibited sectors for majority foreign ownership. The European Community effectively limits Japanese automobiles, through "voluntary" restraints, to only 11 per cent of the market. Many countries provide government aid only to domestically controlled companies. Foreign ownership of banking, insurance, and real estate is frequently severely limited or completely restricted. National security considerations are mentioned by many countries (including the United States) as a reason for restricting foreign ownership and control. Japanese law forbids the takeover of any companies that are at least "25% technologically innovative."

But in Canada we are prostrate. Despite the heavy degree of foreign ownership and control that we have had for three decades, we are constantly told that we have been a closed society, hostile to non-residents. Worse, we are told this by the foreign business community which now dominates so much of the Canadian economy and is increasingly influencing Canada's social policies and politics. Worse still, our own federal politicians, provincial premiers, chambers of commerce, and editorial writers parrot the same song. This despite the fact that year after year in poll after poll, more than 70 per cent of Canadians have said that the country has enough foreign investment and that they want it to be screened much more vigorously in the future.

In the last ten years for which official figures are available, 1978-87 inclusive, foreign-controlled firms took some 40 per cent of the profits in all of Canada's non-financial industries. One wonders exactly what figures would satisfy the C. D. Howe Institute, the *Financial Post*, and the members of the York, Toronto, Mount Royal, Vancouver, and Ranchmen's clubs, and other establishment watering holes across the country. Given their pitiful performance in protecting the integrity and economic well-being of our nation in recent years, one suspects that even if 100 per cent of all profits left the country and even if the unemployment rate went up to 50 per cent, they would still be pleading the case for more foreign investment and relaxed rules for foreign ownership and control. No doubt when future takeover targets such as Inco Ltd., Alcan Aluminium Ltd., Canadian Pacific, Woodward's, the Bay, Stelco, and Canada Trust are completely sold off to non-residents, they will find good reason to defend the sales, as they have done in the past in the takeover of Connaught BioSciences, West Kootenay Power and Light, Bow Valley, Consolidated-Bathurst, Consumers' Gas, and the like.

The nation's pimps are their own best cheer leaders. In other countries they would be regarded as contemptible sell-outs. In Canada they are the establishment. Northrop Frye, one of Canada's greatest citizens, summed it up as well as anyone. In the last speech he gave, shortly before his death, he said: "The Americans made two attempts to occupy the country by military force, both of them beaten off, but violence and the threat of violence continued in the Fenian raids and such things as the 'fifty-four forty or fight' crisis. Then they tried economic penetration in which they were brilliantly

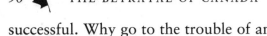

successful. Why go to the trouble of annexing a country that is so easy to exploit without taking any responsibility for it?" (University of Toronto, 23 January 1991).

18

Canada's High Interest Rate Policies

The Competitive Kiss of Death

> *"By early 1990, high interest rates had made a recession virtually inevitable. Under these circumstances, one might have expected the Bank of Canada to lower interest rates sharply. . . . Instead, the Bank of Canada raised interest rates at this point. . . . These increases ensured both that the Canadian economy would go into recession and that the recession would be long and severe."*
>
> *Peters estimates the recession and the continuation of this restrictive monetary policy course will cost the Canadian economy $100 billion in lost output between 1990 and 1992.* ARTHUR DONNER *quoting Toronto-Dominion Bank economist Dr. Douglas Peters, Toronto Star, 25 March 1991*

WHAT CAUSED THE RUINOUS CANADIAN RECESSION of 1990-91? Only a blind and stubborn Adam Smith conservative ideologue would not admit that the Free Trade Agreement was an important factor. Only doctrinaire monetarist ideologues could have implemented and supported the destructive high interest rate policies of John Crow and Michael Wilson. The combined impact of the FTA, high interest rates, and a high dollar has decimated the Canadian economy.

Earlier we looked at the high value of the Canadian dollar and its damaging effect on the Canadian economy, and considered the motivation for maintaining an artificially valued dollar when the harm is so obvious. How legitimate is the speculation that Canada secretly promised to boost the value of our dollar? The graph in Chart 28, comparing Canadian and U.S. interest rates, is taken from the 1991 *Report of the Governor of the Bank of Canada.* Note what happened to the interest rate differential at about the same time that the FTA came into effect.

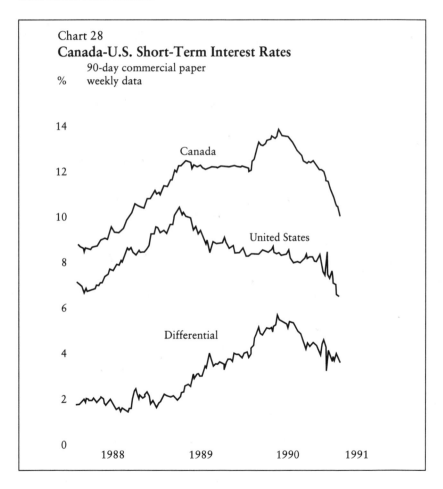

Chart 28
Canada-U.S. Short-Term Interest Rates
90-day commercial paper
% weekly data

But let us assume for a moment that Canada's high interest rates were not the result of a secret behind-the-scenes agreement. Let us even assume, however unwisely, that financing Canada's current account deficit is not a key motivation. For a moment, let us take John Crow at his word — namely, that our high interest rates are necessary in order to hold down inflation.[1] Don McGillivray puts this policy in the right perspective: "The Bank of Canada has been trying since late in 1975 to wipe out inflation by pushing up interest rates. This is the prescription of economic faith called 'monetarism.' There's no proof yet that it works on inflation. ... After 15 years of this monetarist policy the national debt is about $400 billion. . . . Interest on the debt . . . and the central bank's policy is driving the country deeper and deeper into debt." So is the high dollar. And so is the heavy cost of financing foreign investment in Canada. Even before the FTA, Canadians were subjected to years of punitive Bank of Canada high interest rate policy. But since Brian Mulroney became prime minister, real interest rates (interest less inflation) have reached record highs. Chart 29 compares Canada's interest rates in 1990 with those of our chief trading partners.

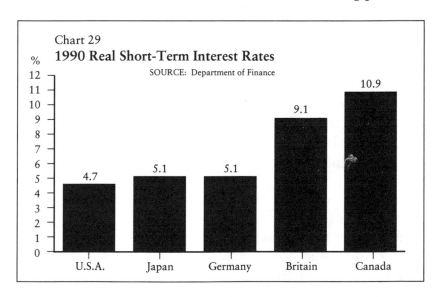

Chart 29
% **1990 Real Short-Term Interest Rates**
SOURCE: Department of Finance

High interest rates are great if you have plenty of money in the bank or in paper investments; but for the average

Canadian and for most businesses, they are damaging if not devastating. Increased costs for business borrowers affect all consumers. High interest rates severely curtail domestic investment. Reduced business investment creates unemployment. At the same time, high interest rates attract large inflows of foreign capital, and this drives up the value of the Canadian dollar. A high dollar, as we have already seen, makes it difficult or impossible for many Canadian industries to compete in the export market. Every increase in the value of the Canadian dollar dramatically decreases exports and increases imports.

The FTA was supposed to be about competing on a level playing field. How can Canadians do so when they have to pay interest rates that are twice as high as those paid by the people they are competing with and significantly higher than those of other people around the world?[2]

The standard line from John Crow of the Bank of Canada, and from the Department of Finance, is that we have high interest rates to fight inflation. The business press and business community, for the most part, blame the federal deficit. Of course, both reasons are valid to a degree, the latter more than the former. The rate of inflation in Canada (until the GST struck) was relatively stable for years, at about 4 per cent. At the same time, the federal government's annual deficit compared with GDP has been declining since 1984. Despite the stable pre-free-trade inflation rate and the declining rate of annual debt, interest rates escalated to produce a deep, protracted, "made-in-Canada" recession. They only began to come down when the degree of suffering became so unacceptable to the business community that even the aloof Bank of Canada felt pressure to reduce them. But they are still far too high, with a spread above U.S. rates proportionally almost the same as earlier in the year and in 1989.

One of the major but rarely mentioned reasons for high Canadian interest rates is the need to finance Canada's balance of payments deficit, which is caused by the huge costs of paying for foreign investment, ownership, and control in this country. To avoid cripplingly high interest rates, we *must* stop the foreign takeover of our economy. We must become far more self-reliant and use our own savings much more wisely. We must make sure that the very substantial annual savings of the Canadian public, deposited in Canadian banks and other financial institutions, are used to benefit Canadians in Canada, instead of being invested outside Canada or being used by large multinational companies to finance the foreign takeover of our country.

The bottom line of high interest rate policies is clear: higher unemployment, misery across the country, more unemployment insurance, more welfare, more poverty, a worsened current account deficit, and the inability of Canadians to be competitive in the world economy. It's an inane policy supported by an inept government — the least popular government in the history of Canada, led by the least popular prime minister since polling began in the country.

Don McGillivray could have gone on to say that it is increasingly foreigners who reap the benefits of Canada's high interest rate policies. Once again, there is a rapidly worsening whirlpool effect. High interest rates in Canada encourage Canadians (including provincial and municipal governments) to borrow abroad. High interest rates in Canada encourage foreigners to put their money into Canadian bonds. In both cases, there is upward pressure on the Canadian dollar; and in both cases, "the net wealth that is available to be passed on to future generations [is reduced]," as the Economic Council of Canada stated in 1989. High interest rates produce a massive transfer of wealth from the poor and middle class to the wealthy and to foreigners. They also exacerbate federal and provincial debts.

John S. McCallum, professor in the Faculty of Management of the University of Manitoba, showed the impact of compounding interest costs when in 1989 he wrote:

The bank rate has been in the 12.5% range of late. At 12.5%, the deficit doubles, because of interest payments alone, in 5.9 years. It takes only 5.9 years for the interest bill on money borrowed to finance a deficit to accumulate to the size of the deficit itself. . . .

At the federal level, the interest bill has almost quadrupled since 1980. . . . Interest now takes more than 75% of federal personal tax revenues. (*Financial Post*, 28 December 1989)

McCallum also spelled out the necessity and consequences of financing the current account deficit:

Since a balance of payments deficit must be financed, the compound interest engine affects a balance of payments deficit exactly as it affects a budgetary deficit.

The net outflow of funds to pay for foreign capital had tripled in a decade, turning a modest balance of payments problem into a deficit that could be $15 billion this year. Would an informed public not prefer remedying a balance of payments problem early rather than endure ever-rising payments for foreign capital? Money paid for foreign capital is not available for use here. (*Financial Post*, 28 December 1989)

As it turned out, the current account deficit was almost $21 billion in 1989.

More and more, Canadians are questioning the Mulroney government's support for Bank of Canada policies. In recent months there have been a number of estimates of the saving on financing the federal debt that lower interest rates would produce. There is general agreement that a 2 per cent reduction in short-term interest rates would save Canadians a huge $7 billion on the federal debt over two years.

High interest rates have numerous side effects. Not only do they hurt Canadian consumers and damage the domestic economy, but the high cost of capital encourages Canadian industry to invest outside Canada. As well, high interest rate policy and the high dollar that goes with it contributes to increased cross-border shopping, which in June 1991 the Conservative revenue minister, Otto Jelinek, estimated "will drain between $4 billion and $5 billion from the national economy in a full year at the present clip."

In sum, Canada's high interest rate policies have left us high up in the air, way out on a slack, wobbly tightrope. The combination of government debt, the high cost of financing foreign investment, and our self-imposed high interest rate policies have left us increasingly vulnerable to the investment decisions of non-residents and a serious balance of payments crisis. The Bank of Canada is terrified that lower interest rates will cause a run on the dollar, and the 1991 budget was a clear signal to foreign investors that interest rates will be used to sustain the high value of the dollar. That means more and more of the same in the future.

As they say, steady as she sinks.

19

Productivity and Competitiveness

The Blind Man with a Hundred Telescopes

Bilateral free trade with the United States is simplistic and naive.
It would only serve to further diminish our ability to compete
internationally. MICHAEL WILSON, PC *leadership race, 1983*

A plethora of studies shows that Canada has had a pitiful
productivity record over the past two decades. Since 1973,
the annual growth rate of Canadian productivity has
slowed dramatically and, when all factors are taken into
account, only Greece turned in a poorer productivity
record than Canada in the 1979-1988 period among the 20
Western industrialized nations ranked by the Organization
for Economic Co-operation and Development.
GLOBE AND MAIL, *29 April 1991*

STUDIES IN ABUNDANCE, DOCUMENTS, REPORTS,
conferences, academic papers, and newspaper editorials in
every part of the country have pointed out Canada's poor
productivity performance. Yet our "blind man" government
cannot see the roots of the problem — or if it can vaguely
make them out, it is totally unable or unwilling to act.

If "globalization" was the buzzword of the last few years
of the 1980s, "productivity" and "competitiveness" are the
current champions. How can we Canadians compete in the
global economy? It is virtually impossible to open an issue of

the *Financial Post* or to attend a Board of Trade or Chamber of Commerce luncheon without being deluged with cliché-ridden sloganeering on productivity and competitiveness. The same corporate geniuses who were such prominent Rotary Club speakers across Canada during the free trade debate, the same blinkered, doctrinaire economists who somehow managed to forget about the exchange rate factor in free trade, are now telling us that we have to be more competitive if we are to survive. We must become much more efficient. We must produce more at lower cost. Wages are far too high. Greedy workers are at fault. The unions are demonic. Canadians are too coddled.

It is true that our productivity growth rate has slowed drastically. Although productivity levels in Canada are still among the highest in the OECD, we are slipping, and slipping badly.[1] Why is this? Is it because Canadians don't work very hard? Since the FTA came into effect, more and more of our business leaders have been implying this. Or is it because Canadians are not very smart? Even the BCNI and the *Financial Post* wouldn't dare suggest that. But — of course! It's Canadian wages that are at fault, and taxes to pay for social benefits. Or so they tell us.[2] In other words, although they don't actually say so, our standard of living is too high. For workers, that is. Management remuneration, which has escalated rapidly in recent years, is rarely mentioned.

The real answer has little or nothing to do with the rantings of corporate executives. In fact, one of the most important reasons for their high-powered campaign to sell Canadians the FTA was to enable them to reduce employee wages and also to reduce social benefits so as to allow them to pay even lower taxes than they now pay. (We shall see shortly how legitimate their claims of overtaxation really are.) The real answer to Canada's declining competitiveness lies with the structural deficiencies that are incorporated into a branch-plant economy. And, of course, the FTA enshrines those inefficiencies through the forever-open-door investment provisions which allow the United States to buy up much of what is still in Canadian hands.

How can Canada possibly be competitive when it has an artificially high dollar that severely inhibits exports? How can Canada possibly be competitive when business in this country faces crippling interest rates that are well above those of our principal competitors? How can Canada possibly be competitive when business in this country is not investing in Canada?[3]

How can Canada be competitive when both government and business spending on job training and on the upgrading of employee skills are a fraction of those of our principal trading partners and are steadily declining?[4] How can Canada be competitive when large sections of its economy are truncated because all major decisions are made outside its borders? How can Canada be competitive when so much of Canadians' savings are being used to finance the purchase of Canada by foreign corporations, and when our own banks are expanding in the United States to the point that Canadian businesses are finding it harder and harder to get the working capital and expansion capital they require?[5]

How can Canada be competitive when its major competitors are constantly looking ahead and planning ahead while in Canada big business has completely convinced government that an industrial policy — of any kind, at any time — is a plague to be avoided?

What use are a hundred telescopes to a government without vision? What are the chances that productivity studies by the BCNI, Kodak Canada Inc., and the C. D. Howe Institute might point to foreign ownership as a serious problem in the Canadian economy? Solutions rarely emanate from the people who are at the root of the problem in the first place.[6]

20

Research and Development

Canada as a Trust Territory

> *You'd think Canada would want its own companies. . . .*
> *Canada is really a Trust Territory of the U.S.*
> MARCIA KAPTUR, *Democratic congresswoman, 1987*

> *The United States and Canada used to be winners because*
> *they had abundant natural resources, more capital than*
> *other countries, superior technology and a better educated*
> *work force. . . . Two of those factors have now dropped*
> *out of the equation, one has turned upside down and only*
> *one remains key. Natural resources are now "irrelevant"*
> *for most countries. . . . A world capital market means Thai*
> *entrepreneurs have access to funds as easily as North*
> *Americans. Technology has distinctly changed the new*
> *emphasis on the means of production.*
> LESTER THUROW, *economist, Globe and Mail, May 1991*

IN THE 1984 FEDERAL ELECTION CAMPAIGN, BRIAN
Mulroney solemnly promised to double research and development spending in Canada to 2.5 per cent of GDP. However, in 1991, real R & D spending will be below the level for 1984.

Here is the prime minister speaking in Ottawa on 25 August 1989, almost five years after his election: "Our goal is an economy that can compete with the best in the world, producing stimulating new jobs and new opportunities for future generations of Canadians. . . . Science and technology are the keys to a modern competitive economy." The prestigious National Advisory Board on Science and Technology repeated the above words as the opening to its *Statement on Competitiveness*, which it presented to the prime minister in November 1990. The statement went on to say: "The fundamental issue is productivity . . . the key to higher productivity is the application of science and technology to product and process innovation. . . . It is surely alarming that . . . R & D expenditure as a percentage of national output has actually been declining for the past four years. . . . The crisis of competitiveness in Canada is so pervasive that . . . it risks permanently eroding the foundation of our society. . . . The future well-being of Canadians is at stake."

In April 1991, when the National Advisory Board presented the prime minister with its eagerly awaited report, *Science and Technology, Innovation and National Prosperity: The Need for Canada to Change Course*, the same warning was present: "One overriding conclusion is inescapable. Canadians will not succeed in meeting international competition, and will therefore face a declining relative standard of living, unless we become much more adept in applying science-based technology to create a continuous flow of innovation and productivity growth. If our economy continues to lose its vitality, all of the fiscal, social and political strains in the federation will become unmanageable."

Some of the main points in the report were as follows:

- There is a "rapidly widening gap between the technological fitness of Canadian industry and that of its industrial country competitors."
- Recent international data indicates that Canada's ratio of gross expenditure on research and development to gross domestic product ranks only seventeenth among twenty-three industrialized OECD countries.

- "Most significantly, Canada's industrial structure has changed very little during the past 20 years, in the sense that the proportion of value added in technology-intensive industries has increased only slightly."
- R & D spending in the Canadian automotive industry is only one-tenth of that of the world auto industry, as a percentage of sales.
- "There is considerable evidence that the low propensity to conduct R & D in Canada is related to the branch-plant status of many of its manufacturers."
- There is evidence that Canadian firms underinvest in R & D because of the high cost of capital in this country.

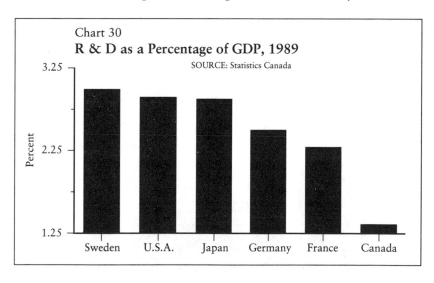

Chart 30
R & D as a Percentage of GDP, 1989
SOURCE: Statistics Canada

There is plenty of "good stuff" in this document but, unfortunately, not nearly enough emphasis on the most important causes of the problem. Chart 30 shows one of the built-in, characteristic by-products of the world's leading branch-plant economy. In the modern world, a nation's future is largely shaped by the research and development it either does or does not do. Canada cannot possibly compete properly or be efficiently productive if it fails to do sufficient research and development.

It is a well-known historical fact that Canada has consistently been near the bottom of the industrialized totem pole when it comes to R & D. Year after year after year, people complain about this chronic problem. And year after year, absolutely nothing changes, despite some of the most generous R & D tax incentives anywhere in the world. When the Liberals are in opposition in the House of Commons, they shout and lament about it. When the Tories are the opposition, they do exactly the same. But year after year, nothing changes. In fact, it is getting worse, not better. In 1985 R & D was 1.42 per cent of GDP; it is now down to 1.36 per cent.[1] Our high-tech products as a percentage of exported manufactured goods are well below OECD and EEC averages.[2]

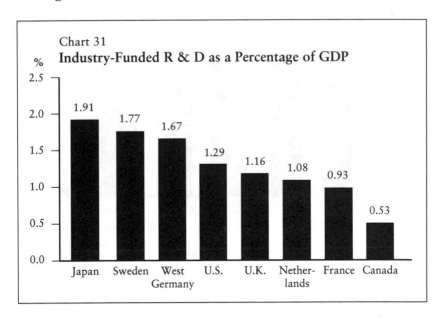

Chart 31
% **Industry-Funded R & D as a Percentage of GDP**

All industrialized nations put public monies into R & D, but in most successful economies, private industry funds the lion's share. Not so in branch-plant Canada. Not only are Canada's overall research and development expenditures among the lowest, but the amount funded by industry is also among the lowest (though government spending on R & D is about average for the industrialized nations). Chart 31 shows industry-funded R & D (as opposed to government or university R & D). Once again, Canada is tucked away down in the lower right-hand corner.[3] In 1989 Canada's industry-funded R & D as a percentage of GDP was only 38 per cent that of Sweden, 36 per cent that of the United States and Japan, and 35 per cent that of Germany.

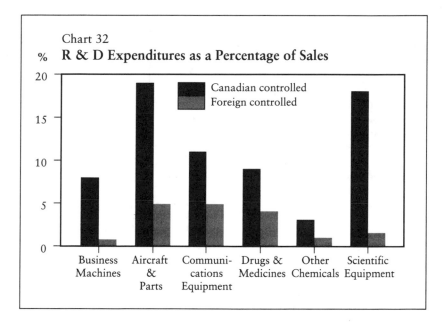

Chart 32
% **R & D Expenditures as a Percentage of Sales**

Chart 32 pinpoints the problem: foreign firms do little R & D in Canada. Although they now make some 35 to 40 per cent of all profits in Canada, they do only 8 to 10 per cent of R & D. As was illustrated in Chart 16, there are many sectors of the Canadian economy in which foreign firms take most of the profits; yet they do little or no R & D in this country.[4] Chart 33, which is based on an Ontario government report,[5] summarizes this dismal situation.

Few countries in the world would tolerate a situation like this. But why *should* foreign firms do R & D in Canada?

Chart 33
Summary of Canada's Science and Technology Performance

Measure of Competitiveness	Canada's Rank among Eight Comparison Countries *
Gross expenditure on R&D as a percentage of GDP	lowest
Industry-funded R&D/GDP	lowest
Government-funded R&D/GDP	2nd lowest
Government-performed R&D/GDP	middle
Higher education R&D/GDP	2nd lowest
Domestic patents granted per 100,000 inhabitants	2nd lowest
International patents granted – by population	lowest
Advanced science degrees and engineering degrees awarded – by population	middle
Scientists and engineers in labour force – by population	lowest
Number of technology-intensive industries with positive trade balance	lowest

*France, West Germany, Japan, Netherlands, Sweden, U.K., U.S., and Canada

Multinationals do most of their R & D in their home country, and if they do pass their front-line technology on to their subsidiaries, you can be certain that transfer pricing is an important element of the exchange. They would not want their subsidiaries to be competing with them for export orders. Nor would they want their branch plants to be so efficient and productive as to steal business away from head office, where the taxes are lower (as are the benefits).

The failure to do adequate research and development is one of the most serious problems that Canada faces. In fact, the term "R & D" holds far more importance for Canada than the current corporate buzzwords "competitiveness" and "productivity." Since 1960, the Science Council of Canada has been warning that foreign ownership is detrimental to R & D. But, as we know so well, Brian Mulroney's government welcomes foreign ownership. So despite all the speeches, despite all the studies, and despite all the warnings, the situation is getting worse, not better — and the investment provisions of the FTA lock this economy-crippling problem firmly into place.

Canada will never be competitively productive unless it vastly increases its R & D; and it will never vastly increase its R & D so long as it is an American branch-plant colony or trust territory. It is becoming more and more obvious that human resources are far more important than natural resources in our modern competitive world. Tying the hands and limiting the minds of Canadians is a tragic mistake.

21

Debt, Deficits, and Deception

Are We Really Bankrupting the Nation?

The cost of servicing the federal debt is stupendous, now $40 billion a year and the fastest growing segment of government expenditures. Unbelievably, the interest bill now takes three-quarters of all federal personal taxes.

NEVILLE NANKIVELL, *former editor-in-chief and publisher of the*

Financial Post, Calgary speech, November 1990

On Canada Day in the centennial year of 1967, the federal debt of the Government of Canada was $18 billion. This year, it will approach $400 billion. Canadians are supporting a public sector they cannot afford.

PETER COOK, *Report on Business, June 1990*

We surely require a new approach to fiscal policy, but it need not be one that panics before the buzzwords "debt" and "deficit." ROBERT HEILBRONER, *economist,*

The Nation, December 1989

CONFUSION ABOUNDS ON THE QUESTION OF DEBT and deficits. Hence, the left is often as confused as the right is ideologically blind.

Canada's national debt exceeded $400 billion in 1990. The debt has more than doubled since Brian Mulroney became prime minister and is now some five times higher than it was in 1980.[1] In 1991 we shall spend more paying the interest charges on the debt than we spend nationally for education — and almost as much as the total of all federal government transfer payments to persons.

Most of the business community and most business writers and economists say that our increasing debt is a menace to the nation and to the standard of living of the citizenry. Much of the government's public policy has been in response to the perception that the increased costs of servicing the public debt clearly show the need to reduce government spending. But some economists, labour leaders, politicians, and many social activists claim the debt is not the main problem — interest rates are.

Who is right? The debate has been long and bitter. Now the Reform party has joined the Conservatives and big business in their demands for billions of dollars in across-the-board cuts to government spending "before the nation is bankrupt." It is clear that social spending is the area where the federal government spends the most. As we are now told on a daily basis, this means that if the public debt is to be cut back, social spending must bear the brunt of the cutbacks.

In the past, the right in Canada cautiously danced around the issue of cutbacks to social programs. After all, Canadians are happy with their social programs and any politicians who attempted to erode them would be in for trouble. But today, in 1991, the attack is massive, sustained, and direct. The dancing around is over. "Obviously," we are told, Canada's social programs are the principal cause of our increasing debt, and this means that we have to start reducing our social spending, by large amounts, quickly.

For those interested in the figures involved, the following analysis should help clarify the situation. (Other readers may wish to skip to the latter part of this chapter.)

Chart 34 shows that the combined debt charges for all three levels of government in Canada have doubled from some 10 per cent of total government spending in 1975-76,

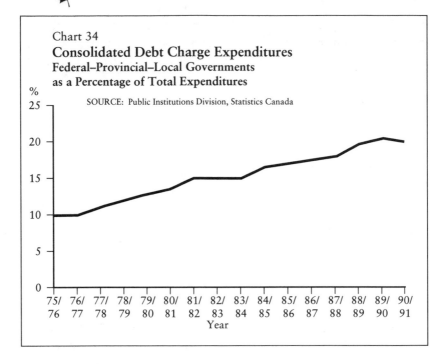

Chart 34
Consolidated Debt Charge Expenditures
Federal–Provincial–Local Governments
as a Percentage of Total Expenditures

SOURCE: Public Institutions Division, Statistics Canada

to twice that in 1990-91. The gross cost of financing the federal government debt has indeed been increasing as a percentage of GDP:

1980	3.2%	1986	5.2%
1981	3.9%	1987	5.0%
1982	4.5%	1988	5.3%
1983	4.3%	1989	5.7%
1984	4.7%	1990	6.0%
1985	5.2%	1991	6.3%[2]

Until the current budgetary cutbacks, the federal government's costs of financing the cumulative debt were escalating
as a percentage of total budgetary expenditures:

1980-81	16.9%	1986-87	22.9%
1981-82	19.9%	1987-88	23.1%

1982-83	18.9%	1988-89	24.9%
1983-84	18.7%	1989-90	27.2%
1984-85	20.5%	1990-91	27.8% estimated
1985-86	22.8%	1991-92	25.7% budgeted

As annual deficits are piled on top of previous accumulated debt, the total debt increases. If the total increases as a percentage of GDP, the problem is real. Here is the federal government's net cumulative debt relative to GDP:

1980	23.3%	1985	41.7%
1981	24.1%	1986	46.3%
1982	26.9%	1987	48.0%
1983	31.6%	1988	48.6%
1984	36.1%	1989	49.5%

Net public debt charges have increased dramatically:

	($ billion)		*($ billion)*	
1980-81	6.249	1985-86	21.780	
1981-82	9.914	1986-87	22.403	
1982-83	12.275	1987-88	24.291	
1983-84	13.811	1988-89	27.622	
1984-85	18.157	1989-90	32.970	
		1990-91	36.478	estimated

Clearly, then, the Conservatives, the Reform party, the BCNI, and the business press are right. Debt and deficit are indeed serious problems. In the past, spending was "out of control"; Mulroney's cutbacks have not been nearly enough, so "much more social spending must get the axe." For fiscal 1990-91, the federal government will have spent three times as much of every dollar to cover debt charges as it did twenty years ago. As more and more is spent servicing the debt, more and more tax dollars are unavailable for social programs and other government spending.[3]

But wait. Let's look again. Rather than increasing, the federal deficit as a percentage of GDP is the same as it was back in 1979-80:

1979-80	4.2	1985-86	7.1
1980-81	4.5	1986-87	6.1
1981-82	3.4	1987-88	5.2
1982-83	6.9	1988-89	4.4
1983-84	7.8	1989-90	4.7
1984-85	8.3	1990-91	4.2

Over much the same period, the federal government's total budgetary expenditures as a percentage of GDP have increased only 1.5 per cent:

1980-81	20.4%	1985-86	23.3%
1981-82	21.3%	1986-87	23.1%
1982-83	23.9%	1987-88	22.8%
1983-84	23.9%	1988-89	22.0%
1984-85	24.6%	1989-90	21.9%

At the same time, the federal government's operating balance (revenue less expenditures, without including interest) has shown a *surplus* for the 1980s:

	($ billion)
1980	– 0.766
1981	+ 6.424
1982	– 3.606
1983	– 7.581
1984	– 9.127
1985	– 6.804
1986	+ 2.490
1987	+ 6.188
1988	+ 10.826
1989	+ 14.254
	+ 12.298

From 1980 to 1989 inclusive, the federal government's program spending doubled, from $51.419 billion to $102.977 billion. However, during the same period, federal government debt charges grew by a huge 277 per cent.

Again, who is correct? The left or the right? Both are. Canada cannot continue to finance deficits that consume more and more of total revenue. While budgetary deficits as a percentage of GDP are expected to drop to the range of 3.5 per cent in the early 1990s, the OECD average of government deficits in recent years has been only 1.5 per cent of GDP. When Brian Mulroney became prime minister in 1984, the federal debt was some $170 billion. Today, it is well over $400 billion. While the operating balance for all the 1980s stood in surplus of some $12.3 billion, public debt charges for the past ten years have been over $236.3 billion, or some 59 per cent of the gross public debt![4]

Clearly, then, Canada's high interest rate policies are a major factor in the huge, escalating debt charges and are in fact the major contributor to the rapidly accumulating debt.[5] Southam columnist Don McGillivray puts it in strong terms: "Canadians are right when they disown the deficit. It has been a creation, almost entirely, of high interest rates. . . . The central bank's policy is driving the country deeper and deeper into debt."

So, in a way, both the left and the right are correct. Our accumulating debt cannot continue to rise so dramatically; but, at the same time, interest rates must not be allowed to continue at the high average levels of the past few years. It is in the solution to these problems that more problems arise. For the right, the answer is clear: big cuts to spending. For the left, the answer is more broadly based: fairer taxes and lower interest rates. (The following chapters on social programs, health care, and taxation provide some fascinating numbers that totally contradict so much of what is said and written on the subject of government spending and debt.)[6]

An important point must be made in relation to government debt held by non-residents. If foreigners hold Canadian government debt, then taxes paid by Canadians end up as money that leaves Canada and is spent elsewhere. A debt is not necessarily a burden if the money is used productively, if interest costs are reasonable, and if the interest payments are widely recirculated within the economy. As economist Robert Heilbroner points out, a deficit that promotes economic growth is a public investment. If government loans for education crowd out private loans for leveraged buy-outs, which is better? "To argue against all deficits on the basis that they restrict funds available to the private sector, is to argue that all private investment should come before any public investment."

However, when deficits simply fund consumption, and when interest rates are high, a serious problem will develop. That problem is compounded by foreign borrowing and the even higher interest rates necessary to finance it. A large foreign indebtedness, as we have seen, severely restricts policy formulation and inevitably damages our standard of living.

Unfortunately, Canada's economic policies encourage increasing foreign investment in the form of both debt and equity. In 1978 only some 15 per cent of Government of Canada marketable bonds, some $4 billion, were held by non-residents. Today, these figures have jumped to 38 per cent — some $53 billion. At the end of 1990, the total foreign holdings of all Canadian bonds amounted to $179 billion. Statistics Canada puts it gently: "The refinancing of such large amounts . . . may create upward pressure on interest rates." *May* create? — like "It *may* snow in winter in the Yukon"?

Statistics Canada recently reported that more than half of these foreign-held bonds will mature relatively soon (*Canadian Economic Observer*, June 1991). Since competition for international investment funds has increased, Canada will be forced to maintain high interest rates. As well, for bonds in foreign currency, if the value of the Canadian dollar falls, then the costs will increase, since more

Canadian dollars will be required to convert into the foreign currencies. Hence, there is all the more reason for the federal government to keep interest rates and the value of the Canadian dollar high. In addition, the millions of dollars that are leaving Canada each hour to pay for this foreign investment will make Canadians infinitely poorer. In 1990, some $17 billion left Canada to service the debt on Canadian bonds. This corresponds to more than 77 per cent of Canada's entire current account deficit for 1990.

There has been much deception and confusion in the whole protracted debate over government debt and deficits, some of it simply through ignorance, but a great deal of it coming from the same forces in Canadian society that lied to the people of Canada during the free trade debate. The deception is self-serving, intended to reduce government spending and hence reduce corporate taxes. But it is a perfectly logical extension of the philosophy that represents so much of the thinking of Canada's establishment: we must become more like the Americans.[7]

22

Down to the Level Playing Field

The Right-Wing Assault on Canada's Social Programs

*There are no changes planned in unemployment insurance . . .
the prime minister has assured me that there will be no
changes.*　　　　JOHN CROSBIE, *St. John's, 14 October 1988*

*There is absolutely nothing [in the Free Trade Agreement]
that will stop the Government of Canada from maintaining
all its social programs, all its regional development programs, but strictly nothing. We are going to maintain all
our social programs.*
　　　　BRIAN MULRONEY, *televised election debate, 24 October 1988*

*I would go after regional development and universality. . . .
You've got to get into the social programs. You've got to
go through a whole list of really ugly things. This is not
pleasant stuff. You've got to say "Atlantic Canada, you're
on your own; northern Ontario, you're on your own."*
　　　　MARSHALL (MICKEY) COHEN, *Financial Times, 28 November 1988*

BRIAN MULRONEY REPEATEDLY LIED TO CANADIANS
about free trade and its impact on Canada's social programs.
So did his friends in big business. Before the free trade deal
was signed and throughout the 1988 federal election cam-

paign, Canadians were assured by the prime minister and his cabinet ministers, and by the Canadian Alliance for Trade and Job Opportunities, that we need have no worries about our social programs, and especially not about medicare. Without question, these programs would be enhanced, not harmed, by the agreement. The federal government and big business spent millions of dollars (much of it from sources that have still not been disclosed) reassuring Canadians that there need be no worries of any kind in this respect. The level playing field would not level Canada's social benefits.

The Alliance ran many expensive four-page ads in newspapers across Canada during the election campaign. The ads were grossly misleading. Here, for example, are some of the comments relating to social policy:

> Question: But won't our social benefits add up to higher labour costs than in the U.S.?
> Answer: It's a myth to say that the costs of our total compensation packages are uncompetitive with the U.S. because of our social benefits.
> Question: What about our social programs like Pensions and Medicare?
> Answer: The free trade agreement is about trade. Period. Not social programs. . . . Services such as health and welfare, day care, education and public administration are not in the agreement and *are not threatened in any way by it.*

Mickey Cohen[1] ("You've got to go through a whole list of really ugly things") was a member of the Alliance that ran those ads. So were scores of other representatives of big business who have been demanding massive cuts in Canada's social spending ever since the last election. As soon as the election was over, the chorus began: "Canada is uncompetitive because of the huge costs of our social programs" . . . "We Canadians spend far too much on our social programs." Or, in the words of newly appointed, ultra-right-wing editor of the *Financial Post,* Diane

Francis: "Canadians support one of the world's most overgoverned and foolishly generous welfare states."

Here is Laurent Thibault, who was then president of the Canadian Manufacturers' Association, in a letter to then finance minister, Michael Wilson, less than four months after the election: "[The Free Trade Agreement] makes it more urgent that we tackle the outstanding issues that affect our competitiveness. . . . Because 60 per cent of program spending is tied up in statutory programs, with most of this in social programs, this is the spending area that must be reduced."

In March 1989 the Canadian Manufacturers' Association called for deep cuts in social spending. Soon afterwards, the Canadian Chamber of Commerce joined in, as did think tanks funded by members of the BCNI; and so did the Royal Bank of Canada, one of the foremost proponents of the FTA. For the past three years, our newspapers have been inundated with regular reports of speeches by leading CEOs, bank presidents, business association executives, and other representatives of big business, telling Canadians exactly the same thing: "We can't be competitive unless we stop this reckless spending, which is bankrupting the nation." This is some contrast to "It's a myth to say that the costs of our total compensation packages are uncompetitive with the U.S. because of our social benefits" and to the promise that social programs "are not threatened in any way" by the agreement.

How can we explain this? Were they simply lying to us? Were they perhaps just incredibly stupid? Or were they themselves deceived? How is it possible that Canadians are being told today that we cannot afford our cherished, much-admired social programs if we are to compete head-to-head with Americans, when we were repeatedly told exactly the opposite before the last election?

We can rule out stupid. Whatever else they may be, the members of the BCNI are not stupid. On the contrary, many of the chief executive officers of our major corporations and big banks and the heads of the foreign transnationals in

Canada are very clever. So were they themselves deceived? Not likely. And deceived by whom? After all, the leading members of the BCNI were both the instigators and the main advocates of a bilateral FTA with the United States.

If not stupid, if not deceived, then there can be no other explanation than that Canadians were lied to. Canada was betrayed by big business and by its representative, Brian Mulroney. The proponents of the FTA, who now so vociferously complain about excessive government spending, high taxes, and "cradle to the grave" social benefits, are neither inherently evil nor incompetent. What, then, are their motives? No one describes it better than Eric Kierans:[2]

> These [free trade] negotiations have one object, to smooth the path of Canadian corporate wealth into American markets and citizenship. . . . Employment in Canada, sovereignty and political independence are not goals of the Canadian corporate community. . . . The principal beneficiaries of this agreement will be the less than 200 major Canadian conglomerates who have amassed such surpluses in Canadian markets, under Canadian laws and political stability, that they believe that they must cross into continental and global markets to pursue their own expansion and growth. . . . The corporation uses the surpluses drained from its home economy to finance its expansion abroad, leaving behind a weakened nation and escaping, at the same time, political, social and economic responsibilities. Corporations have no interest in people, in the value of politics, in the social and cultural dimensions of living. . . . The corporate goal is accumulation and nothing else. ("Giving In to Corporate Giants," *Policy Options*, May 1988)

Not stupid. Not deceived. Not evil. Not incompetent. Simply selfish and greedy.

The Alliance asked this question in its four-page ads: "But won't the agreement gradually force us to align our policies along the lines of the larger and stronger partner? Won't

Canadian business lobby to reduce spending on social and other programs?" The answer was "Not at all."

Read now the words of Mickey Cohen from the same *Financial Times* interview that was quoted at the opening of this chapter: "If you're going to compete, we have to look more like the guys we're competing with."

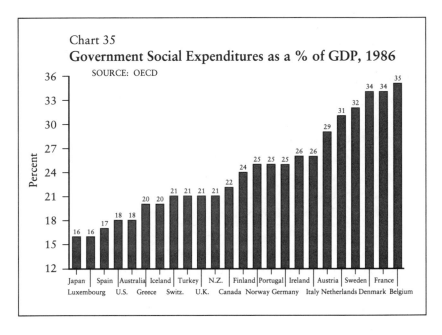

Chart 35
Government Social Expenditures as a % of GDP, 1986

SOURCE: OECD

Does Canada spend too much on social programs, as both the Mulroney government and big business are telling us? If so, too much compared with where? Chart 35 shows that of all twenty-four OECD nations, Canada has been right in the middle in terms of social spending, and in fact just-published OECD figures for 1988 show that Canada's social spending is actually slightly below average for the industrialized nations. Of the G7 nations, during the past ten years, Italy, France, Germany, and the United Kingdom all spent considerably more than Canada on social programs as a percentage of GDP; only the United States and Japan spent less. It would be interesting to know how many Canadians would like to have social programs similar to those in Japan and the U.S. The next time you hear some representative of big business or some ill-informed politician saying that we Canadians spend too much on social programs, ask two questions. First, "We spend too much compared with where?" And secondly, "Do we get good value for the money we spend on social programs?" Clearly, the answers, by all valid international comparisons, must be that we Canadians are blessed by our comprehensive social-care policies and that these policies are the envy of most of the world both for their quality and for their comparatively low costs.

This is not to suggest that we do not have problems in some areas or that we cannot make improvements. We do and we can. But decimating our social programs and forgetting the generations of cross-party, cross-Canada support for the caring and compassionate society that we have evolved is a tragic mistake. Our social programs are one of the most fundamental and cherished cornerstones of our nation. If we follow the advice of the same people who sold Canada the FTA, we shall move quickly to the same level of social conditions found in the United States.

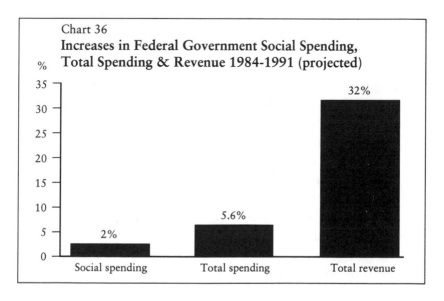

Chart 36
Increases in Federal Government Social Spending, Total Spending & Revenue 1984-1991 (projected)

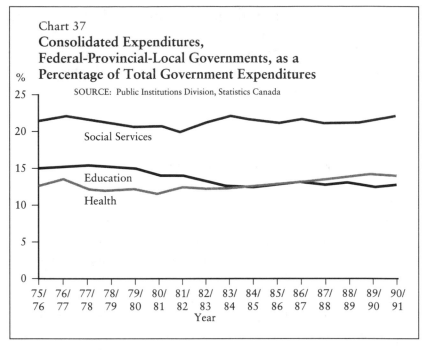

Chart 37
**Consolidated Expenditures,
Federal-Provincial-Local Governments, as a
Percentage of Total Government Expenditures**

SOURCE: Public Institutions Division, Statistics Canada

Instead of heeding the Mickey Cohens of Canada, we should look carefully at Charts 36 and 37. The former shows federal government spending and revenue since Brian Mulroney became prime minister. Total spending increased at almost three times the rate of social spending; but, at the same time, Ottawa's revenue increased at sixteen times the social-spending increase. Obviously, social-spending increases have not been the villain responsible for our large deficits and accumulating debt. So where did all that extra revenue go? Look back to Chart 34 for the answer. It is high interest rates, not social programs, that are at fault.

Chart 37 demolishes the skewed propaganda coming from Bay Street and from the likes of Diane Francis that our escalating social costs are at the root of our economic problems. Combined federal, provincial, and local government social-services costs remain at virtually the same level they were at fifteen years ago.[3] In fact, the federal government's share of social-services expenditures is actually lower than it was fifteen years ago.[4] Its expenditures on social programs as a percentage of GDP are only marginally higher than they were at the beginning of the last decade.[5] But, at the same time, mostly because of our high interest rate policies, public debt charges as a percentage of GDP have tripled in the last fifteen years.[6]

Despite all the "sacred trusts" and solemn promises, Canadian social programs are now being slashed. Despite John Crosbie's promises in St. John's, unemployment insurance benefits have been substantially reduced — and this was done just at the time when unemployment was going up to its highest level in over five years. Both benefits and entitlements have been cut, leading to large increases in provincial and municipal social-assistance costs. Despite Brian Mulroney's promises to improve social benefits, clawbacks have ended universality in family allowances and old-age security, and more important and more damaging cuts are likely yet to come.

Perhaps most important of all, the Mulroney government has cut back transfer payments to the provinces by billions of dollars. The decision to put a ceiling on federal contributions to the Canada Assistance Plan hurts the poor and disadvantaged. Once again, the burden falls on the provinces and municipalities. Their choice is simple: raise taxes or reduce services and erode standards. Moreover, transfers to the provinces will be cut to such a degree that funding for some social programs will actually disappear entirely in some provinces, with enormous potential ramifications for preserving national portable programs with national standards, and with enormous ramifications for national unity.

Since Brian Mulroney became prime minister, federal government major transfers to other levels of government have declined by 0.7 per cent of GDP.[7] In 1990 alone, that amounted to reduced transfers of some $4.8 billion of badly needed funds for hospitals, health care, social assistance, and postsecondary education. Meanwhile, the federal government is paying excessively high interest rates to wealthy Canadian and foreign bond holders. Duncan Cameron, editor of *Canadian Forum*, summarizes it well: "Social needs may go unmet, but money is found to pay bond holders a premium of some five percentage points more than they would get for holding American government securities."

Most of the Canadians receiving social assistance are children, women who are single parents, the disabled, people in ill health, and the unemployed (who are very familiar with the declining help-wanted index). Rather than being a cause of economic problems, Canada's social programs have helped create a good, compassionate, healthier society that has far less violence than that of the United States. There is abundant evidence that the prosperous countries which top the list of per capita GDP (with one notable exception) also have the strongest social-assistance programs. A closer look at the one exception follows in the chapter on health care in the U.S., as well as in the later chapter on whether Canadians will become Americans.

Do we need to cut social programs? Look again at the past few charts. Rather than cutting social programs, we need a national economic strategy that will allow sharply reduced interest rates and, as we shall see in the chapter on taxation, an infinitely fairer tax system.

23

Health Care in the United States

The Tragic and Costly Disgrace

The American health system is slowly eating its way through the country's GNP. *Its share has now reached 12 per cent. A dreaded word, rationing, now looks more likely than reform to stop the growth.* ECONOMIST, *23 March 1991*

Your [Canadian] solution wouldn't be appropriate here where the individual is king. No one wants to pay higher taxes to help somebody else.
JAMES TODD, *vice-president, American Medical Association,*
Toronto Star, 7 January 1990

IT IS NO SECRET THAT THERE ARE A GREAT MANY similarities between Canada and the United States, but there are also many vitally important differences. Perhaps nothing better exemplifies the basic differences that Canadians wish to preserve than the health-care systems in the two countries. Once again, despite Brian Mulroney's unctuous reassurances, we now find a concerted assault against medicare in Canada both by the Mulroney government and by the right-wing elements of Canadian society that it represents.

Canada has developed health-care policies that are admired around the world for both the quality of treatment and their comparatively modest cost. In the United States, health care is a growing national scandal and a growing economic burden.

The *Calgary Herald* (11 May 1991) sums it up well:

> When Freed Little showed up at the Texas Heart Institute with chest pains, he didn't have to worry about going on a waiting list. The 64-year-old oil consultant only had to guarantee he could pay before his operation was scheduled for the following day.
>
> Robert Huff, 57, an Atlanta house painter, wasn't so lucky. He died last January, shortly after X-rays revealed a tumor in his lung the size of a fist. Because he didn't have health insurance, he had delayed seeing a doctor for a cough for 13 months.
>
> These are the two faces of American health care. For the rich the U.S. system responds to the clink of cash with health care that's often superior to anything else in the world. For those unable to afford increasingly expensive insurance, illness too often means bankruptcy or death. . . . Some [of the poor] have waited since 1988 for operations for hernias, cancer, orthopaedics and other elective surgery. . . . A heart disease victim covered by U.S. government Medicaid is 40 per cent less likely to receive needed surgery than a privately insured heart patient.

John Saunders, writing from Washington, D.C., in the *Globe and Mail* (18 May 1991) noted that millions of Americans have no health care insurance whatsoever:

> Millions more have some insurance, but not enough to see them through such catastrophes as cancer, heart disease or acquired immune deficiency syndrome. And some U.S. health plans are like auto insurance: people who run up big bills see their rates balloon, or simply find their coverage cancelled. . . . Part-time workers are seldom covered. . . .
>
> Insurers adjust rates to reflect claims. In a small group, the rate may suddenly double if one or two workers suffer expensive ailments. In some circumstances, an insurer may insist a worker in poor health be barred from the plan, leaving him or her unprotected. . . .

In Washington, one outfit that advertises heavily on television asks $339.50 a month for a healthy family of four. . . . Medicaid, the government plan . . . pays doctors and hospitals at far less than standard rates, which means Medicaid patients often get a chilly welcome. . . .

Some hospitals have been caught "dumping" uninsured and Medicaid-insured patients; that is, finding excuses to transfer or discharge them.

Saunders quotes an assistant professor of medicine at Harvard University who writes on health economics: "In some ways there's no waiting list in the United States, because the poor never get on the waiting list." For example, uninsured patients rarely get coronary artery bypass grafts except in some larger centres that have public hospitals.

Bob Hepburn, the *Toronto Star*'s former bureau chief in Washington, D.C., had a first-hand experience of the American system. He wrote the following account in one of his columns:

It's a shock at 6 a.m. to be bluntly told that you can't enter the hospital unless you hand over a check for $600 right on the spot.

Still groggy with sleep and nervous about a scheduled outpatient test on my right kidney, I wrote out that check to Sibley Memorial Hospital here recently. My check was accepted, I was admitted and by 10:30 a.m. I was on my way home. I thought that was the end of my medical bills. Foolish me: my nightmare was just starting.

Within days, a flood of bills arrived in the mail. Doctors I had never seen billed me. Medical labs sent more bills. My main doctor chipped in with his statement. The hospital wanted more money. It billed me for everything in sight, right down to $1 for a sniff of oxygen.

Final tab for a 270-minute hospital visit: $2,083.50. That comes to $2,562.09 Canadian.

And what would happen if I didn't have a check when I appeared at the hospital? No problem: Visa, MasterCard and American Express accepted here.

If you didn't have a check or a credit card? Simple: you don't get in.

That nasty experience was a brutal reminder for a Canadian . . . that medical care in the U.S. is big business. Profit is the key word in the American medical profession. Doctors gouge patients; hospitals charge outrageous fees for beds (I was billed for each of the three rooms I was in); laboratories issue bills for tests a patient has no idea he ever authorized.

In short, paying for health care in America is a horror show.

Eventually, I got a second medical opinion in Toronto. I decided to have the operation performed at Toronto General Hospital after the surgeon there said the kidney might be saved. It was an alternative never suggested by the American doctors, who are notorious for their quick and easy "cut-it-out" approach to medical problems. To date, the Toronto doctor says the operation has been a success.

But as I wrote out the $600 check that dark morning to the Washington hospital, I thought of the 37 million Americans who have no health insurance.

How can they afford a relatively common operation such as I had to have? How can they even afford the pre-surgery tests? Or a visit to a doctor's office?

Every day, American newspapers carry stories about middle-income families driven into poverty by medical bills. In Washington, for instance, local residents are holding bake sales to raise money for a two-year-old girl who needs a heart transplant. Her father works full-time but can't afford health insurance, and no hospital will perform the operation without a down payment of $150,000. In view of its wealth, the United States should be the healthiest nation in the world — it spends more on health than any other country in the world — but, in fact, its health-care system is a disgrace.

Two years ago, when I was flying to Regina for a speaking engagement, I sat next to an Edmonton doctor who was on his way to Manitoba for a funeral. His uncle, a farmer, had moved from Saskatchewan to Minnesota in the 1970s and in 1986 contracted cancer. Before long, the costs of chemotherapy, hospitalization, doctors' bills, and other expenses were eating up the entire savings of the family. They took out a second mortgage on their home, but still the bills mounted. Eventually, the farmer discharged himself from the hospital, walked out onto his farm, put a shotgun in his mouth, and blew the top of his head off.

Janie, a nurse in her twenties, worked in the bone-marrow unit of the famous UCLA hospital in Los Angeles. Many of the children in the unit were required to use exercise bicycles, for which they were charged $75 a day. A shot of Demerol cost $80. Blood transfusions cost between $400 and $500. Two aspirins cost a dollar. Some of the children required private rooms, and the charge for those was $1200 a day — $36,000 a month! Janie saw many children who were not admitted to the unit simply because their parents couldn't pay such enormous sums. Janie also suffered personally from the high costs of the U.S. system. She left the bone-marrow unit to have her first child, and during her pregnancy she had a mild kidney complication and was hospitalized for two days. The total cost of having her child came to more than $13,000.

Now let us make some comparisons between this system and health care in Canada:

- In 1989, per capita health-care spending in the U.S. was $2196 compared with $1570 in Canada.
- In the U.S., some 34 million Americans (the majority working at full-time permanent jobs) have no health-care coverage whatsoever. Many millions more are seriously underinsured. In Canada, all Canadians are covered by medicare. The number of uninsured Americans increased by some 20 per cent in the 1980s. It is estimated that more

than 1 million Americans are denied health care every year because they cannot afford it.

- Canada spends some 8.7 per cent of GDP on health care. The U.S. reached 12 per cent in 1989 and is headed for 15 per cent within a few years (see Chart 38).
- In the United States there are ten infant deaths per thousand live births in the first year, compared with seven in Canada. Many poor women in the U.S. even have difficulty finding an obstetrician who will see them.
- Some 89 per cent of Americans say fundamental reform is required to the U.S. health-care system. By contrast, 86 per cent of Canadians say they are happy with Canada's system.
- In the United States, powerful well-funded lobbies for huge private health-care companies have a stranglehold on government policy. In Canada (at least until now) private health lobbies have been lacking in influence, except in the pharmaceutical industry.
- In the U.S., if you become ill, your private health-care policies are often cancelled. The sick, the infirm, and people who are likely to need prolonged medical care can find themselves turned down as a bad risk or offered such a costly plan that insurance is out of the question. If you become ill in Canada, you receive good quality care. If you have money in the United States, you also receive good quality care. But in the United States, illness is one of the leading causes of bankruptcy. Polls show that 50 per cent of Americans say that they cannot afford a serious illness. One estimate suggests that one in four Americans do not seek medical assistance because they cannot afford it. "An illness away from financial ruin" is a common phrase in the U.S.
- Doctors in the U.S. frequently charge more than twice as much as Canadian doctors, and the average doctors' fees are 2.4 times higher, despite the fact that American doctors provide fewer services per person.
- An operation in Canada that costs $3000 might cost as much as $20,000 in the United States. On average, fees for

surgery are more than 300 per cent higher than they are in Canada, and American doctors charge on average five times as much for visiting patients in the hospital.

- Medicaid, the U.S. government's program of health care for poor people, actually provides assistance for only some 40 per cent of those living in poverty. Millions of poor Americans are ineligible for assistance and too poor to purchase insurance. Since Medicaid pays only $11 for a visit to a doctor, the poor that are eligible often find that doctors refuse to see them.

- The average American household spends about 4.3 cents in every dollar on health care; in Canada the average cost per household is 1.8 cents in every dollar.

- The maternal mortality rate per 100,000 live births in the U.S. in 1980-87 was eight. In Canada it was only three.

- Life expectancy in Canada at birth is 77.0 years; in the U.S. it is 75.9 years.

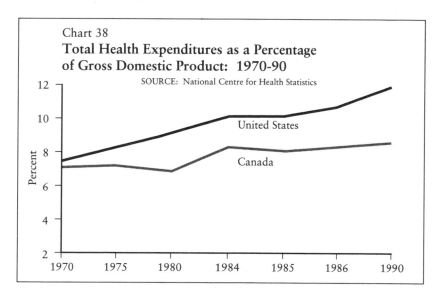

Chart 38
Total Health Expenditures as a Percentage of Gross Domestic Product: 1970-90

SOURCE: National Centre for Health Statistics

In the United States those who have no insurance and cannot pay the hospital bills have markedly lower hope of treatment. Some U.S. doctors stop providing chemotherapy if the patient runs out of money. More than 320,000 Americans were denied hospital emergency service in 1989 because they had no health insurance. Incredibly, eleven Los Angeles hospitals have decided to close their emergency wards rather than accept the growing number of patients who have no health insurance and consequently cannot pay for hospital services.

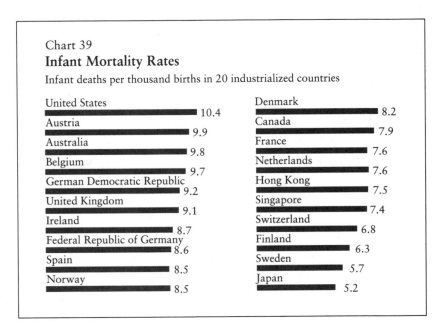

Chart 39
Infant Mortality Rates
Infant deaths per thousand births in 20 industrialized countries

Country	Rate	Country	Rate
United States	10.4	Denmark	8.2
Austria	9.9	Canada	7.9
Australia	9.8	France	7.6
Belgium	9.7	Netherlands	7.6
German Democratic Republic	9.2	Hong Kong	7.5
United Kingdom	9.1	Singapore	7.4
Ireland	8.7	Switzerland	6.8
Federal Republic of Germany	8.6	Finland	6.3
Spain	8.5	Sweden	5.7
Norway	8.5	Japan	5.2

The result of all this is that the poor die instead of being cured. The United States has one of the highest infant mortality rates of all developed countries (Chart 39). In 1988, 40,000 babies in the United States didn't live to see their first birthday. The evidence is clear: over half of these deaths could have been prevented with proper prenatal care for poor mothers. In some areas, one-third of maternity patients arrive for delivery having had no advance care. Compare this with the regular visits most Canadian mothers make to their doctor before having a baby. And even the poorest Canadian mother can have prenatal tests in hospital if necessary, including ultrasound and other procedures.

Canadians wishing to have an informed American comparison with Canada's health-care system should consult the *New England Journal of Medicine* of 2 May 1991. Here, Dr. Steffie Woolhandler and Dr. David Himmelstein look at "The Deteriorating Administrative Efficiency of the U.S. Health Care System":

> In 1987 health care administration . . . in the United States . . . amounted to 19.3 to 24.1 per cent of total spending on health care, or $400 to $497 per capita. In Canada between 8.4 and 11.1 per cent of health care spending ($117 to $156 per capita) was devoted to administration. Administrative costs in the United States increased 37 per cent in real dollars between 1983 and 1987, whereas in Canada they declined. The proportion of health care spending consumed by administration is now at least 117 per cent higher in the United States than in Canada. . . . If health care administration in the United States had been as efficient as in Canada, $69.0 to 83.2 billion would have been saved in 1987. . . . The administrative structure of the U.S. health care system is increasingly inefficient as compared with Canada's national health program.

The following table is reproduced from the article:

Cost of Health Care Administration in the United States and Canada, 1987		
	Spending per Capita ($ U.S.)	
	U.S.	*Canada*
Insurance administration	106	17
Hospital administration	162	50
Nursing-home administration	26	9
Physician's overhead and billing expenses:		
Expense-based estimate	203	80
Personnel-based estimate	106	41
Total costs of health-care administration:		
High estimate	497	156
Low estimate	400	117

The article points out that, in contrast to the U.S. system, "Canada has evolved simple mechanisms to enforce an overall budget, but it allows doctors and patients wide latitude in deciding how the funds are spent. Reducing our administrative costs to Canadian levels would save enough money to fund coverage for all uninsured and underinsured Americans. . . . The fragmented and complex payment structure of the U.S. health care system is inherently less efficient than the Canadian single-payer system. . . . The scale of waste among private carriers is illustrated by Blue Cross/Blue Shield of Massachusetts, which covers 2.7 million subscribers and employs 6682 workers — more than work for all of Canada's provincial health plans, which together cover more than 25 million people."

Another edition of the journal notes that, in general, elderly Canadians are "as likely, if not more likely, than their U.S. counterparts to have access to acute-care hospitals and high-technology services." Yet elderly Canadians spend 4.5 times less on health care than their U.S. counterparts. American senior citizens end up paying almost half of their doctors' bills even if they are covered by U.S. Medicare (the U.S. government's insurance plan for those over 65), and they have to make monthly insurance payments. Compare this with the Canadian situation. In Ontario, for example, senior citizens are exempt from insurance payments and they get much of their medication free.

There is no question that in almost every way, Canada's health-care system is superior. Canadians pay substantially less than Americans for health-care, yet despite this they live longer, are healthier, and have far greater overall access to medical services. In Canada, there is no two-tiered system for rich and poor as there is in the United States. Canada's publicly funded and publicly administered non-profit health-care system is comprehensive, universal, portable, and accessible to all. And Canadians like it and want to keep it.

So why are Americans not moving to the Canadian system? Ask the congressmen and senators who receive huge political donations from the big U.S. drug and health-care companies. Or ask the 82 per cent of American CEOs who say they are opposed to a national health insurance plan in the United States.

24

Medicare

Taking It from People Who Really Need It

> *I give you the assurance that I gave my mother, and that I*
> *would give my mother if she were on the blower to me right*
> *now . . . "Ma, your medicare is okay, your pension is okay,*
> *everything is protected." What free trade is going to do is*
> *give Canada more money so we can do more for all of you.*
> *And God bless you all.*   BRIAN MULRONEY, *3 November 1988*

> *What about our social programs like Pensions and*
> *Medicare? The Free Trade Agreement is about Trade.*
> *Period. Not social programs, not culture, not the environ-*
> *ment. . . . Services such as health and welfare, daycare, edu-*
> *cation and public administration are not in the agreement*
> *and not threatened in any way by it.*
> CANADIAN ALLIANCE FOR TRADE AND JOB OPPORTUNITIES,
> *election campaign advertisement, 3 November 1988*

How incredibly ironic! Just as health care in the United States is becoming a national scandal, and just when more and more Americans (including the U.S. government's General Accounting Office) are praising the Canadian system, the Mulroney government and its troglodyte friends are attacking Canadian medicare: it costs too much; we can't afford it; it's one of the main reasons our taxes are so high; the costs are skyrocketing; and so on and so on. Diane Francis recently referred to "the cancerous $56 billion medical tab this country suffers under each year."

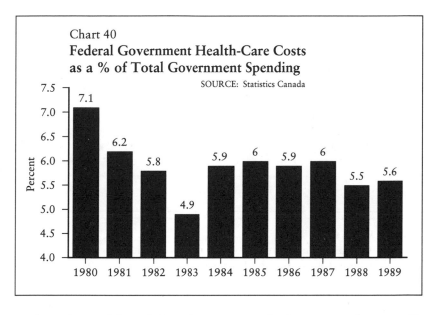

Chart 40
Federal Government Health-Care Costs as a % of Total Government Spending
SOURCE: Statistics Canada

Are the critics right about costs being out of control? Hardly. We have already seen that this is definitely not the case when the Canadian situation is compared with that of the United States. Chart 40 shows that Canadian federal government health-care costs were certainly not skyrocketing in the 1980s, and new figures show that in 1990 federal costs were only 5.2 per cent of total federal government spending. From 1979 to 1988, Canada's average annual growth rate of real per capita health spending was only 1.4 per cent, well below the OECD average of 2.1 per cent. As noted earlier (in Chart 37), health expenditures have risen only modestly as a percentage of all spending by all three levels of government since 1975.[1] Chart 41 shows that hospital costs in 1989 were below the average of the 1980s, and Chart 42 shows who it is that is paying for any increased health expenditures in Canada. In 1980 provincial govern-

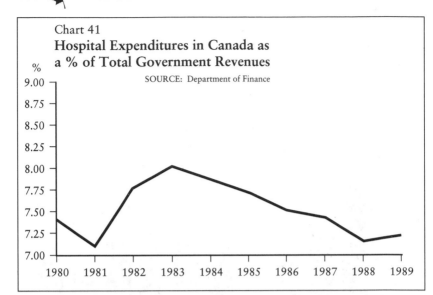

Chart 41
Hospital Expenditures in Canada as a % of Total Government Revenues

SOURCE: Department of Finance

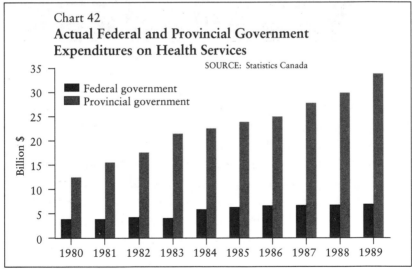

Chart 42
Actual Federal and Provincial Government Expenditures on Health Services

SOURCE: Statistics Canada

- ■ Federal government
- ■ Provincial government

ments spent 23.2 per cent of total expenditures on health care; in 1991 it will be 27.3 per cent.

The major problem is that Ottawa is cutting back its health-care funding. At a press conference in Ottawa in June 1991, Canadian health-care groups said that the survival of Canada's health-care system is in jeopardy because of

Ottawa's reduced funding. The president of the Canadian Medical Association, Lionel Lavoie, said that "in every part of the country a sense of frustration, fear and anger seems to have pervaded the health-care system." Cutbacks by the federal government will reduce transfers from Ottawa to the provinces by some $30 billion between 1986 and 1996. Unilaterally, the Mulroney government has changed the rules. Instead of 50-50 funding, the provinces are now expected to fund an ever-increasing share. In Ontario, the federal contribution is already down to 32 per cent and is heading even lower.

The Mulroney government's Bill C-69 will curtail federal contributions even further. Inevitably, with declining contributions come inferior standards, cutbacks in services, user fees, extra billings, pressure for privatization, and a two-tiered health system closer to the current American mess. With declining contributions, the federal government's ability to set and enforce standards will evaporate. In a statement issued in June 1991, the National Council of Welfare said: "Medicare will be effectively dead as a national health-insurance scheme." Patchwork health care and privatized health care are on the horizon. To see the future for Canadian health care under Brian Mulroney, one need only visit the United States.

Canada's first medicare scheme was introduced by Tommy Douglas's provincial government in Saskatchewan in 1962. It met with fierce opposition, notably from the establishment and the medical profession, yet the benefits soon became apparent, especially to the thousands of Saskatchewanians who had not previously been able to afford medical treatment. In 1966, the Medical Care Act was passed by the federal government, introducing medicare at the national level.

Federal policy is the key to the fate of medicare. In the 1966 Medical Care Act, the federal government guaranteed to contribute to provincial medical-care insurance plans on condition that the provinces fulfilled certain provisions. These included universal coverage for a comprehensive range of medical services, which were to be available to everyone equally, regardless of ability to pay. Thus, by the terms of the act and by its crucial funding support, the federal government gained a strong influence over the provincial administration of health care. By 1971 all provinces were participating in the scheme. This brought a marked improvement in health care throughout the country and a notable improvement in the health of Canadians.

Dr. Marc Baltzan of Saskatoon, a past president of the Canadian Medical Association, summed up the situation as follows:

In 1974 the annual death rate in Canada, adjusted to 1986 age and sex distribution and cancer incidence, was 0.92 per cent. In 1987 it was 0.71 per cent.

This is astounding. In scarcely more than a decade, the annual chance of dying from illness and accident has fallen nearly 25 per cent. The result is a massive life saving: 45,000 Canadians live who otherwise would be dead. This equals all the Canadian servicemen killed in the Second World War, or one-third the population of Prince Edward Island. . . .

The annual cancer fatality rate has declined considerably, more than 20 per cent. This improvement can be due only to better clinical medicine.

The abrupt decline in death rates in the early 1970s correlates with the widespread introduction of major advances in clinical medicine. These include the broad availability of intensive-care units, many effective new drugs, new surgical techniques, and advanced diagnostic technology. . . .

So, improved clinical medicine is the most probable principal cause of the decline in death rate, with preventive medicine making a lesser contribution. . . . Morbidity reduction is another. Implanted lenses, replaced hips and knees, angina relieved and so on reduce the chance of death and improve the quality of life. . . .

The Hall Commission of 1965 produced the medicare plan. It also projected its future cost, estimating the long-term annual

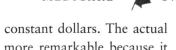

increase at 4 per cent per capita in constant dollars. The actual rate is 3.8 per cent, which is even more remarkable because it includes technological change and population aging, both of which weren't foreseen. . . .

The benefits are increasing. Costs as a percentage of GDP have not changed in the past five years. . . . Cost and quality are better than we have dared to predict. (*Globe and Mail*, 15 October 1990)

As we have seen, it is largely because of the public nature of medicare that costs have been kept so well under control. Canada's health-care costs, as a percentage of all national spending, have remained relatively stable for almost twenty years.

Had there been a Free Trade Agreement in place when Tommy Douglas was premier of Saskatchewan, Canada would never have had medicare. The FTA requires compensation to the United States for any Canadian action that is seen by U.S. corporations to be depriving them of potential revenue. U.S. health-care corporations would certainly have blocked any attempt to introduce a national public health-care plan, just as U.S. auto-insurance companies will move to scuttle any attempts by the Ontario government or by any other government to introduce public automobile insurance or other public insurance in the future.

In May 1989, the head of the Canadian Medical Association's ethical affairs committee said that the Free Trade Agreement would "undoubtedly" erode universal health care in Canada and would lead to a two-tiered medical system. As well, he said, it "will put pressure on the commercialization of health-care services in Canada, and this will affect the quality of services." Monique Bégin, who was federal minister of National Health and Welfare from 1977 to 1984, was of much the same opinion:

One fact is evident to me in the free trade agreement: it's dangerous to the Canadian medicare program. It strains credibility to imagine that Trade Minister John Crosbie or Prime Minister Brian Mulroney sincerely believe there are no dangers from free trade to the Canadian health-care system.

. . . Canadians fought against the Alberta, and the British Columbia, and then the Ontario governments when they started dreaming of American companies running Canadian hospitals. And so we now have only a very few cases of privatization. In other words, without free trade, only constant vigilance and warnings prevented the privatization of our hospitals.

The Canadian Health Coalition, an organization concerned about medicare and the health-care system, held similar views, stating in August 1988 that "the Free Trade Agreement undermines some of the basic principles on which our Medicare system was founded"; and the Canadian Council on Social Development warned that "the agreement threatens a wide range of health and social services."

There is no doubt that despite the Mulroney government's assurances, the future of Canadian health care now looks bleak. There will be a growing trend towards privatization, with more contracting out of management to large U.S. health-care corporations. Under the terms of the Free Trade Agreement, these large U.S. companies must be treated exactly as if they were Canadian companies. Once they are well entrenched in Canada, it is not inconceivable that they will complain that the Canadian health-care system is an unfair subsidy because of its government-funded programs. That will be the final nail in the coffin, the end of medicare. This is highly ironic, considering that the area in which Canada has so much expertise is health care. We should be expanding this expertise and exporting it, rather than importing vastly inferior U.S. policies and values.

The above scenario is not hypothetical — a gloomy forecast of what *may* happen. Already, the Province of Alberta has shown signs of wanting to move towards a two-tiered system of medical care. On a national level, the Mulroney government has long demonstrated itself attracted to American values, catering to them even when they conflict with long-established Canadian traditions.

Take, for example, Bill C-22, which in 1987 created the Patented Medicine Prices Review Board in the face of strong opposition from the Consumers' Association of Canada, senior citizens' organizations, and numerous other interest groups. This unpopular Act of Parliament was the result of enormous pressure from the Reagan administration and a well-funded campaign by the transnational drug companies, which disliked the competition they were getting in Canada from generic drug companies. As the U.S. lobby desired, and as the U.S. government insisted before entering the FTA talks, the new Canadian legislation effectively limited the sale of less expensive generic drugs — to the great advantage of the American pharmaceutical companies and to the great disadvantage of the Canadian public.

The inevitable result of Brian Mulroney's current policies will be a dozen different health-care schemes, all moving in the direction of privatization and all vastly inferior and much more expensive than the universal, comprehensive, portable, and accessible system we now have. Health care in the less affluent provinces will deteriorate sharply; and in all provinces, privatization will create a vastly inferior quality of treatment for all but the wealthy.

Of all the relatively affluent nations in the world, the United States is the only one that does not have a comprehensive national health-care system. With Brian Mulroney and big business in charge, Canada seems destined to be country number two — a giant step backwards by all standards of compassion and civilization, and a tragic abandonment of widespread and long-held Canadian principles.

Clearly, the greatest threats to health and health care in Canada are not cancer, heart disease, and pollution of the environment. Nor are they even such underlying problems as poverty and lack of education. No, the greatest threats to Canadian health and health care are Brian Mulroney, Bay Street, and the Canada-U.S. Free Trade Agreement.

In the months ahead there will be many more intensified attacks on Canada's social programs, including medicare. Big business, right-wing think tanks, Conservative and Reform politicians, chambers of commerce, and business organizations dominated by the giant corporations will all escalate the attack. Every time you read or hear of these ideologically based efforts to undermine our social programs, remember the charts in this book and consider the comments of Canada's chief statistician, Dr. Ivan Fellegi: "Should long-term economic growth continue as it has in the past and unit costs evolve, as assumed, the public expenditures in health, education and pensions would represent fifty years from now about the same claim on the economy as at present . . . in spite of the aging of the population." (*Canadian Economic Observer*, October 1988).

Finally, it is interesting to compare federal government debt charges with all Health and Welfare Canada expenditures (hospital insurance, medicare, extended health care, family allowances, old-age security payments, Canada Assistance Plan, Medical Research Council, etc.) in recent years:

Federal Budgetary Expenditures Percentage Distribution for Fiscal Years Ending March 31

	Health & Welfare	*Public Debt Charges*
1988	25.2	25.2
1989	24.9	27.2
1990	24.2	29.6
1991	22.3	28.6

Note that in 1988 the Health and Welfare and debt charges were the same percentage of total federal budgetary expendi-

tures. Had they continued in a similar ratio in 1991, an additional $9.632 billion would have been available to relieve pressure on the provinces and municipalities, to reduce the accumulated debt, and to reduce taxes. Compare this one-year figure with the $9.5 billion that Ottawa plans to cut from provincial government health care transfers to the provinces over the next five years.

Dr. Baltzan has pointed out that "a one per cent increase in the interest rate equals the total doctor cost of medicare to all Canadian governments. . . . When the Bank of Canada inflates interest rates three or four percentage points beyond norm [they are] making governments carry the equivalent of three or four extra medicare programs. . . . On the other hand a relatively teensy weensy increase in health-care costs sends them into a frenzy" (*Globe and Mail*, 15 October 1990). Our health-care costs also upset directors of the BCNI and the C. D. Howe Institute, such as Mickey Cohen, who stated, "This issue isn't going to be resolved merely by cutting out universality. That is only the beginning; that is only the painless stuff. It simply won't be enough to take money away from the people who don't need it. You are going to have to get at the people who really need it as well. That is not so much a question of political courage as having the stomach to do it, because it is going to be very, very painful." Corporate Canada wants to get at Canadians who really need health care. Perhaps a better alternative would be for all of us to stop drinking Molson's.

Canada's social programs are the envy of the world and are supported by the vast majority of Canadians.[2] They are comparately efficient and their costs are reasonable by all international comparisons. Canadians must not allow a terrible prime minister and the corporate elite who fund and advise him to destroy our social heritage.

25

Canada's Unjust Tax System

The Myth of "Tax Reform"

> *The overall balance of tax reform can be summed up in a nutshell. People will pay less; corporations will pay more.*
>
> MICHAEL WILSON, *Financial Post Conference on*
>
> *Tax Reform, 25 June 1987*

Shortly after Brian Mulroney came to power in 1984, Michael Wilson became his finance minister, and he held the post until April 1991. Let us now look at his promise of "tax reform" and his assurances that "people will pay less" and "corporations will pay more." You can then decide for yourself how much faith to put in Michael Wilson's promises.

From fiscal years 1984-85 to 1991-92, personal taxes in Canada increased at an average annual rate *three times faster* than corporation taxes. Since Michael Wilson's *Financial Post* promise of people paying less and corporations paying more, personal income tax payments to the federal government will have risen some $17 billion (1987-88 to 1991-92) and corporation taxes some $2 billion. The following are figures from Mr. Wilson's own Department of Finance.

Personal and Corporate Income Tax as a Percentage of All Federal Government Budgetary Revenues

	Personal Income Tax	Corporate Income Tax
1980-81	40.6	16.6
1981-82	39.9	13.5
1982-83	43.4	11.8
1983-84	42.0	11.4
1984-85	41.0	13.2
1985-86	42.9	12.0
1986-87	44.1	11.5
1987-88	46.2	11.1
1988-89	44.2	11.3
1989-90	45.6	11.5
1990-91	46.9	10.4

Another way of measuring the corporate share of taxes in Canada is to compare it with GDP:

1950	4.4%
1960	3.3%
1970	2.6%
1980	2.7%
1990	1.9%

This represents the largest rate of decline in the corporate share of taxes of any industrialized nation in the world.[1]

In terms of being honest with the people of Canada, Michael Wilson and Brian Mulroney are good company for each other.

We constantly hear from the business press, the tall towers of Toronto, and chambers of commerce across the land that Canadians are overtaxed. Overtaxed compared with where? What these people are really saying is that we Canadians pay more tax than Americans do. In fact, we do so mostly because of the much more compassionate and caring society we have developed — a society which, as a result, is different in many important ways from that of the United States. It is also a society which the vast majority of Canadians would like to preserve.

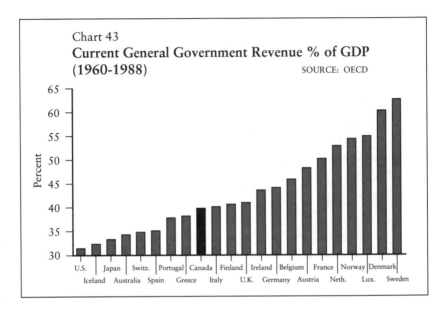

Chart 43
Current General Government Revenue % of GDP (1960-1988)
SOURCE: OECD

Chart 43 once again contradicts so much of what we constantly hear from the continentalist right in Canada. Of the twenty-two OECD countries shown here, thirteen have governments that take in a greater share of the GDP than Canada does. Only eight take in less. Note that this graph represents a very long period — twenty-nine years, from 1960 to 1988 inclusive. Contrary to all the propaganda, government revenue in Canada is well below the average of OECD and EEC countries. When looking at this chart and the one that follows, bear in mind how superior Canada's social programs are compared with those in the countries to the left of Canada on these graphs.

Chart 44 shows tax revenue as a percentage of GDP for 1989, the last year for which reliable comparative statistics are available. In that year, seventeen OECD countries had

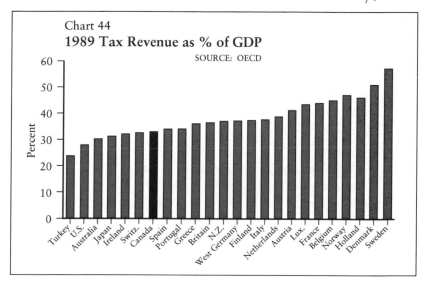

Chart 44
1989 Tax Revenue as % of GDP
SOURCE: OECD

higher overall tax revenue as a percentage of GDP than Canada, and only six countries had a lower rate. In the previous year, 1988, Canada's overall government taxes, including social security contributions, were 34 per cent of GDP, well below the OECD average of 38.4 per cent. By 1989, they had dropped to 33.4 per cent. Clearly, by all comparisons with the world's leading industrialized nations, Canadians pay less tax than the average, not more.

There is a problem, though, and a serious one. The problem, on any broad comparative basis, is not that Canadians pay too much tax. It is, rather, the unjust tax system that Mr. Mulroney and Mr. Wilson have punished Canadians with in the name of "tax reform." In Canada, individuals and families pay far too much tax, while large corporations pay far too little. The system is thus unfair to the vast majority, while benefiting the small minority of individuals and the giant corporations and conglomerates that already own and control most of Canada. International comparisons clearly show that individual Canadians bear too much of the tax load, and the GST makes things even worse. (The unpopular, regressive GST is a direct spinoff of the Free Trade Agreement, both as a means of replacing the manufacturing sales tax and as a money raiser to replace lost tariffs. In March 1991, Statistics Canada reported that the introduction of the GST had increased imports and that exports had declined. This is ironic to the extreme!)

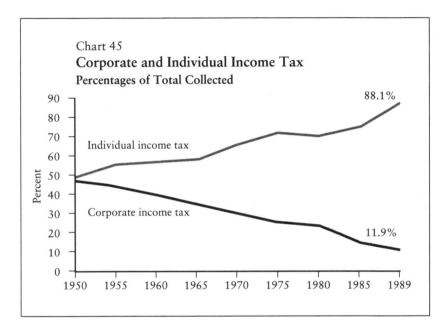

Chart 45
Corporate and Individual Income Tax
Percentages of Total Collected

Now let us take a look at the long-term trends in individual and corporate income taxes. Chart 45 shows that back in 1950 individuals and corporations paid about the same share of total income taxes collected in Canada. By 1989, in percentage terms, the individual share was 7.4 times the corporate share. Most Canadians are totally unaware of the consistent long-term trend lines on this graph — the steadily rising income tax share assumed by individuals, and the steadily declining rate assumed by corporations. Amazing as it may seem, until very recently there had been virtually no public debate on this process. Is it in the public interest to have corporations assume such a small percentage of the total income tax burden? The institution of the GST transfers billions of dollars of additional tax burden away from the corporations onto the backs of families and individual Canadians, despite the fact that the tax system has already been drastically altered to discriminate against individuals and families in favour of corporations.

In the introduction to the tax paper I presented to the Canadian Senate in 1990, I said:

> The Canadian tax system has been characterized by enormous tax concessions for giant corporations, conglomerates and wealthy individuals. Huge, very profitable and powerful banks, trust companies, insurance companies, petroleum companies and mining companies have been paying remarkably low real rates of taxation, on real profits, rates of tax well below that of average Canadian individuals, families, and well below the rates of most small and medium-size Canadian businesses.
>
> The Mulroney government "tax reform" has increased the tax burden for the overwhelming majority of individual Canadians and their families and decreased it for the very wealthy. At the same time, effective corporate tax increases for the largest, most profitable corporations have been modest and the government's own projections of corporate tax revenue for 1992 show small increases.
>
> The result is a shocking concentration of wealth and power in Canada and an excessive tax burden for the overwhelming majority of Canadians. (Presentation to the Senate Standing Committee on Banking, Trade and Commerce, 26 July 1990)

Here are a few of the examples and comments from the Senate submission:

> From 1980 to 1987, inclusive, Canada's banks made profits of over $7.64 billion and paid federal income taxes at the rate of 2.48%. These figures can only be described as appalling. It is completely beyond comprehension that any government, any elected officials, or any senior civil servants could have allowed

such a situation to occur. Few Canadians are aware of these figures. Few taxpaying Canadians could comprehend how such a travesty could have been allowed.

It is safe to say that the vast majority of bank tellers in Canada, including the lowest paid, paid a far higher rate of tax, throughout the entire decade of the 1980s, than the bank that she or he worked for. The low effective rate of tax paid by banks, trust companies, insurance companies — in fact the entire financial sector — should be a scandal. But few Canadians know of it. The financial press in Canada does not tend to dwell on such matters.[2]

From 1980 to 1984 life insurance companies in Canada made total profits of $3.076 billion, and paid federal income taxes at the rate of 4.3%.

From 1981 to 1984 seven large trust companies in Canada made profits of $775 million and paid federal income taxes at the rate of 7.6%.

The metal mining industry made profits of $2.355 billion in 1986 and 1987 and paid federal and provincial income taxes at the total combined rate of only 7.7%.

The petroleum and coal products industries during the same years made profits of $6.216 billion and paid taxes of only 9.5%.

During these same two years, the financial sector, including banks, trust companies and insurance companies made profits of over $54.818 billion and paid taxes at the rate of only 11.2%.

Chart 46 compares the tax burden for individuals in Canada and in the other G7 nations. There is not much doubt about which country's citizens are carrying the largest burden. In 1988, taxes on personal income in Canada were 39.1 per cent of all tax revenue, while the average for all OECD countries was only 30.8 per cent. If one considers all levels of government in Canada, in 1990 individuals contributed 90.1 per cent of all direct taxes, and corporations only 9.9 per cent.

Simply put, the Canadian tax system represents a dismaying portrait of corporations in control of society. While the

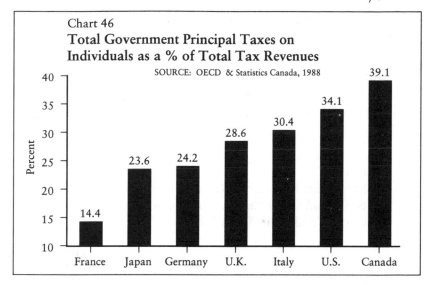

Chart 46
**Total Government Principal Taxes on
Individuals as a % of Total Tax Revenues**
SOURCE: OECD & Statistics Canada, 1988

tax load on individuals and families increased rapidly, corporations increased their profits (until the FTA) yet paid less
tax. And if government subsidies to corporations are taken
into account, the net corporate tax share drops to what can
only be described as scandalously low and unjust real rates
of taxation.[3]

One very important point needs to be made about corporation taxes. Again, it is a point that is rarely mentioned in the
financial press and one that is ignored by publications financed
by BCNI members. We constantly hear complaints about the
high corporate tax rates in Canada. Canadians should disre-
gard these complaints. First of all, as we have seen, corporations are not bearing anywhere near their fair share of the
tax load. Secondly, as we shall see, in terms of actual taxes
paid, corporations in Canada do very nicely compared with
those in other countries. The statutory tax rates so often
complained about have little relationship to the real effective
rate of taxes which corporations in Canada actually pay.

A recent Revenue Canada report, released under the Access
to Information Act, noted that aside from getting the write-
offs, exemptions, deferrals, and other concessions that

Canada's tax laws allow corporations (which, of course, substantially reduce the actual taxes paid), "very large corporations tend to be chronic noncompliers [who] take the most favourable interpretation of tax laws and force the department to find and resolve contentious issues, often through the courts." The report estimated that the amount owed but not paid by large corporations in 1987 was some $10 billion.[4]

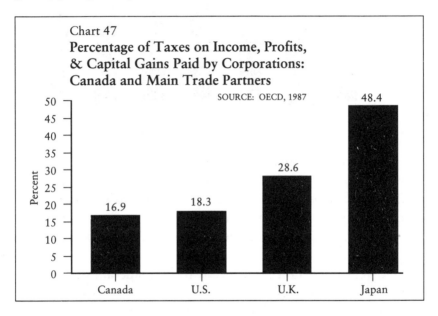

Chart 47

Percentage of Taxes on Income, Profits, & Capital Gains Paid by Corporations: Canada and Main Trade Partners

SOURCE: OECD, 1987

The argument is made, over and over again, that we must not tax corporations in Canada too much, because that would inhibit them from competing in the global market. But as Chart 47 shows, in 1987 corporations in Japan contributed almost three times as much, as a percentage of total taxes, than corporations in Canada did. The last time I looked, Japan was a pretty good trade competitor. Other international comparisons between Canada and its principal trading partners show similar results (including taxes on corporations as a percentage of total government principal tax revenue, taxes on profits and capital gains, and top central government tax rates for corporations).

Canada's tax system is a rip-off for the average Canadian. Individuals pay far too much; corporations and the well-to-do pay far too little. This needs to be changed, and, as we shall see in the next chapter, changed very quickly. But one more important point must be made in relation to the mindless annual reports of the Fraser Institute (which are unfortunately so eagerly and unquestioningly absorbed by the media in Canada). Yes, as we have seen, taxes on individuals and families in Canada are far too high, but when one considers the taxes that individuals and families pay and the benefits they receive back from government, then clearly Canadians have long had one of the highest net results (take-home pay plus transfers from government) of all the OECD countries. (Has anyone noticed that the Fraser Institute does not dwell on the pitifully low taxes the big corporations in Canada pay? The Fraser Institute refuses to release a detailed list of its sources of funds.)

Small and medium-sized businesses really have little latitude when it comes to avoiding taxes. But, in Canada, if you are big enough, it is infinitely easier. If you are a transnational corporation, it's easier still. In Brian Mulroney's Canada, it is the huge corporations and conglomerates that have the ear of the government, not small and medium-sized businesses. The same large companies that fund the research institutes (which hold press conferences to espouse public policies which further their corporate interests) are the principal beneficiaries of the effective lobby that has so dramatically reduced the corporate share of income taxes.

Despite its abundant rhetoric to the contrary, most big business is not too serious about a free market economy. For example, most members of the BCNI would be strongly opposed to more effective federal competition laws and tougher laws regulating concentration of ownership.

Much of what you have read in these pages is an attack on big business in Canada, both Canadian and foreign, but it is not an attack on free enterprise. Monopolies and oligopolies are not supposed to dominate a free market economy. Corporate concentration is not in the best interests of competition or of the consumer. Economist Paul Samuelson says it well when he asks: "Are you in favour of big business or free enterprise?"

In many ways, generations of Canadians, from all political parties, have developed a remarkably wise balance between public and private, between free enterprise and government intervention for the public good. Nothing I know of leads me to believe that there is a better system than a free enterprise society regulated by an aware and intelligent government, with some public participation where logical, such as in areas of transportation, communications, and energy, for example. Mostly private, some public. This was the heritage of all three major political parties in Canada, until Brian Mulroney. It was, after all, the Conservatives who introduced Ontario Hydro, the CBC, the Bank of Canada, and the Canadian Wheat Board.

The Mulroney government is a radical government, not a Conservative government in the true tradition of the Progressive Conservative Party of Canada and the history of our country. Its privatization agenda, its attacks on Canada's social programs, its economic and foreign policy leap into the arms of the United States, and its goal of harmonization with U.S. fiscal and other policies — all these are a radical departure, not only from the historical development of Canada but from traditions stretching from John A. Macdonald to John Diefenbaker. Perhaps two recent back-to-back press reports put it in the right perspective:

PM INVOKES GHOST OF SIR JOHN A IN NATIONAL FIGHT
Kingston, Ont. — Standing beside Sir John A. Macdonald's grave site, Brian Mulroney invoked the spirit of Canada's first prime minister Thursday as the guide to his fight for national unity.

MACDONALD WOULD BE DISPLEASED

Winnipeg, Manitoba — The great-grandson of Sir John A. Macdonald says Canada's first prime minister would be "turning over in his grave" if he could see what the country has become.

The unjust tax system is at the base of much of what is wrong with Canada. And one of the most important things wrong with Canada is a direct result of the tax system, as we shall see in the next chapter.

26

Corporate Concentration

Who Owns and Controls Canada?

*Ours is a mixed economy, and the concept has produced
many beneficial results for Canadians. . . . We can still
meet the [economic] targets . . . provided Canadian corporations are prepared to stop investing so much of the country's scarce resources in the unproductive game of corporate takeovers. I've yet to see a takeover that has created a
single job — except of course, for lawyers and accountants.*

BRIAN MULRONEY, *Where I Stand*, 1983

*The name of the game in the Free Trade Agreement is
money. Not money for real investment in creating new and
better goods and services, but money for takeovers, mergers . . . money for accumulation and concentration of
wealth and power.* ERIC KIERANS, *House of Commons Committee
on External Affairs and International Trade, 3 December 1987*

*Now that we've proven we can't really play hockey very
well, take-overs are the only genuine Canadian sport left.*

CONRAD BLACK, *quoted by Peter C. Newman in
The Establishment Man*, 1982

CHART 48 SAYS A GREAT DEAL ABOUT ONE OF THE
most fundamental and serious problems we have in Canada,
a problem that almost everyone seems to have forgotten

Chart 48
Corporate Concentration in Canada (1987)

- 25 enterprises control 1116 corporations and own 41% of all assets

- The top 1/100th of 1% of all enterprises control 56% of all assets

- The top 1% of all enterprises control 86% of all assets and make 75% of all profits

Put another way:

- 99% of all corporate enterprises own 14% of assets and make 25% of profits

about, including most of the press and almost all our parliamentarians. When these shocking numbers were published by Statistics Canada in 1990, there were no front-page headlines even in the business sections of newspapers. There was no debate in Parliament. There was hardly a stir in the nation. Yet these are the numbers that really count in any discussion of tax policy, free trade, the workings of the political process, or public policy of any kind — and especially in discussions about the future of our country.

By any standards of fairness and competition, by any comparative levels, by any measurements employed to determine how a free enterprise economy should function, these numbers are unacceptable and appalling. Canada's excessive corporate concentration should be a public policy scandal. Our tax system and our hopelessly inadequate anticompetition laws have resulted in a situation in which a small number of huge corporations and powerful conglomerates (both foreign and Canadian) and a small number of families own and control Canada. Since the Mulroney government is clearly an extension of big business, the ramifications are self-evident. In an editorial in January 1989, the *Toronto Star* almost got it right: "The powers of the people — the power of government — has, for the first time in our history, joined forces with the power of Canada's corporate elite, and with the awesome financial powers of the United States." Almost right, because the people in Canada now only have power during an election, and even then, as discussed earlier, that power is in danger of being overwhelmed by cartons of corporate cash.

The figures in Chart 48 are for 1987, *before* the huge mergers of 1988, 1989, and the first part of 1990. All the evidence suggests that when the figures for 1990 are available (which, unfortunately, will be after the next federal election), the picture will be much worse. Canada's hopelessly weak antitrust laws, the very low effective rates of corporate taxation, and tax laws allowing the write-off of interest payments related to acquisitions — plus a government that wouldn't recognize corporate concentration if Parliament Hill itself was acquired by a conglomerate — have combined to produce a situation which a former deputy minister of finance described to me as "outrageous."

As we have seen, the tax system in Canada clearly benefits the wealthy and the largest enterprises, to the disadvantage of small business. For example, in 1987, in the manufacturing industry, 33,338 corporations with assets of less than $1 million paid income tax on 91 per cent of their book profits. In the same year, 958 large manufacturing corporations, with assets of $25 million or more, paid income tax on only 57 per cent of their profits.

Now take a look at the cumulative percentage of assets, as shown in Chart 49. It is one of the most dramatic charts in this book. The bottom line represents 646,174 corporations in Canada, and the vertical line on the left gives the percentage of assets they own. The Lorenz curve shows that a tiny number of corporations own most of Canada — and remember that this was *before* the $57 billion in mergers in Canada in 1988 and 1989.

The growth of the assets of the top twenty-five enterprises in Canada is remarkable. In 1975 these groups owned some 29 per cent of non-financial industry corporate assets. By

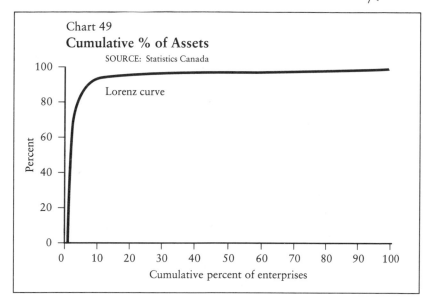

Chart 49
Cumulative % of Assets
SOURCE: Statistics Canada

Lorenz curve

Percent

Cumulative percent of enterprises

1985 this had increased to about 33 per cent, and by 1987 it had jumped all the way to 41 per cent. As was noted in Chart 48, in 1987 the top twenty-five enterprises controlled 1116 corporations in Canada and the top one-hundredth of 1 per cent of all enterprises controlled 56 per cent of all corporate assets. Put another way, 2393 large corporations, with assets of $25 million or more, shared 69.6 per cent of profits, while 447,726 corporations got to share 30.4 per cent of profits. Large corporations with assets of more than $25 million owned 71.8 per cent of all non-financial industry assets. (And in case there is any doubt about the nature of the foreign control of Canada, note that large foreign corporations made 90.3 per cent of all foreign profits and owned 89.8 per cent of all foreign assets in Canada. Big business dominates foreign ownership in Canada.)

Compare the above figures with the business situation in the United States, Japan, and West Germany, the home bases of most of the world's largest and wealthiest multinationals. In these three giant economies, the top hundred corporations control some 25 to 28 per cent of non-financial assets. In

Canada it was 55.8 per cent back in 1987, before mergerma-
nia. Yet, incredibly, we are constantly told that big is beauti-
ful and that we need more mergers in order to compete glob-
ally. In June 1991, as this chapter was being written, there
was talk of the desirability of having fewer and bigger banks,
of merging the two railways, and of having only one national airline in Canada. Big business loves monopolies and
oligopolies. Big business loves the Mulroney government.

Canada has the weakest competition and antitrust laws of
any of the large industrialized economies. The Canadian
competition act does not even deal with corporate concentration. In contrast, two of the largest exporting nations,
Germany and Japan, have very much tougher laws, and so
do most of the nations of the European Community. Even
the U.S. standards make ours seem a joke by comparison.

It is revealing to note that some of Canada's leading advocates of the FTA are at the same time prominent senior officers of the largest corporations and enthusiastic supporters
of takeovers and mergers. Trevor Eyton, chairman of Brascan
(and now a senator), Tom Kierans, the head of the C. D. Howe
Institute, Conrad Black of Argus *et al.*, and Mickey Cohen
of Molson all support the "bigger is better" philosophy.
(Amusingly, William Stinson, chairman of Canadian Pacific
Ltd. and co-chairman of the BCNI's constitutional task force,
recently said the country should take a lesson from business
and decentralize. Canadian Pacific controls 167 companies.)

The big business lobby in Canada has effectively opposed
strong competition laws for decades, and it is now saying
that large corporations should be allowed to own banks,
trust companies, and insurance companies, and vice versa.
The already unacceptably high levels of corporate concentration would then go straight through the roof. But, with the
Conservative government, what big business wants, big business gets. According to Brian Mulroney, "If the marketplace
is increasingly global and the capacity to compete internationally requires enormous strengths, growth and bigness of

themselves are not necessarily deleterious." Once again, here is another reversal — a total change in policy from the quotation at the beginning of this chapter.

Even after the huge takeover of Texaco Canada by Imperial Oil, the mergers of Molson and Carling O'Keefe, and the takeover of Wardair by Canadian Airlines International, Consumer and Corporate Affairs Minister Harvie Andre said, "Mergers to enhance company strength through increased efficiency, consolidation, rationalization and so on — hallelujah." Perhaps someone should explain to the minister what has happened to airline fares recently. Incredibly, the minister went on to say that there is a false impression that just a few companies controlling an industry is necessarily bad. Who would you say has Harvie Andre's ear — the Consumers' Association of Canada or the BCNI?

Stephen Jarislowsky, the well-known pension-fund manager, has a different perspective. He suggests that the growing number of takeovers and mergers has created massive debt loads, has decreased competition, and has created a slowdown of investment in modernization and a weakened economy.

Writing in *Inside Guide* in June 1991, James Gillies, former senior policy adviser to the prime minister, put it this way:

> While anti-combines legislation to prevent the restraint of trade has been on the books in one form or another since the 1880s, the laws have never been seriously enforced. Unlike the United States where anti-trust legislation has usually been vigorously enforced, in Canada there have been few if any mergers turned down by government agencies because they might result in restraint of trade. The degree of concentration, or in other words the lack of competition, in many markets in Canada is the greatest in the world and the concentration of economic power is enormous. Indeed, approximately 80 per cent of all companies in the Toronto Stock Exchange Composite Index have a controlling shareholder with the balance widely-held; in the United States it is almost exactly the reverse — about 80 per cent of the

firms in the Standard and Poor's Index are widely-held and only 20 per cent have a controlling shareholder. . . . With a few exceptions, Canadian businessmen have never wanted or encouraged competition. Indeed, the reaction of many to competitive inroads has been to sell the business; as a result there is a higher percentage of foreign ownership in Canada than any country in the world.

One of the exceptions James Gillies refers to is Hal Jackman, chairman of National Trust Company:

Since 1987, Canadian corporate debt has grown at twice the rate of government debt, with net interest costs as a percentage of pretax profits rising from 22 per cent to 45 per cent. What is tragic about the mortgaging of corporate Canada is that too little of this increased debt resulted in any net increase in productive investment. Where are the new factories? The new jobs or the new industries in this country? The vision that motivated the business leaders in the 1950s seems to have been lost. Instead, needed resources were used for takeovers, leveraged and management buyouts, the building of corporate empires at the expense of the tax system — empires which seem to have no social or economic purpose. In the 1980s it became fashionable to justify this activity by equating 19th century utilitarianism with 20th century cupidity and greed. While the business world, or large parts of it, was indulging in an orgy of self-gratification, our industrial plants deteriorated, the necessary retooling and restructuring necessary to compete in global markets was neglected, research and development expenditures were postponed, and concern for environmental issues ignored.

Greed and cupidity are, of course, not unique to the 1980s. They have been with us throughout history. However, what made the 1980s different from the years that preceded our most recent gilded age has been the unseemly worship or toleration of standards of conduct which in previous ages would not have been considered acceptable. (*Inside Guide*, June 1991)

It is amusing the way the financial press applauds the increasing takeover of Canadian business by foreign owners as a sign that the FTA is working to Canada's advantage. Or, rather, it would be amusing if it was not so sad.

The president of a steel fabricating company in Edmonton said that the problem with the FTA and increased competition from the United States is that it is causing *less* competition in Canada. Four or five suppliers he once dealt with have gone out of business or been taken over. According to the *Edmonton Journal*, "His costs rose immediately, reducing his competitiveness; he's now in a position where office and store fixtures can be made in the U.S. and shipped north for half his costs. 'I will stay another two years at the most. Most other people (small business) are in the same position. . . . I think it's going to be a catastrophe for the small guys.'"

Michael McCracken, of Infometrica Ltd. in Ottawa, believes the FTA was a key factor in the merger boom and the takeover of huge companies (such as Consolidated-Bathurst Inc. by Stone Container of Chicago). In 1985 acquisitions totalled about $8 billion. By comparison, mergers and acquisitions in 1989 were more than $30 billion, according to Investment Canada.

When is the last time you heard of a merger or takeover *creating* new jobs in Canada? If it happens, it's very rare. The reverse is usually true; many thousands of jobs are lost each year. When is the last time you saw mergers and acquisitions lead to lower prices? Ever? The increased debt loads invariably produce higher prices. And what about efficiency? As U.S. economist Walter Adams notes, if the enormous size of U.S. auto and steel companies was a key factor in competitiveness, such companies "should be the efficiency and innovation marvels of the world. Clearly they are not."

Not only is the Canadian economy foreign-dominated on a scale that would be unacceptable virtually everywhere else in the industrialized world, but it also has levels of corporate concentration that would be unacceptable elsewhere — a deadly combination.

Since Brian Mulroney became prime minister, big business has had effective control of the political and economic agenda, and hence the social and cultural agenda as well. Paul Desmarais provided much of the money for Pierre Trudeau's campaign, Brian Mulroney's campaign, and Jean Chrétien's campaign. The Desmarais group controls 69 corporations in Canada, including Power Corporation, the Great-West Life Assurance Company, and Investors Group Inc. The Irvings, with their tax haven in Bermuda, control 113 corporations and much of New Brunswick. The Weston Group has 126 corporations, including George Weston Ltd., E.B. Eddy, Loblaws, Kelly Douglas, Westfair Foods, and B.C. Packers Ltd. The Reichmann family controls Olympia & York, Block Bros., Abitibi-Price, Gulf Canada, and Hiram Walker Resources Ltd. The Edward and Peter Bronfman group controls more than 360 companies, among them Noranda, Labatt, MacMillan Bloedel, Trizec, Bramalea, and Brascade Resources. B.A.T. Industries of the U.K. controls 64 companies, including Imasco, Canada Trust, Genstar, and Imperial Tobacco. Charles Bronfman's trust controls 118 companies, and the K.R. Thomson Group controls 85.

Yet Conrad Black says, "The last thing our economic system needs is yet another outlet for our dreary national tendency to punish success." Poor Conrad. Perhaps he has missed out on something.

A look at the actual rates of return on capital in the business sector provides a totally different picture of profits in Canada than we receive from either the business community or the financial press. Recently released OECD figures show that, contrary to what we have been told so often during the past three years, business in Canada was doing very well indeed, in fact remarkably well, until the recent recession. In every year from 1980 to 1990, the return on capital in Canada exceeded both the OECD average and the European Community average, and in every year but one it exceeded the average of the G7 nations. Furthermore, the rates of return were well above OECD averages for the entire decade of the 1980s:

	1980-1986	1987	1988	1989	1990
Canada	16.8	18.6	18.9	18.3	16.7
OECD average	13.8	15.3	15.9	16.4	16.3

Invariably, the result of mergers and takeovers is reduced competition, higher prices, poorer service, and job layoffs. The champions of "market economics" are also champions of acquisitive control. For instance, when was the last time you saw real competition in bank interest rates? Or between banks or trust companies in mortgage rates? Or among oil companies in gasoline prices (except for the few token, periodic skirmishes intended to fool the press and public)?

Is it a healthy situation when 99 per cent of the hundreds of thousands of corporations in Canada get to share only 14 per cent of all non-financial industry assets? And when five big banks and a handful of large trust companies dominate the vital financial sector?

Finally, is it any wonder that time after time, when public opinion polls clearly show how Canadians strongly feel about various issues, the Mulroney government does exactly the opposite? For Mulroney, the polls from Rosedale, Forest Hill, Westmount, and Mount Royal are the polls that count.[1]

Part II

LAST CHANCE FOR CANADA

27

The Americanization of Canada

Gobbling Up the Neighbour

> The moneyed classes, having so many of the levers of
> national power in their hands, easily lose the distinction
> between personal and public interest. They thus convince
> themselves that their acts of national betrayal are actually
> for the people's good.   JOHN RALSTON SAUL, December 1987

> The Business Council on National Issues (is) the federal
> Progressive Conservative government as a numbered
> company.   MICHAEL VALPY, Globe and Mail, February 1991

> Canada must mesh its economic and tax policies with those
> of the United States or lose big under free trade, says the
> president of Dow Chemical Canada Inc. David Buzzelli
> said salary and benefits, interest rates, tax policies, social
> costs and inflation "all must be kept in line. . . . Free trade
> is a terrific, tremendous opportunity and we have to seize
> that opportunity."   CANADIAN PRESS, 2 June 1990

CANADA'S TAX SYSTEM, EXCESSIVE CORPORATE
concentration, and foreign ownership are three of the most
important reasons why our country is now in very big trouble. Many of the largest corporations care little for Canada;
they are ready to move to wherever they can generate the
most profits. Money is pretty well all that counts. Their

sense of community responsibility — their concerns about the economic, social, and cultural environment which they might leave behind — are minimal or nonexistent. Having engaged in a massive reduction of investment in Canada since the FTA, they now blame the election of an NDP government in Ontario for their "capital flight."

Simply put, the big corporations like no government if the government interferes in any way with their plans for expansion or with the maximization of profits. If leaving Canada is the goal, a Free Trade Agreement is the catalyst that allows the corporation flexibility. Profits from Canada will fund expansion in Georgia. Canadian tax laws will have facilitated the accumulation of capital for a new plant in the Mexican *maquiladoras*.

With the Mulroney government in power, the large corporations are in power. Their goals become the goals of the government and hence the goals of the society. The elected Tory politicians are the agents for the corporate society. Jobs don't count; profits do. Equity and fairness are irrelevant; corporate priorities are first and foremost. Responsibility to shareholders is low in priority compared to growth and greed, expansion and power. If you already own most of Canada, it is only natural that you will want to expand into other countries. If, in the process, the FTA allows you to close plants in Canada, so be it.

Those who oppose the policies of the large corporations are labelled protective, inward-looking, small-minded, afraid to compete, or as hiding behind closed doors or being narrow nationalists. How remarkable! Of all the nations in the industrialized world, Canada has always been one of the most open and receptive in terms of trade and investment. We managed large merchandise trade surpluses and a good standard of living without an FTA. But now the proponents of the FTA tell us that the only way they will stay in Canada is if we make all the other changes to bring us completely into line with American economic and social policies. To compete on the level playing field, we must reduce taxes, chop social programs, and do things exactly the way they do them in the United States. Harmonize. Integrate. Capitulate.

The major difference between those who led the support of the FTA and those who opposed it can be summed up in one sentence. The FTA means the Americanization of Canada; the supporters of the FTA approve of this, and the opponents strongly disapprove. Or, as George Grant put it, in *Lament for a Nation*, "In its simplest form, continentalism is the view of those who do not see what all the fuss is about."

The elite who own and control most of Canada have a very different view of the United States from that of most Canadians. Most Canadians like the U.S., but, as mentioned earlier, the vast majority don't want to become Americans and don't like a great deal about certain aspects of American society.

Not so the Canadian establishment. They like the lower taxes and they love the *laissez-faire* political and economic environment. When they visit the United States, they stay in expensive hotels or at posh resorts, and they live in walled, guarded compounds in Palm Desert or Palm Beach. The people they play tennis or golf with are very nice, very well-to-do Americans who pay less in taxes than they do. By and large, the Canadian elite like and admire Americans, their values, and their standards. They tend to watch the American television news and to rely on *Time*, *Forbes*, *Fortune*, the *New York Times*, the *Wall Street Journal*, and other American magazines and newspapers as their principal print sources of news and information. Many of their most valued business associates or bosses are American, and they regard the differences between Canada and the United States as minimal and as certainly not worth worrying about if Canadian practices have to be sacrificed to facilitate corporate expansion.

The pro-free-trade campaign was very well financed and brilliantly manipulative. Hundreds of large corporations on both sides of the border warned about the cataclysm that would inevitably occur if the Mulroney government was defeated. One well-known economist even suggested that Canada would become another Beirut. The federal government spent almost $13 million in taxpayers' money on free trade promotion. External Affairs sent out some 10 million pieces of literature. Media giant Maclean Hunter, the beneficiary of so much protective legislation and public subsidies, gave $50,000 to the Canadian Alliance for Trade and Job Opportunities; and its head man, Ron Osborne, sent a memo to 6000 employees saying, "The deal makes sense for Canada. . . . "[1] Powerful U.S. companies met secretly with government and business leaders in Washington, Toronto, and Ottawa to discuss the election in Canada. The Canadian Bankers' Association warned against rejecting the agreement. In Hamilton, Ontario, some 12,500 employees of Stelco received letters from their president, urging support for the deal. The Canadian Manufacturers' Association sent letters to 3000 members, and the Canadian Chamber of Commerce urged its 170,000 members to "go out there and shake the trees for free trade."[2] Loblaws, the Ford Motor Company, and other large corporations organized campaigns to convince their workers, and Ford distributed a video of its president defending the FTA in front of staff. The Alliance and others frequently quoted an Economic Council of Canada study which concluded that 375,000 new jobs would be created by 1995 and that Canada's gross national product would increase by 3.6 per cent.

In Canada it was David Culver, Thomas d'Aquino, Peter Lougheed, and Donald Macdonald who led the way. Thomas d'Aquino is president of the Business Council on National Issues (BCNI), which includes the big oil companies, the big auto companies, the major chemical companies and insurance firms, and, of course, the big banks. The heads of some 150 large corporations, with assets of close to a trillion dollars, make up the organization. One of the main initiators in setting up the BCNI was continentalist W. O. Twaits, former CEO of Imperial Oil. The organization was patterned after the very influential Business Round Table, which consists of 200 of the largest corporations in the United States. The BCNI hoped to "contribute . . . to the development of public policy and to the shaping of national priorities." And so it did.

Writing about the BCNI, political economist David Langille observed, "What is shocking is that Canadian business leaders met with American businessmen, with the U.S. ambassador, and with Vice-President George Bush, to solicit their endorsement for the deal, long before the Canadian government was even ready to discuss it." As some indication of the influence the BCNI has with the Mulroney government, Langille says that the "Business Council wrote its own weak competition legislation designed to regulate against monopolies and price-fixing and the government finally accepted it with a few amendments." Rowland Frazee, former Royal Bank head and one of Canada's leading continentalists, was an early BCNI chairman.

Among the members of the Business Council on National Issues are many of the most powerful and wealthiest transnational corporations in the world:

General Motors	Mobil Oil	Continental Can
General Mills	Quaker Oats	General Foods
Ford	Union Carbide	IBM
Du Pont	General Electric	Exxon
Sears	Campbell Soup	Lloyds Bank
Bechtel	Kraft	Merrill Lynch
Cargill	Procter & Gamble	Nabisco
Control Data	Honeywell	Texaco
Goodyear	Shell Oil	Imperial Oil
Xerox	ITT	Celanese
Kodak	American Express	Fletcher Challenge
3M	BP	Mitsubishi

Senior executives of Du Pont, Imperial Oil, Ford, Shell, ITT, and IBM are on the BCNI policy committee. So are leading Canadian continentalists such as David Culver, the Royal Bank's Allan Taylor, and Mickey Cohen, to mention only a a few. Some 30 percent of BCNI members are foreign-controlled corporations, and many others have extensive foreign ownership.

The BCNI was instrumental in setting up the Canadian Alliance for Trade and Job Opportunities, which spent millions of dollars selling Canadians the free trade deal. Setting aside the whole question of its deceptive media campaign, the Alliance, led by Culver, Peter Lougheed, and Donald Macdonald, lied to Canadians. Over and over again, they promised the press that they would reveal their source of funds. Shortly after the 1988 federal election, Tom d'Aquino said, "I look forward to reading a public retraction from Mr. Hurtig when the list of donors is made public next year." The full list of donors was never made public.

Alliance spokesman and Alcan employee Lorne Walls assured Canadians, "We don't have the big American corporations backing us," and promised that "not one cent came from one American company."[3] More lies. Large U.S. corporations funded much of the expensive Alliance campaign. Furthermore, when the Alliance was confronted, it didn't even have the decency to apologize for misleading the people of Canada. Contrast this with Tom d'Aquino's statement that, "in the free trade debate, you try to be as factual as possible."

No one should underestimate the role and effectiveness of David Culver in making certain that the Free Trade Agreement became a reality. The chairman and CEO of Alcan Aluminium Ltd. played a major role in masterminding the pro-free-trade campaign and setting up the Alliance, which many opponents regarded as essentially a front for the BCNI. Culver was chairman of the Alliance, most of whose funds came from BCNI members, and Alcan supplied staff services and offices for the new organization. One of the most amusing quotes during the debate came from Culver's right-hand man, Lorne Walls, who acted as spokesman for the Alliance: "We have nothing to do with politics. . . . We've always kept a long arm's-length distance from all governments and all parties and we're a little apprehensive about being active during the election campaign because now it's a partisan issue." One year later, during the election campaign, the Alliance was spending millions of dollars in ads that were clearly intended to benefit only the Conservative party.

The profiles of David Culver and Alcan are worth looking at because of what they represent. Alcan's profits in 1988 were an enormous $1.108 billion. Only about one-quarter of Alcan's employees work in Canada, and as reported in the *Wall Street Journal* in 1989, Alcan planned to double capital spending in the United States. In December 1987, Statistics Canada told me that over 56 per cent of Alcan was owned outside of Canada. As for David Culver, as well as being chairman and CEO of Alcan, he is honorary chairman of the BCNI and sits on the boards of several American companies, including American Express, Shearson Lehman Hutton, American Cyanamid, and J. P. Morgan & Co. Culver is a tough, confident guy. Witness his statement that Canada needs "more people who revel at the sight of their competitors' blood running down the streets." (For similar pleasantries, try that great democrat Conrad Black: "Those who claim Mulroney has given the national store away deserve to have their tongues plucked out with hot tongs, wielded by Mounties in red tunics.")

Anyone who has read Ronald Reagan's recent autobiography knows that Reagan was not in charge of the formulation of U.S. policy.[4] One tip off as to who was came from the relatively rapid passage of the free trade empowering legislation through the U.S. Congress. Clearly, everything had been orchestrated well in advance. There is good reason to believe that the U.S. Round Table (in other words, big business) developed the free trade initiative, just as it developed and controlled almost all of the legislative program during the Reagan years.

Paul H. Robinson, Jr., former American ambassador to Canada (1981-85), takes credit for pushing the idea of free trade with Thomas d'Aquino and others in 1983. In an interview with Peter Newman, Robinson explained: "I realized, of course, that the public initiative had to come from Canada, because if it came from us it would look as if we were trying to gobble up our neighbor. . . . We were afraid to call it free trade, so we referred to it as 'freer trade' which was kind of silly." Robinson went on to say that Brian Mulroney "is one of the finest men I've ever met. . . . I agree with him on just about everything."

So, more deception. The initiative came from the United States, but it was made to look as if it had originated in Canada.

In the United States it was American Express that led the way, hiring four high-powered political consulting, public relations, and lobbying firms to orchestrate its campaign. They spearheaded the Coalition for Free Trade with Canada. (Prominent in the coalition was Robert Strauss, the powerful lobbyist who so terrified former Canadian Ambassador Allan Gotlieb with his threats of "scorched earth" if Canada dared to try to regain more control of its book-publishing industry.) Meanwhile, many of the same corporations that are members of the BCNI had their parent companies in the U.S. championing the agreement in Washington: IBM, Du Pont, Goodyear, Honeywell, AT & T, Procter & Gamble, and many others. More than five hundred U.S. corporations were involved in the U.S. coalition.

As a sequel, it should be noted that on election day, 21 November 1988, the Mulroney government quietly passed an order-in-council giving American Express the right to operate as a commercial bank in Canada, even though American Express is not legally a bank in the United States.

The time has come to stop using muddy terms like "continentalists." Canadian political scientists have been woefully weak in not coming up with a more accurate description. So many of the voices heard from Canada's elite today are not the voices of continentalism; they are the voices of those who advocate the Americanization of Canada, though they never have the courage to say so. As much as separatists in Quebec, they are the anti-Canadians. They are the harmonizers, the integrationists, the capitulators, the abandoners of a nation. They are the "Canada-lasters." It seems as if many of them don't give a damn for our country, its welfare or its survival.[5]

28

Globalization

Walking All Over Governments

If we have free trade agreements like Canada-U.S., where the concept of national treatment enters or dominates, we'll see the demise of multinationals and the rise of what might be called transnationals, because you'll no longer have to be a multinational in the sense that the host country has any impact on you . . . you'll be able to walk over [national governments] because they have to treat you like their own nationals. THOMAS COURCHENE, *Queen's University, 1990*

Companies need to use free trade as a catalyst to mobilize employees to cut costs. Nothing clears the mind so much as the spectre of being hung in the morning.
RAY VERDON *of Nabisco Brands Ltd., Toronto Star, 10 April 1989*

Regional economies . . . will look outward to the global economy, rather than to national capitals, as the main force in shaping their economies. MARSHALL (MICKEY) COHEN,
speech in London, England, June 1991

N<small>O WORD HAS BEEN MORE COMMONLY USED IN</small> defence of the FTA than "globalization" (or "globalism"). And with globalism comes "the borderless world." Globalism is a very fashionable term in Canada. Hardly a luncheon or dinner speech goes by without it being saluted. But how many people, aside from the big transnationals, have thought through its consequences? Apparently not very many.

The global world of Ronald Reagan, George Bush, Margaret Thatcher, and Brian Mulroney is a world of deregulation and the overall weakening or abandonment of the powers of the nation-state. Most Canadians are still unaware of the fact that one of the most significant results of the FTA was a very large decline in the powers of not only the federal government but also provincial and local governments. This weakening of government was one of the unstated but foremost goals of the corporations that were behind the agreement.

Who should determine the goals and rules of a society? Most people would answer that it should be the society's elected representatives. In a true democracy that functions as it is intended, the elected representatives of the people are meant to govern in the best interests of the society — to help facilitate opportunities in an equitable manner, to regulate resource utilization, to improve educational, health, and other social policies, to protect the environment, and to respond to the many other concerns and priorities of a civilized society. As well, they are expected to restrict or abolish monopolies and oligopolies.

It is argued (though not very convincingly) that the process of globalization brings society benefits by breaking down barriers and destroying the powers of nation-states. But the obvious question must then be: In a world of weakened nations and of strong transnational corporations, who looks after the egalitarian aspirations of society? In a world without world government, who is responsible for regulating the growing wealth and power of the corporations, and who is responsible for justice? In short, are corporations or the people to be in charge of our future?

Gradual and imperfect as it has been, the evolution of modern society has put more power in the hands of people and taken it away from monarchs, dictators, and the baron kings of industry. Until recently. The world of the Round Table and the world of the BCNI is a world of concentration of wealth, with little or no sense of social responsibility, and with matters relating to independence, the welfare of the citizenry, the distribution of income, cultural aspirations and the like, all taking second place to the goals of the corporation. The corporation is first, foremost, and supreme.

The theory of globalism is simple: trust the large corporations to make the right decisions, which will inevitably benefit society. Allow them to accumulate ever more and more wealth ("or else we'll move production to Mexico or Taiwan or Kuala Lumpur"), to lower wages and social standards ("or you'll be hung out to dry in the morning") and to weaken all governments so that they don't interfere with corporate goals. No doubt about it, some of the wealth will eventually manage to trickle down to some of the people.

But above all, the corporation must be free to be competitive. The corporation must make the key decisions about where new economic activity will take place. In the name of free enterprise, mergers and acquisitions must be allowed, even if they reduce competition, even if they increase prices and concentrate more ownership and power. Yes, the massive debt loads that result will require even higher prices and even lower wages and benefits, but, after all, the corporation must keep up with the competition.

As the concentration of wealth increases, as more markets are captured through eliminating competition, the power of the corporations in society grows and the power of people declines. Uninhibited corporate growth becomes the goal; human values are submerged. National aspirations are denigrated and shunted aside, and the nation-state becomes a fossil of the past. After all, "economies will look outward to the global economy, rather than to national capitals, as the main force in shaping their economies."

Let's run that by again. Look outward to exactly whom? To the boards of General Motors or Mitsubishi? Or will we

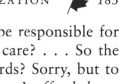

be looking to Exxon? Exactly who will be responsible for schools, for the environment, for health care? . . . So the people want better environmental standards? Sorry, but to be competitive in the global economy, we can't afford them; remember, we're going to be competing on a level playing field with the cesspool environmental standards in Mexico. You want better working conditions in the factories or pregnancy leave for women? Forget it. They don't have such unnecessary frills in South Korea. You want to tax corporations fairly? No way! If that happens, we'll move to Buffalo.

In other words, the constitution of the corporation becomes the constitution of the population. Do we really want to live in a world run by the giant transnational corporations? Most Canadians would answer emphatically no. Yet that is exactly the direction we are heading. From the beginning, the name of the game for the big American corporations was a continental deal guaranteeing cheap Canadian energy and resources and cheap Mexican labour. Brian Mulroney gave them the first two, and a corrupt Mexican government is about to give them the second.

All this is extremely ironic in view of the repeated complaints, mostly from the right, of overcentralization. Who will the people in the Reform party appeal to in a globalized world? To exactly which elected representatives? If we are too centralized already, imagine the supernational clusters now being fostered by the transnationals — a world in which faceless and nameless bureaucratic servants of the corporations run society as a collection of corporate, borderless host states. Ultimately, as the transnationals become more and more dominant, their huge factories in low-wage, low-benefit countries will serve the world.

Today, many people seem to be confused by the two dominant political themes of the 1990s, globalism and the emerging new nationalism. They would be less confused if they remembered how remarkably well Canadians, the kings of compromise, had succeeded in balancing some of the basic concerns of modern society before Brian Mulroney arrived on the scene. The balance, while far from perfect, was between centralized decision making and ample powers for the provinces, between being an open society and protecting our own priorities, between an outward positioning to the world and introspection, between the evolution of our own standards and the absorption of those of others. To be sure, it was not perfect, but in such a large country and still such a young country, it was a remarkable achievement.

The advantage of the nation-state is that it allows the people the freedom to determine their own future to the best of their ability. People of common values and inclinations build traditions and develop a legal framework for the society they have evolved . . . for the preservation of their heritage, their culture, their moral standards, their ethics, and their customs. Different nations have different standards and values; and to the extent that democracy functions properly, these standards and values are reflected in the way the society functions.

Living next door to the world's most nationalistic and patriotic superpower, Canadians, probably the least nationalistic people on earth, were repeatedly warned not to be too chauvinistic or too nationalistic. With an $81 billion five-year merchandise trade surplus as one of the world's great trading nations, we were warned that we had better stop being inward-looking and should become more competitive. In a world where the nation-state will continue to be the basic unit of human organization, we were told that we should prepare to abandon national powers and get ready to wipe out all borders. In a nation with a remarkably high real standard of living[1] combined with a very good quality of life, we were told that we had to change everything and become much more like Americans, if not actually becoming Americans. In a world where more and more people are returning to "small is beautiful" as a desirable human creed, we were told and sold that only big counts.[2]

Globalization is the new religion of big business. It is a Darwinian religion with the undemocratic standards and values of centuries past.

29

Lougheed and Hearst Are Happy

And Pop Is Pleased Too!

> The momentous move towards uniting the two countries economically is very gratifying to me. For more than a decade my pop urged in his newspapers that Canada become part of the U.S.   WILLIAM RANDOLPH HEARST, JR.,
> 11 October 1987

> The Canadians don't understand what they have signed. In 20 years, they will be sucked into the U.S. economy.
> CLAYTON YEUTTER, U.S. trade official, Toronto Star, 22 October 1987

> The trade remedy laws cannot apply to Canada, period!
> BRIAN MULRONEY, New York Times, 2 April 1987

> [Such a dispute settlement] mechanism without a formal agreement is like a court without laws; if we have not settled by formal agreement such matters as what constitutes acceptable subsidies, there is nothing for a dispute-settlement body to settle.   RICHARD LIPSEY, economist, 8 August 1985

THE SAME FORCES IN CANADIAN SOCIETY THAT SO cleverly plotted the campaign which gratified U.S. publishing magnate William Randolph Hearst, Jr., are now hard at work finishing the job of uniting U.S. money and control with Canadian resources and cheap Mexican labour. The

Canadian compradors are loyally doing their full share. And, once again, Brian Mulroney is chief factotum.

Now, almost three years after implementation of the Free Trade Agreement, a number of things are very clear that were in murky dispute in 1987 and 1988. So before we look at the ramifications of a trilateral FTA with Mexico, let us briefly review a few more of the consequences of the bilateral deal.

Despite Brian Mulroney's protestation to the contrary in the *New York Times*, all U.S. trade laws do indeed continue to apply to Canadian exports to the United States. Not only is Canada not exempt from U.S. trade laws, but in the FTA implementation legislation, the U.S. Congress insisted that there should be special scrutiny for Canada on an annual basis, with a mandatory detailed report on "unfair" Canadian practices as interpreted by U.S. law.[1] And as economist Richard Lipsey pointed out, since there was no agreement as to what constitutes subsidies, U.S. trade law is the basis of almost all disputes, since most of them stem from U.S. protective actions.

Given the long list of current impediments for Canadian exporters who attempt the promised "guaranteed access" to the U.S. market, the recent hoopla over the pork ruling, as a vindication that the FTA is working, is a sad commentary on how desperate the Mulroney government and the financial press are for any news to balance the many disastrous effects of the agreement on Canada. The pork "victory" followed several dispute settlement defeats. The final decision took more than twice as long as a GATT decision would have taken, and it cost millions of dollars that the industry would not have had to pay if the case had gone to GATT. These millions of dollars and almost two and a half years of legal dispute managed to produce the great triumph of reinstating the pre-FTA status quo and removing a countervail duty of the kind that the prime minister said "cannot apply to Canada, period!" We now find that live hogs shipped from

Canada to the United States may face double the current U.S. duties by the fall of 1991, retroactive to 1988.

What is abundantly clear is that Canada did not achieve its principal objective in entering into the free trade talks — namely, guaranteed access to the U.S. market. The many continuing trade disputes between Canada and the United States, the falling investment and increased unemployment in Canada, the deindustrialization of our economy, and our declining balance of payments position with the U.S. all speak for themselves.

Some of the industries in Canada that have been hurt or seriously harmed since the FTA went into effect are appliances, machinery and equipment, flour mills, food processors, trucking, steel, power boats, lobster fisheries, limousine manufacturers, ice cream and yogurt producers, fish processors, plywood manufacturers, auto parts, canola crushing, grape growing, textiles, clothing, commercial printing, furniture, forestry, sugar, and beverages. The forest industry, one of Canada's leading exporters, has lost thousands of jobs. The auto-parts industry faces steadily declining sales to the United States. Canada's once-proud steel industry is in a crisis and expects that exports to the U.S. will diminish by one-third. And some 6000 jobs have been lost in the furniture industry, where a $268 million trade surplus has been turned into a $135 million deficit.[2]

Since the FTA, there has been a long and growing list of protectionist U.S. actions against Canadian exporters: anti-dumping charges, countervailing duties, meat inspection obstructions, the tightening up of numerous rules that were not previously enforced, border auto inspections for Canadian content, import quotas (sugar products), long border delays (auto parts and clothing), and so on. For a number of Canadian industries used to exporting into the U.S. market, harassment at the border is an increasing and serious problem.

A child of the FTA — and of its handmaidens the GST and a high Canadian dollar — is cross-border shopping, with its devastating impact on retailers in Canada and the multiplier effect this has on manufacturing and on the service sector of the Canadian economy. There are many other areas where the true impact of the FTA is now only beginning to sink in. Regional programs are severely constrained. Marketing boards and all forms of supply management are under attack.[3] Export taxes to ensure Canadian processing or upgrading are no longer possible. Local content regulations, local sourcing policies, and policies of import substitution are either threatened or impossible.

The agreement freezes Canadian cultural policy in place. In what was trumpeted as a great victory for Canada, the Mulroney government effectively agreed that the heavy U.S. dominance of Canada's cultural industries would be forever written in stone as part of the agreement and that any important future attempt to implement Canadian cultural initiatives would have to be approved first in Washington. Canada, the colony.

Today, some 77 per cent of all magazines sold in Canada are foreign, as are 83 per cent of records and tapes, and 96 per cent of videocassette sales; 76 per cent of all book sales in Canada are of foreign titles; 96 per cent of movie screenings are of foreign films, and virtually all of the revenue from our movie theatres leaves Canada. Over 90 per cent of all English-language television drama shown in Canada is foreign. The vast majority of the revenue from all of these cultural areas goes straight south to the United States. *Ottawa Citizen* columnist Marjorie Nichols summed it up well: "Those who believe that cultural industries . . . will be preserved under free trade . . . must also believe in the tooth fairy."

The question of subsidies was not resolved for two reasons. First, the United States understood how vulnerable to failure of the negotiations the Mulroney government was, with its oft-stated public position that Canada "had to" get an agreement. (The U.S. demands regarding subsidies were so outrageous that even Simon Reisman had to leave the negotiating table temporarily.) Secondly, the United States never really wanted an agreement on subsidies once it had obtained agreement to virtually all of its important objectives. Why should it want a clear definition of subsidies included in the FTA? The U.S. uses massive defence industry subsidies to stimulate its high-tech industries and to create new domestic employment and export products. Since defining subsidies might constrict U.S. trade negotiations with Japan and the European Community, the decision was made to "delay" the definition resolution for from five to seven years. Perhaps one of the greatest ironies here is the huge amount of subsidies that U.S. states are now employing to lure eager Canadian entrepreneurs to move their businesses south of the border.[4]

If the investment provisions of the agreement were ill-conceived, if the failure to consider the exchange rate was a foolish and fatal flaw, and if the abandonment of control over our ability to institute a wide variety of new public programs was a grievous error, what the Mulroney government did in energy constitutes such a blatant sellout of the Canadian public interest that it is difficult to imagine how any citizens of this country could have negotiated and signed such an agreement without forever hiding their faces in shame.

It is impossible, in a few paragraphs, to do justice to the dimensions of the Canadian sellout on energy in the FTA. In the future, entire books will be written on this single aspect of the agreement. Here, I shall give simply a brief list, together with one more comment on the press in Canada. The abandonment of Canada's control over its energy supplies and energy policies should have been front-page headline news. Instead, today not one in a hundred Canadians understands how much we gave away and how serious the implications are for the future of our country. Only one newspaper, the *Toronto Star*, gave Canada a comprehensive, objective, and accurate description of the dimensions of the energy sellout.

Let us turn to two enthusiastic supporters of the FTA for their comments on the energy provisions. First, former Alberta premier and Alliance leader Peter Lougheed. In an interview published on 5 November 1987, he proudly proclaimed, "It will no longer be possible to set a new made-in-Canada oil or natural gas price." A few days later, on the television show *Crossfire*, he exulted, "I think the deal made was better than I expected."[5] David Yager, publisher of the oil industry magazine *Roughneck*, who is another fan, said, "We can't have a made-in-Canada price. That's what the free trade agreement is all about."

From a somewhat different perspective, here is a branch of the Consumers' Association of Canada: "We are at a loss to understand how a government which has the interests of Canadians at heart, would enter into an agreement with a foreign power, which would provide that power even greater access to the diminishing supplies of essential commodities."

Articles 408, 409, and 904 of the Free Trade Agreement contain provisions that no self-respecting government anywhere in the world would have accepted. In summary:

- Canadians no longer have the ability to set the prices for their own vital energy supplies.
- Canadian oil prices will be determined not by Canadians but by OPEC and the U.S. market.
- Canada gave away the ability to charge Americans higher prices than Canadians for its own oil and natural gas. (Whatever happened to "comparative advantage"?)
- Canada abandoned the ability to ensure a reasonable minimum price for oil and gas exports (in a country where most of these exports are sold by foreign-controlled corporations to other foreign-controlled corporations!).
- Canada agreed to continue to sell the United States the same proportion of resources that it has supplied to the U.S. over the previous 36-month period, even if Canadians are running short.

- Even if resource exploration, development, or pipelines have been heavily subsidized by Canadian taxpayers, Canada agreed not to charge Americans a higher price for resource exports than the price Canadians pay.
- Canada agreed to abandon all mechanisms which might encourage or ensure the upgrading of resources before they are exported.
- Canada agreed to pricing arrangements and resource-sharing arrangements that would forever make it impossible to employ Canadian resources and energy strategically as a stimulus for industrial development in this country.
- Canada agreed that it would drastically curtail the ability of the National Energy Board to protect the interests of Canadians with surplus tests, pricing requirements, or net benefit measurements.
- Whereas under GATT provisions Canada could control resource exports for reasons of conservation, for domestic refining and processing requirements, and in order to achieve price stabilization, Canada signed away these abilities under the FTA.

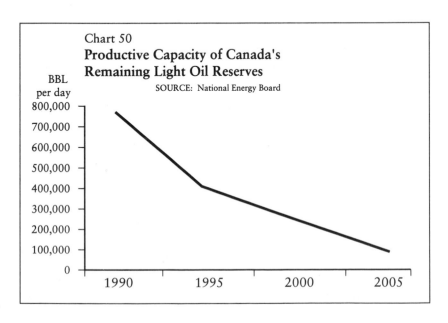

Chart 50
Productive Capacity of Canada's Remaining Light Oil Reserves

BBL per day

SOURCE: National Energy Board

Chart 50 provides a good picture of how, in only a few years, all Canadians will realize what a serious blunder the energy provisions of the FTA are. Canada's conventional oil reserves peaked in 1969, producing some 1.7 million barrels a day, and have since declined by almost 60 per cent.[6] Productive capacity was 734,000 barrels a day in 1990; in less than four years from now it will be below 400,000 barrels a day, and Canada will have become a net importer of oil by 1993. By 2005, our conventional production is expected to be only 145,000 barrels a day.

Meanwhile, contrary to all promises of both the industry and the government, energy exploration in Canada has dropped since the FTA went into effect, falling to well below the levels prior to 1989. Employment in the industry is down some 40 per cent from the levels of the early 1980s, and frontier energy exploration has almost stopped. With the FTA has come deregulation. Natural gas export prices are now down to one-half of what they were in 1985 and about only 40 per cent of what the regulated prices were in 1980. The graph of Canadian gas exports to the United States forms an almost perfect X. The line for the quantities exported goes straight uphill to the right, and the line representing the selling price goes straight downhill. Today, we export some 40 per cent of all natural gas production to the United States, much of it at very low prices and on long-term locked-in contracts. (By the way, the GST now ensures that we Canadians will pay even more for our oil and natural gas than Americans do.)

To sum up . . .

Do you want to charge Americans higher prices because Canadian taxpayers footed the bill for energy exploration and development, or because of "free enterprise" market demand? There's no problem about that — as long as you charge Canadians exactly the same higher prices.

Are you worried that in a cold northern country we are beginning to run short of oil and could be left in a dangerous and vulnerable position? No problem. We can cut back exports to the U.S., provided we also cut back sales to Canadians.

Do you want to reduce production of a resource because prices are too low or because you wish to ensure that your province's industries don't run short? No problem. British Columbia can be cut off, Ontario can be cut off, Manitoba can be cut off — but not our buddies, the Americans.

Do you want to encourage new industrial development, attract new investment, diversify your economy, or provide your industries with a competitive advantage through lower energy prices than offered to Americans? Forget it; you can't.

Do you think that as market conditions change we can alter the FTA energy provisions accordingly to take advantage of the new changing conditions? No way! — except that we *can* sell for lower and lower prices any time we want.

Do you think that Canada might have been wise to have aimed for a policy of energy self-sufficiency when it had ample opportunity to do so? You can say goodbye forever to such foolish ideas. The name of the game now is to export as much of our resources as quickly as possible, with no regard to price or security of supply.

Do you want to establish a national electric power grid? Sorry, too late.

Do you think it was all worth while anyway because we gained guaranteed access to the U.S. market for our resources? No way! U.S. trade remedy laws and state legislation are still obstructive whenever Americans find it to their advantage to play hardball. But it's not a total disaster, is it? The United States did get guaranteed access to Canadian resources. So we'll have many more Hibernias in the future — expensive megaprojects ($5.6 billion for Hibernia), largely financed with Canadian taxpayers' money ($3.175 billion for Hibernia), producing comparatively small quantities of energy (a total of about one year's supply of oil for Canada from Hibernia), which will likely all end up going to the United States anyway (as will almost certainly be the case with

Hibernia). Good old Canadian taxpayers will pump billions of dollars into frontier and offshore projects and new oil-sands plants, whose subsidized product can then be purchased by Americans simply by outbidding Canadian buyers. Or, as Shell Oil says: "If we can make a fair deal with Canadians, we'll sell it to them." (In case there is any doubt, "it" is Canadian oil and natural gas.)

How utterly, utterly stupid!

How stupid to say we will sell energy at below replacement costs! How absurd to agree to supply non-Canadians even if Canadians are running short![7] How nonsensical to weaken and abandon our standards measuring future Canadian requirements! How preposterous to turn our energy regulating agency, charged with protecting the future needs of Canadians, into yet another federal government charade! How incredibly irresponsible to agree that our future elected representatives will no longer be able to ensure premium fees for energy exports! How plain dumb, in a huge, cold, northern country, to say that we cannot, from time to time as we may wish, limit the exports of our energy and other resources! How bloody incompetent to take a vital comparative advantage and turn it into a competitive disadvantage!

But it can't be all bad, can it? After all, Peter Lougheed is happy.

30

On the Road to Mexico

Free Trade Part Two: The Three Amigos

> Profit means money. Money has no heart, no soul, no con-
> science, no homeland.
>
> FRANK STRONACH of Magna International Inc., announcing plans to
> establish manufacturing operations in Mexico, 11 June 1991

> Michael Wilson has said he wants to see Canadian firms
> get the same access to the inexpensive Mexican labour pool
> as U.S. firms while protecting Canada's unique market
> access in the U.S.   FINANCIAL POST, 12 June 1991

> What happens if you (Canadians) go back to the bargain-
> ing table and the U.S. says we want more?
>
> PETER MURPHY, former U.S. trade negotiator,
> Toronto Star, January 1990

WHAT HAPPENS INDEED! WE ALREADY KNOW
from sections 304 and 409 of the U.S. implementation legislation for the Canada-U.S. Free Trade Agreement, as well as
from numerous public statements ever since from Carla
Hills, Jules Katz, and other senior U.S. trade officials, that
the U.S. has a well-established priority hit list for future discussions with Canada. It includes:

- the elimination of any remaining restrictions on U.S.
  investment, ownership, and control in Canada;

- the elimination of any and all protection for Canadian culture industries — in particular, book publishing, television, magazines, and films;
- the elimination of any agricultural rules and regulations that impede U.S. access to the Canadian market;
- the elimination of autopact safeguards;
- the elimination of any restrictions for U.S. participation in the service sector of the Canadian economy;
- the elimination of any remaining restrictions relating to U.S. access to Canadian natural resources and energy;
- the abolition of any Canadian standards which the U.S. regards as unfair impediments to access to the Canadian market (such as packaging and labelling, etc.);
- greater access by American firms to Canada's telecommunications industry;
- an increase from 50 to 60 per cent in the amount of North American content required for duty-free automobile sales;
- greater U.S. access to the Canadian plywood market via reduced plywood standards;
- a clarification that water sharing is indeed part of the Canada-U.S. deal; and
- the removal of Canadian restrictions on the import of eggs, chickens, and other poultry products from the U.S.

As far as the Americans are concerned, "everything is up for negotiation." And what does the Mulroney government want? It wants whatever the BCNI and Canada's big banks want — a North American Free Trade Agreement. Why? Look again at the first two quotations at the opening of this chapter. But there are also two other reasons. First, Canada's big banks see the trilateral talks as an opportunity for them to move much or most of their banking activities to the United States. That is the unstated reason why the Mulroney government is now one of the three free-trade amigos. The other unstated reason is fear. Ottawa is terrified that the FTA has placed Canada in a totally untenable position. Having been promised an exclusive deal with the United States, having trumpeted to the nation the expected benefits of an exclusive deal, having a good understanding of the motivations of the BCNI and the large banks, a confused and panicked government is at the table because it believes that it has no other choice.

And, once again, we are the supplicant. The U.S. has *allowed* us to be present. Even though, by a two-to-one margin, Canadians are against a trilateral deal, that doesn't matter, as Michael Walker of the Fraser Institute says, so long as you have a majority in the House of Commons.

In the Mexican *maquiladora*[1] areas just south of the U.S. border, there are already some 1800 plants and some 500,000 workers, mostly women. *Maquiladoras* wages go from 50 cents an hour to $1.60 on average in the Mexican auto-parts industry. Most workers in the *maquiladoras* corridor earn 60 cents to $1 an hour, and child labour is paid $4 a day. One plant pays 50 cents an hour for a ten-hour day; the average age of the workers in the plant is eighteen. Overall, the average Mexican wage is some 15 per cent of the U.S. rate, but in the *maquiladoras* it is only some 7 per cent. In 1989, the average wage rate in manufacturing was $1.90 in Mexico, $14.71 in Canada, and $14.32 in the United States. However, with the growing popularity of the low-wage *maquiladoras*, real wages in Mexico have fallen some 50 per cent during the past decade,[2] and 40 per cent of the work force now earn less than the official minimum wage.

Not only are wages by far the lowest in the Western world (and much lower than in Taiwan, Singapore, and Korea, for example) but the benefits are virtually nonexistent and the working and housing conditions are abysmal. Health and safety standards are often appalling, and toxic waste disposal is a serious and growing problem that receives little attention.

More than a thousand U.S. manufacturers are already located in the *maquiladoras* corridor along the Mexican-U.S. border. The Mexicans advertise a saving of $25,000 a year per assembly worker. Canadian companies such as Mitel,

Northern Telecom, Fleck Manufacturing, and Custom Trim Ltd. are there, too, along with U.S. companies which moved from Canada to Mexico, such as Bendix Safety Restraints of Collingwood, Ontario. The wages are low, the standards are low, the corporate taxes are low. Is it any wonder that big business in the United States is already spending millions of dollars lobbying for the new deal?

Michael Wilson's promises about the current talks are about as reliable as all of the many promises made during the Canada-U.S. talks. In other words, they are worthless. Canada will pay dearly for whatever access the Royal Bank and friends get to the U.S. banking system. After giving the Americans so much already in the bilateral talks, our bargaining position is nonexistent. But, more important, a Canada-U.S.-Mexico free trade deal would be the final nail in the coffin for Canadian industry. The deindustrialization process would soon be complete, unemployment would skyrocket, and our standard of living would plummet. Ronald Reagan's "economic constitution for North America" would be a reality.

In Europe, the European Community's Social Charter helps poorer countries to raise their standards towards those of the better-off nations. The North American Free Trade Area will do exactly the opposite. Witness Michael Wilson's ready endorsement of the U.S. administration's position on environmental standards:

> Trade Minister Michael Wilson threw his support Tuesday behind the Bush administration's position that environmental issues be excluded from negotiations on a North American free-trade zone. . . .
>
> U.S. environmental groups, backed by organized labour, say free trade with Mexico should be made contingent on its environmental and enforcement standards conforming to those north of the border. Otherwise, they argue, American and foreign companies will shift their manufacturing operations to Mexico to take advantage of less onerous standards. The results

would be that Mexico's pollution problems would get worse and thousands of American manufacturing jobs would be lost. (*Globe and Mail*, 1 May 1991)

Mexico's labour laws, its environmental standards, and its attitude towards the working poor are right out of the dark ages. Clearly, the workers are as exploited as anywhere in the world. The *maquiladoras* factories have been in operation for more than twenty years, and rather than serving to raise the standard of living, they have placed women, children, and whole families in bondage.

The *Wall Street Journal* (18 April 1991) put it very well:

During the past decade, hundreds of U.S. companies, lured by Mexico's rock-bottom wages and lack of effective government regulations and enforcement, have shut down factories and relocated in the maquiladora areas. While American workers were losing their jobs, more than a half-million Mexicans working in maquiladora plants were joining the ranks of the most crudely exploited humans on the planet. The result has been conditions along the Mexican side of the border that rival any of the well-publicized disasters of the worst Stalinist regimes. Yet the maquiladoras continue to be lauded as a godsend to Mexican workers — a source of desperately needed jobs and economic development. As for the prospect of American workers finding new jobs in industries that produce goods for the Mexican market — what do they propose to sell to people who earn $27 a week? The fact is that trade is good for workers only when it is carried out side-by-side with minimum standards of wages, benefits, safety and environment.

Canadians who are bent on helping the tens of millions of miserably poor Mexicans can do much better than perpetuate their poverty and deny them the opportunity for self-betterment in an agreement which will essentially benefit enormously wealthy transnational corporations.[3]

31

Industrial Policy

Marching Blindfold into the Twenty-first Century

> *While the rest of the world is getting its act together,*
> *Canadians are still arguing over whether they should com-*
> *mission a script.*   GERALDINE KENNEY-WALLACE, *president,*
> *McMaster University*

> *National prosperity is created, not inherited.*
> MICHAEL PORTER, *The Competitive Advantage of Nations, 1990*

> *The critics of "industrial policy" usually fail to distinguish*
> *between those remedies that have outlived their usefulness*
> *— and hence deserve criticism — and those, perhaps still*
> *undiscovered, that are needed to cope with today's radically*
> *changed and dynamic world. The contemporary challenge is*
> *to create new policies to ensure that Canada reaps the full*
> *potential . . . [of] a more productive economy and society.*
> NATIONAL ADVISORY BOARD ON SCIENCE AND TECHNOLOGY,
> *Science and Technology, Innovation and National Prosperity, April 1991*

JAMES GILLIES, THE RESPECTED FORMER CONSERVATIVE
member of Parliament who was once senior policy adviser to
the prime minister, is probably the leading proponent of an
industrial strategy for Canada. Gillies believes that support

for the concept of an industrial strategy is building, but there seems to be little evidence of this in Canada's business press, and there is staunch, unrelenting opposition from the dominant Canadian business groups. In a world of growing corporate concentration, with increasing centralized corporate control and strategic long-term planning, big business prefers the invisible hand, the mythical, magical market, to any government actions to look and plan ahead. However, the record is clear. Countries that have adopted an industrial strategy have been very successful. Gillies points to Taiwan. It is because of public policy that Taiwan, with a population of about 20 million, exports the same amount as 154 million Brazilians and about four times more than 85 million Mexicans, even though Mexico is located next door to the world's largest market and Taiwan is 6000 miles away.

Gillies also cites leading industrial nations such as West Germany and Japan: "They rely on well-planned and -executed skill-training systems. They foster stability in the workplace and in social programs, and they understand that manufacturing is a significant engine of growth. They create sophisticated regulatory environments that support policy for favoured industry sectors, without having to resort only to simplistic tax breaks and outright subsidies." And here is a key consideration: "A country should have national goals and its corporations should regard themselves as citizens as much as any individual — with obligations as well as rights. It is nonsense to separate the economy of a country from the overall well-being of its people."

The above statements by the founding dean of York University's School of Administrative Studies speak volumes about what is fundamentally wrong with our country. Canada, the world's leading branch-plant nation, also has enormous corporate concentration, but unfortunately it does not have many Canadian or foreign corporations that regard themselves as having a responsibility for the well-being of the people of the country. In fact, since the implementation of the FTA, we have seen exactly the reverse — a blatant disdain for corporate responsibility to the community.

But why should huge transnational corporations feel a responsibility to Canada's national goals or to the overall well-being of its people? Similarly, Canadian corporations that pull their trucks up to factory doors in the middle of the night — and load their machinery for a one-way trip to Mexico or North Carolina — obviously do not believe they have many obligations to Canadians.

It is ironical that although industrial strategies have been so remarkably successful in other countries, the FTA makes it totally impossible for Canada to pursue such policies. The strategic tools employed by so many developed countries and now used so well by the newly industrialized countries — the investment regulations, the incentives, the government procurement strategies, and the bulk of the sophisticated arsenals now being employed by so many other countries — are simply no longer available to Canadians.

The fundamental question is this: Is there a national interest? If there is, then planning to protect the national interest is clearly mandatory. If not, then there is no need for national planning.

Is it important for Canada to have east-west transportation and communications systems? Is it important to use our resources in a prudent manner, with some consideration for the future? Is it important that we equip our citizens with the skills and resources that will allow them a good standard of living and an environment that will help them enjoy a good quality of life? Is it important that we own and control our own country?

If the answer to these questions is yes, then Canada must have a well-thought-out industrial strategy. But we should no more want a new national industrial strategy put in place by government alone than we would want business alone or labour alone to put it into place. We should therefore do what so many countries around the world do (but not the

United States) — we should have a permanent mechanism for close consultation and close working relations, in a spirit of cooperation rather than antagonism, between government, business, and labour. That is what is done in Germany, Austria, Norway, Sweden, Denmark, Switzerland, and Japan.

In Canada, alone among all industrial nations,[1] the invisible hand of Adam Smith and the fairy tales of Milton Friedman rule. As the rest of the word plans, priorizes, and prepares, Canada prepares for only one thing: to march blindfold and empty-handed into the twenty-first century.

If I had to summarize, as succinctly as possible, a new industrial policy for Canada, it would be this: Canada should become infinitely more self-reliant, much less dependent, and hence far less vulnerable. Only in Canada has business convinced government that an unregulated market should rule and that the market rules fairly and wisely. Only in Canada has business convinced government that, unlike business, government should not plan ahead and should not evolve strategies for the future. Big business hates "industrial strategies" and "industrial policies" — except those developed by big business for the benefit of big business.

32

Principles and Policies

Alternatives and Solutions

> *Only nationalism could provide the political incentive for planning; only planning could restrain the victory of continentalism. . . . No such combination was possible and therefore our nation was bound to disappear.*
>
> GEORGE GRANT, *Lament for a Nation, 1965*

> *It's high time Canadians began to interfere in their own internal affairs.* ABRAHAM ROTSTEIN, *economist, quoted by*
>
> *Andrew H. Malcolm in The Canadians, 1985*

THERE IS NO QUICK CURE FOR THE SERIOUS ECOnomic problems we now have in Canada, no single new policy, no magic panacea to turn our country around. But there are many excellent alternatives, many good solutions to the serious problems we face. A comprehensive, multifaceted set of new policies will have to be put in place.

First, there are some basic steps that must be taken if Canada is to survive in the short term and thrive in the future.

Priority number one: we must get rid of the terrible, inept, nation-destroying Mulroney government in the next federal election.

Next, as soon as we possibly can, we must abrogate the Free Trade Agreement. There will be no Canada left if the FTA remains in place much longer. If Jean Chrétien, Paul

Martin, Jr., or any other politicians tell you that they will renegotiate the agreement, tell them they are naive and consequently you have no confidence in them. The Americans will never agree to renegotiate the agreement — unless, of course, Canada agrees to make even more major concessions. The FTA must be abrogated, not renegotiated.

Next, we must stop the growth of foreign ownership in Canada. There is far too much already and it is damaging our productivity and competitiveness and seriously threatening our standard of living. Foreign ownership can be curtailed in a variety of ways, all beginning with a new government. Many countries around the world employ a key sector approach to protecting various areas of their economies. Some simply prohibit foreign ownership above designated percentages. Others prohibit any foreign participation except for joint ventures with domestically owned and controlled firms. There will be no need for Canada to adopt a costly buy-back approach. Tough limits on the growth of foreign ownership in the future will solve the problem.

We also need vastly improved, effective legislation that will provide for much closer monitoring of the activities of foreign corporations in Canada and much greater disclosure of their operations, especially the details of parent-subsidiary-affiliate business relationships in connection with transfer pricing and non-arm's-length purchases of business services. Foreign investment is like a martini. One martini may be great, but two can be dangerous and three can be deadly. Canada has had a pitcherful. While selective, limited foreign investment can be beneficial, majority foreign ownership and control of a large number of important sectors of the economy is a guaranteed recipe for disaster. Joint ventures, when required, can and should be allowed on a selective basis, but only when majority ownership and truly effective control resides in Canada.

Canada must put into place tough laws limiting corporate concentration in this country. It is far too high at present and is not only seriously damaging our economy but is also threatening our political system. By changing the tax system to eliminate interest deductibility on corporate takeovers, we could discourage more corporate concentration instead of encouraging it, as the tax system currently does.

Overall, we need to develop a far fairer and more progressive tax system which would be more broadly based and much more effective than our present grossly inequitable system. There are in fact many viable alternatives to the GST. Imposing more effective taxes on large corporations would be a good place to start. An increase in the personal income tax rate for the top one-fifth of Canadian taxpayers would be another. As well, there should be more corporate audits and far more attention to transfer pricing; this would yield billions of dollars in tax revenue. The number of Revenue Canada's tax audits on corporations has dropped dramatically in recent years, from almost 7.5 per cent of corporations to less than 2 per cent. Revenue Canada has stated that in 1988, for every dollar spent on audits, more than $17 in tax revenue was collected.

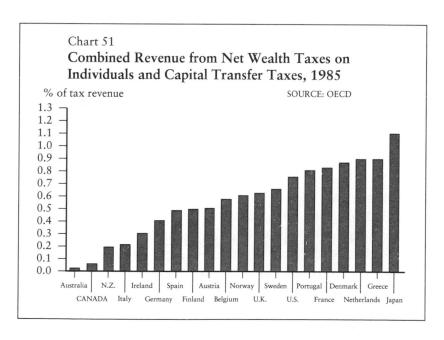

Chart 51

Combined Revenue from Net Wealth Taxes on Individuals and Capital Transfer Taxes, 1985

% of tax revenue   SOURCE: OECD

If Canada had a wealth tax (Chart 51) and if it was set at the same rate as the OECD average, this would raise almost $2 billion. Of the industrial nations, Canada, New Zealand, and Australia are the only countries that now have no wealth tax.[1] Progressive but relatively small inheritance taxes could produce another $2 billion. As well, taxes to curtail land speculation should be introduced, and there should be luxury taxes on such things as expensive cars, expensive jewellery, and expensive homes. Even the United States has recently introduced new luxury taxes. There should also be full taxation of capital gains, as in the United States and United Kingdom, and artificially high depreciation allowances should be eliminated. At the present time, over half of capital gains exemptions in Canada go to the richest 1 per cent of Canadians.

A large number of corporations pay no taxes on many millions of dollars of profits; a minimum tax rate should therefore be introduced on all corporate profits. Every year, too, many wealthy individuals still pay no income tax on large incomes, despite the recent reforms. Consequently, there should be a further tightening up of tax loopholes to correct continuing avoidance by those with high incomes. Also, consideration should be given to charging interest on future deferred corporation taxes.

Finally, the entire tax system should be revamped to make it much more progressive; that is, it should be based on the ability to pay, and there should be more categories, on a sliding scale. Where business incentives are deemed desirable, they should go to small and medium-size businesses.[2] While such businesses should continue to be taxed at the current lower rate on their first $200,000 in annual profits, gradually increasing progressive tax rates should be applied to all corporation profits above that amount. The present corporate tax system is not based on progressive tax rates, and this should be a top priority for change in the first budget after the next federal election.

In addition, two further measures would be beneficial. Even a modest 2 per cent reduction in short-term interest rates would save some $7 billion in federal debt charges over two years. And a reduction in the artificially high value of the Canadian dollar would aid exports, increase profits, and produce substantial additional tax revenue.

Canada has one of the highest poverty rates of the major industrialized nations, with some 14 per cent of the population living below the official poverty line. This compares with some 7 per cent in West Germany, 9 per cent in Great Britain, and approximately 5 per cent in Norway and Sweden. The poverty rate among children in one-parent families in Canada is close to 50 per cent — shocking for a nation that is one of the most affluent in the world. The recent United Nations *Human Development Report* was very critical of Canada. Jean Fabre, United Nations information officer, stated that "Canada is one of the worst countries in the world" in terms of the income gap between rich and poor. "It's not as bad as the United States. But it's still nearly twice as bad as the best countries in the industrialized world."

Since 1986, there have been more than 1 million Canadian children living in poverty. Hundreds of thousands of children rely on food banks, including many thousands under the age of five. Somehow, Canada has become a nation that accepts soup kitchens and food banks as a normal condition of society while happily giving giant corporations like General Motors and Exxon hundreds of millions of dollars in taxpayers' money. While one in five Canadian families that rent live in substandard dwellings (some 560,000 families) and while over 50 per cent of families headed by women are poor, and 50 per cent of unattached women over 65 live in poverty, income distribution figures for the high-growth decade of the 1980s show more inequality at the end of the decade, not less. Policies to reduce poverty, including affordable housing and adequate day care, should be a Canadian priority.

By far the best way to reduce poverty in the future is through improved education. Yet the Mulroney government has been cutting transfers to the provinces for post-secondary education and also cutting funds for job-training programs. While unemployment has risen and is expected to stay above 10 per cent through 1992 at least, unemployment benefits and R & D have been curtailed. We should, of course, be increasing these funds instead of curtailing them. Job training in Canada is like R & D in that everyone talks about it but nothing happens. Canadian businesses "train half as much as firms in the United States, and the United States does a fraction of what Japan and Germany do," according to the deputy chairman of the Economic Council of Canada.

The *Globe and Mail*'s Jeffrey Simpson is direct and to the point: "The Canadian private sector does a lousy job on training. The private sector's expenditure on training and education as a percentage of gross national product in Canada is 0.25 per cent, compared to 0.48 per cent in France, 0.66 per cent in the United States, 1.40 per cent in Japan, 1.96 in West Germany and 2.17 in Britain. (The Germans and the Japanese also have superb apprenticeship programs not counted in these numbers.)" This is the same private sector that worries so justifiably about Canada's competitiveness. Far too much public money has gone to corporations for job training, with poor results. The innovative new Quebec government program, which gives money for education and upgrading to individual workers, is likely to be more productive.

During the past two decades, Canadians have been among the world's highest per capita savers. (Canada's personal and net household savings have been much higher than those in the U.S., for example.)[3] A substantial portion of these savings have been regularly deposited in Canadian banks, mostly in the five large banks: the Royal Bank, the Canadian Imperial Bank of Commerce, the Bank of Montreal, the

Toronto-Dominion Bank, and the Bank of Nova Scotia. We shall never know exactly how much of these savings have gone to fund the foreign takeover of our country and the enormous expansion of foreign corporations here. Remarkably, neither the Bank of Canada nor the Department of Finance — and not even Statistics Canada — bothers "to keep information of that kind," as two ministers of finance told me. They simply don't know or want to know. A large amount of Canadian savings also goes to fund Canadian and foreign corporate activities outside Canada; and, of course, a much larger amount is used to finance rapidly growing corporate concentration within Canada.

Our substantial savings must be far better employed in ways that would benefit many more individuals and bring more substantial benefits to our country. Policies should be put into place that would increase the amount of Canadian savings available to small and medium-size Canadian-owned companies and to individual Canadians. Such policies would produce a far better return in terms of our standard of living than the financing of billions of dollars in leveraged buyouts and speculative real estate transactions in the United States. A top policy priority must be to impose strict limits on the amount of Canadian savings that are available to non-Canadians and on Canadian savings employed outside of Canada.

Making more savings available in Canada would drive down interest rates, reduce the high Canadian dollar, increase exports, and create more competition and many more jobs. The banks would yell and scream, of course, but the big banks in Canada have had a virtually free rein for far too long. They are much too powerful, both politically and economically; and now they are concentrating on expanding in the United States. For Canadian banks, the Canadian national interest is well down the list of priorities. Their own bottom line is what counts, and for them that means their ability to grow outside Canada. Their basic philosophy is simple: what is good for the banks is good for Canada.

Since the end of World War II, Canada has been one of the world's greatest trading nations. Without question, this trade has helped bring us prosperity. But in recent years, especially since the election of Brian Mulroney, through organizations like the BCNI and the C.D. Howe Institute we have developed an obsessive fixation with trade while ignoring our most important engine of prosperity, the domestic economy. Certainly our foreign trade has done very well through the gradual GATT removal of tariff barriers. But somehow we have developed a tunnel-vision compulsion to concentrate on trade at the expense of other policies. For this we can mostly thank big business and its motives (as described on previous pages). The tail has been wagging the dog. Instead of allowing industrial policy to dictate trade strategy, we have made trade policy number one and have ignored industrial policy. We need to improve Canadian innovative ability, to develop more domestically controlled, competitive firms, and to see that our own industries have access to adequate working capital at competitive interest rates, all of which will then lead to new trade initiatives.

We also have to stop being the world's leading goody-goody-two-shoes of trade. Any examination of the trade policies of the United States, Japan, and the European Community makes Canada look like a naive finger-in-the-mouth dolt. Canada plays in the fast, tough, hardball world of trade, with a slow-pitch mentality. While the Europeans and Americans impose "voluntary" limits, while the Americans violate international law with the notorious section 301 of the U.S. Trade Act, while the Japanese protect rice, their computer chip, their automobile parts, and their high-tech industries in general, as well as restricting access to their markets with scores of written and unwritten exclusionary practices and preferential buying, while every country in the world has political policies designed to protect key or vulnerable sectors of their economy, and while voluntary export restrictions remain the name of the game in many areas of trade, the boys in

External Affairs have not yet been able to figure out what economist Lester Thurow explains so well: "Europeans do not want to give up their economic way of life — their long vacations, high minimum wages and generous social welfare system — for the sake of an open economy. If they want to protect their cash wages, they will have no choice but to keep out of the products of Japan and the Pacific Rim. . . . [Europe] will not try to eliminate trade with the rest of the world, as the trading blocs of the 1930s did, but it will try to manage trade between itself and the rest of the world."

Why should we Canadians give up our way of life so that BCNI companies can locate abroad? Why should our trade and foreign investment policies leave us so totally exposed that we are now being warned that we have to change the very basic and fundamental values of our society? We should not have to. We are *not* vulnerable in trade terms. Some 27 million Canadians buy almost exactly the same amount of U.S. exports as the 320 million people do in the twelve nations of the European Community. And Canada buys more from the United States than 122 million Japanese do. During the 1980s, American exports to Canada grew twice as fast as U.S. exports to the rest of the world.

I mention all of this because of the pervasive underlying fear that if we take any policy initiatives in our own best interests, we risk offending the Americans — and then we are in for big trouble. Isn't it time we Canadians stopped being so timid? Millions of Americans work in industries that have huge exports to Canada. If we become more self-reliant, as we must, will they stop selling to their best customer? Will they seek to harm their largest market? Yes, there will be many threats and attempts at intimidation, but if we keep our backs straight, we have little to fear.

Beyond the real and the practical economic questions, there are the basic questions of sovereignty and self-interest. If Canadians cannot adopt policies which they determine to be in the best interests of the nation, what is the use of even having a country? We have far too many timid Canadians, and far too many of them are ensconced in the Langevin Block, in the Pearson Building on Sussex Drive, and in the offices of the leaders of the BCNI. Many Canadians now regard with utter dismay the pitiful collapse of our once-proud Department of External Affairs and its long tradition of defending Canada's national integrity.

On previous pages I described the damaging high interest rate policies and the resulting high dollar — the destructive duo which, along with the Free Trade Agreement, produced the 1990-91 recession, which has harmed so many Canadians. In 1990, Canada's central bank average discount rate was 11.78 per cent, compared with 6.50 per cent in the United States and 6 per cent in Germany and Japan. Canada has had the highest real interest rates of all the industrialized nations. As Doug Peters points out, "The . . . goals set by the Bank of Canada and the Minister of Finance ignore the more important goals of full employment and economic growth." Peter Cook of the *Globe and Mail* puts it this way: "Plainly, when public policy has to hammer the productive economy so continually, it is being inexcusably and inhumanly wasteful."

Other nations, for instance Japan, Austria, Switzerland, Norway, Sweden (and what was West Germany), have full employment as their basis for all economic policy. In Canada, our obsessive-compulsive basic economic policy is a preoccupation with inflation. The human and financial costs of the high interest rate policies of Michael Wilson and John Crow far outweigh any benefits. Even before the job-destroying Free Trade Agreement and the made-in-Canada recession of 1990-91, Canada still had almost a million citizens who desperately wanted jobs but were unable to find them, even after six years of an expanding economy. Incredibly, many of Canada's well-tenured think tank and academic economists seem to regard as attractive and desirable an unemployment rate of 7 per cent.

Full employment strategies would save billions of dollars in unemployment insurance costs and welfare payments and in the abundant multiplier costs caused by the waste of human beings and the misery that accompanies high unemployment. Cutting unemployment in half would increase Canada's GDP by some $30 billion and would decrease our deficit by billions. The increased economic activity of a full-employment strategy would produce greater tax revenue, would help eliminate deficits, would avoid wasting so much of our money in paying so much interest on our debts, and would yield substantial overall benefits to society in economic, social, and cultural terms.

From 1978 to 1987, firms in Canada with less than 100 employees created 93 per cent of all new private industry jobs in Canada. Almost all of these firms were owned and controlled by Canadians. During the same years, large firms with more than 500 employees reduced their employment by 14 per cent. A full-employment strategy should concentrate on creating jobs in small and medium-size Canadian firms by transferring to these businesses many of the enormous benefits and concessions that are now going to foreign transnationals and to Canadian conglomerates.

Trade will always be important for Canada, but the more self-reliant nations whose economies are based on full-employment strategies are much less inclined to find themselves down on their knees in trade negotiations. As this book was going to press, only Ireland and Spain had higher unemployment rates than Canada. Australia, Belgium, Finland, France, Germany, Holland, Italy, Japan, Sweden, Switzerland, the United Kingdom, and the United States had lower rates, most of them much lower rates.

Economic policy in Canada has been standing on its buried-in-the-sand head with its rear end in the air. As long as the likes of Brian Mulroney, Michael Wilson, Don Mazankowski, and John Crow are in control, it will continue that way. The first thing a new government should do is to make a careful study of the economic policies of full-employment countries and then go to work putting Canadians back to work. Among other things, this will certainly mean changes in government procurement policies, which at present are tilted to foreign suppliers. Of the top fifteen corporations which shared much of the $8.5 billion in contracts from the federal government in the last fiscal year, nine were foreign and only six were Canadian. "Buy Canadian" policies should be used as an industrial tool until the economy is functioning closer to capacity, even if this means abandoning our bare-knees Boy Scout uniform and temporarily replacing it with a more protective outfit.

Interest rate policy should be changed so that an overheated provincial or regional economy does not penalize an entire nation, as has happened so often in the past. Higher regional mortgage rates, slower depreciation rates, and larger home or automobile down payments are all measures that could be employed temporarily in overheated areas. And surtaxes could be imposed on the interest payments on selective categories of new bank loans. In some situations, the Bank of Canada could increase the mandatory reserves of the chartered banks. The banks would, of course, oppose all these policies. But they make infinitely more sense than our current policy of penalizing an entire nation whenever a single province or region is bursting at the seams.

Hand in hand with a more logical interest rate policy, the Canadian dollar should be allowed to find its own level, without intervention by the Bank of Canada and with restrictions on the inflow of foreign direct investment and foreign portfolio capital. Despite the somewhat higher inflation that would come with a lower and more realistically valued dollar, the overall benefits to the economy would overwhelmingly outweigh the costs.

Interest rate policy is far too important to be left in the hands of the Bank of Canada. Canadians have been paying a terrible price for this policy for much of a generation.

Instead of the bank making these vital decisions, interest rate policy should be set by the government, in consultation with the bank and with industry and labour. As well, the board of the bank should have a regional balance. And the buck should stop at only two places: on the desk of the prime minister and on the desk of the minister of finance. Only elected representatives of the people should ultimately be responsible for interest and exchange rate policies.

In 1971 the Science Council of Canada suggested that we should have a national industrial policy based on better education and more research and development. During the 1984 election, Brian Mulroney promised to double the research and development budget to 2.5 per cent of GDP. As we have seen, this was yet another in a long list of broken promises. Our major trading partner and competitor spends twice as much on R & D per employed person as we do. Canada's high-tech trade deficit alone translates into the loss of between 150,000 and 200,000 jobs. Alas, as economist Arthur Donner has written: "The major public-sector thrust in the high-technology field makes good sense because, on a global basis, these industries represent the fastest growing product areas. . . . Our industrial structure is heavily tilted towards natural resources, our industry is heavily foreign-owned. . . . But a significant public sector thrust in this worthwhile direction will run smack up against the new Canadian-U.S. free trade treaty; the spirit . . . is to dampen important government levers that have helped develop embryonic high technology industry."

After we rid ourselves of the FTA, we must dramatically increase research and development through a carefully conceived combination of selective incentives and withholding taxes. But we should also do much more of what all countries do — all but Canada, that is. We should study what others are doing, we should copy, we should improve, and we should innovate. This is what the Japanese did after World War II, and it is what the newly industrialized countries have been doing. We should go after products and processes that would suit us — in transportation, communications, mining equipment, and machinery. We should choose products we need, especially those we can improve on and especially those in which we have a heavy trade deficit, and then (but only if necessary) we should enter into joint ventures. The Americans scream blue murder if Canadians have a mere third of their softwood market or tiny percentages of their steel market. It is high time that we reserved part of our own market for companies that create new jobs in this country.

If the parochial provincial premiers continue to resist the removal of interprovincial trade barriers, we should throw the whole myopic bunch out of office until we get agreement on the removal of barriers to the movement of services, people, and capital within Canada. It is typical of the colonial mentality of many of our premiers that they so ardently opted, through the FTA, to allow American companies a multitude of special privileges which are not available to Canadian companies from other provinces. Selfish, self-centred, petty, and power hungry provincial potentates, with visions that extend no farther than the steps of their own legislatures, are a contemporary Canadian plague.

We should stop regarding our natural resources as being commodities only for export. Other countries, even those with very few trees, have sophisticated wooden-furniture export industries; other countries successfully use their natural resources to attract new labour-intensive industries, rather than shipping their nonrenewable resources out of the country as quickly as possible, at low prices, and with little or no value-added. Instead of concentrating so much on the export of newsprint, pulp, and lumber, our forest industry should follow the advice of the Science Council: it should double its spending on R & D and should develop forest machinery, furniture, fine paper, chemicals, and glues both for domestic consumption and for export, as the Scandinavian countries have done. Canada has almost 10 per cent of the world's forests, but we are not taking advantage of this wonderful resource the way we should be.

As so many people have recently pointed out, it is becoming increasingly clear that much more attention must be paid to the government regulation of forest management. But from the way some of our provincial governments have performed of late (most notably British Columbia and Alberta), perhaps it would be best for the federal government to appoint a national forest ombudsman who would report to the people of Canada annually. Only some 4 per cent of Canada's forest budget is spent on forest management — about one-tenth of the figure in Sweden.

Resource exports will be important to Canada for as far as we can see into the future. But instead of concentrating so much on rushing resources out of the country, we should use the comparative advantage we have inherited to create jobs in Canada. Instead of adopting an attitude of "Please take our resources, at low prices, as quickly as possible" (as we have with natural gas), we should be much more adroit at using our resources as strategic bargaining tools rather than as fire-sale commodities. Instead of following Simon Reisman's advice and exporting our fresh water to the United States, we should use our wonderful water resources as a means of attracting more jobs to Canada. But we should not do it the way the Alberta government has done — ruining magnificent rivers for the benefit of foreign forestry companies that are heavily subsidized by Alberta taxpayers.

That is typical of the way a balkanized colony behaves. Canadian provinces bid against one another to see which of them can give away the most cash, the greatest tax concessions, and the largest forgivable loans and infrastructure investments to lure enormously wealthy foreign corporations to come in and cut down or dig up Canadian resources. Invariably, neither job creation nor royalty revenue come anywhere near the taxpayer's total subsidies; and, invariably, few long-term jobs are created, environmental standards remain lax, and the profits flow out of Canada. Huge resource megaprojects, in which the bulk of the product is destined for export, are often self-defeating for Canadians in the exchange-rate factor alone. If billions of dollars in foreign equity or debt capital are required, the inflow of foreign capital drives up the value of the Canadian dollar, harming more labour-intensive exports. If the capital is raised domestically, more labour-intensive industries find it more expensive and more difficult to raise working capital.

Please note that this is not an attack on resource development. It is an attack on excessive or too rapid development of resources for export, by foreign corporations, subsidized by Canadian taxpayers.

Canadians should be leading the world in research to create liquid fuels from coal and for converting natural gas into economic transportation fuels. There is no lead in natural gas; it is relatively non-polluting, and it is also relatively cheap and abundant.

Instead of building our feeble economic strategy on the export of vast quantities of electricity and natural gas, we should use our comparative advantage in energy to create new employment for Canadians. The strategy of selling cheap hydro power and cheap natural gas to our principal trade competitor boggles the mind, though it is certainly a wonderful way to create employment — in the United States.

Canada should be much more aggressive in going after unfair U.S. trading practices. For every Canadian countervail or other trade action, there are a dozen launched by the Americans. U.S. Defense Department subsidies would be a good place for us to start the next time some backwoods U.S. politician forces action on Canadian pork, potatoes, lumber, shingles, steel rails, lobsters, or other exports, or suggests that Canada's social programs invite countervail.

By concentrating far too much on trade and not enough on our domestic economy, we not only play into the hands of the transnational corporations but we also leave ourselves overly dependent, overly vulnerable, and frequently driven by the dictates of interests very different from our own. In trade, as a percentage of GDP, we far exceed such famous long-time trading nations as Britain, France, the United States, Italy, Australia, and many other countries. Instead of 25 or 30 per cent of GDP being devoted to trade, a much more normal 10 or 15 per cent would be beneficial. Not only would we reduce our dependency and vulnerability, but we could also employ our financial and natural resources to great overall benefit. In our trade with the United States, our goal should be at least a trade balance in jobs and in the current account, instead of our decades-long obsession only with the numbers in our merchandise trade balance.

There has been much discussion over the years about "a third option" and other attempts to diversify Canadian trade. But it is impossible to diversify our trade when there is so much American ownership of the Canadian economy. As we have seen, U.S. branch plants in Canada buy most of their parts and components and their services from their parent companies or affiliates, and rarely, if ever, do they buy them at arm's-length prices. When they export, they sell most of their finished products to their parent companies or affiliates. And most branch plants have no export mandate: the parent corporation would never allow them to compete with head office for export markets.

By doing so much of our trade with one country while at the same time sanctioning a strategy that concentrates on trade and allows growing American ownership of Canada, we have left ourselves in the vulnerable position that helped produce the FTA. A more logical approach would be to have more trading arrangements with countries such as Japan, Brazil, Korea, Australia, New Zealand, and the Soviet Union, and with Europe and the Caribbean. Our greatest trade growth in the future should be with the Pacific Rim, the fastest-growing economic region in the world.

First and foremost, we should build our own domestically based industries in areas where we already have experience and advantages as well as the resources, and then we should go out into the world and compete. We should do what Japan has done: open up sectors of the economy where we are strong and protect sectors where we are weak but which are clearly capable of improvement in the future. And we should *not* let the "free market" propaganda of transnational corporations put our workers in bread lines.

Is Canada's health-care system perfect? No one claims that it is. There would be many problems to be solved even if Ottawa were not reducing transfer payments. In recent years, the number of doctors practising in Canada has increased at four times the rate of population growth, and some health-care economists suggest that "doctors are creating their own demand" and that the number of billings is increasing in proportion to the increased number of doctors rather than according to the much smaller increase in the population. Figures from Health and Welfare Canada show that while the population grew by 10.5 per cent from 1979 to 1989, the number of active physicians increased by 41 per cent, and the medical services supplied increased by 42 per cent.

Waiting lists for treatment are a problem, though they have been overstated by critics of medicare. Drug costs have increased since the Mulroney government bowed to the pressure from Washington and the U.S. pharmaceutical lobby. Another problem is that aging and chronically ill patients occupy too many acute-care hospital beds. More alternative convalescent facilities are required. And more attention should be given to preventive programs, such as reducing smoking and controlling pollution.

Canada has great expertise in many areas of health care. We should be expanding and refining that expertise and sharing it with the world instead of importing inferior American policies and practices. Similarly, instead of reducing social programs, we should be improving child-care and nursing-care facilities; and as soon as we can right the economy, we should introduce a national denticare program for all children at least.

Canadians should become world leaders in good environmental policies and technologies: we could do this by reducing contamination of the environment, by cutting down on the wasteful use of resources, by planning rational polices of conservation, by moving towards sustainable development (with good and, where necessary, tough environmental laws, including recycling and reduced speed limits) and by halting the discharge of foul and dangerous materials into our rivers, lakes, and oceans.

Instead of cutting back on east-west transportation, we should be investing in modern rail services and improved communications. During periods of high unemployment, we should improve our highways and rail lines, build sewage-treatment plants in the many communities that do not have them, build and improve airstrips in the North, and engage in other public-works projects. Investment in the restoration and upgrading of municipal infrastructure — particularly water and sewage-treatment facilities — is badly needed and would be an important aspect of any national environmental program. Such investments could also be an important component of regional programs.

Employee share-ownership plans are increasingly popular and work especially well when the corporation contributes, as in the case of Bell Canada, which provides $1 for every $3 invested by the employee (to a maximum of 6 per cent of base annual salary). Almost a quarter of all Toronto Stock Exchange companies now have some form of employee share-ownership plan. Several countries have tax legislation encouraging "worker capitalism." In the United States, more than 12 million workers now belong to some form of profit-sharing or employee stock-ownership plan. Policies that facilitate greater worker ownership usually produce good results, especially when they involve more worker participation in decision making. The extra incentives produce better productivity, lower rates of absenteeism, and a higher quality of work. Worker capitalism also encourages better relations between management and labour, the best partnerships being like those in Germany and Sweden, where it is common to have workers on the board of directors.

What we do not need are more poorly-thought-out plans providing unproductive tax shelters, such as the $3 billion tax rip-off which Marc Lalonde and Mickey Cohen foisted on Canadians in an attempt to pump money into science and technology development in Canada.

I have many reservations about stock savings plans that benefit only the well-to-do or that lead to the political pork barrel. Any investment incentives should not be overly generous and must not lead to greater corporate concentration. But they should and can be designed to pull dollars from socks, mattresses, and bank accounts for careful, prudent investment. At the same time, tougher rules for policing the investment industry should be developed.

Canada has one of the world's largest perennial deficits in trade in machinery and equipment. Compared with all the Group of Seven industrialized nations, we are consistently at the bottom in terms of the contribution of capital goods to GDP, and this share has been declining. From a $5 billion trade deficit in machinery and equipment in 1976, our deficit in 1990 was almost $32 billion. As one of the world's most important mining nations, we do not have a significant mining-equipment industry; and as one of the world's leading forestry-products nations, we rely on imported forestry equipment. Clearly, any new restructuring of our economy should encourage the development of machinery and equipment production for industries in which our domestic and export production give us large enough volumes to warrant competitive development.

Much more effort in Canada will have to go into biotechnology, microelectronics, and the development of new generations of industrial materials. In country after country around the world, government works with business and labour to support the strategic evolution of new industries where common sense indicates they can be competitive. Similarly, we need more agriculture research into potential alternate crops and, obviously, better conservation of agricultural land. There should also be more research and development in hydropower technology, resource management, cold-weather drilling, health-care technology, computer-assisted design and manufacturing, new railway equipment, and petroleum industry equipment. Rather than trying to get enhanced access to the U.S. market, we should have been concentrating on enhanced Canadian content to create more jobs in Canada and more wealth in our own country.

Where will all the dollars come from for these new policies? I have already mentioned several possibilities, but primarily the money will come from four sources: first, a fairer, more broadly based and far more effective tax system; secondly, from the additional tax revenue accruing from a more fully employed and more productive economy; third, from the substantial savings from the punitive costs of our high interest rates and artificially high dollar; and, lastly, they will come from much better access to and utilization of our own savings and resources.

33

The Most Important Principle of All

Canada's Flawed Democracy

> *Immediate. Private. I must have another ten thousand. Will*
> *be the last time of asking. Do not fail me. Answer today.*
> SIR JOHN A. MACDONALD'S *telegram to the lawyer for Sir Hugh Allan*
> *of the Canadian Pacific Railway, 26 August 1872*

T HE MOST IMPORTANT PRINCIPLE OF ALL IS DEMOC-
racy. Politics should be democratic. Politics should be controlled by citizens, not by corporations. Canada will never
function as it should, in the best interests of the majority,
unless we make important changes in our political system.

Our present political system is far from democratic.
Most Canadians suspect this (witness the many comments
to this effect to the Spicer Commission's Citizens' Forum),
but few understand just how tilted and how unrepresentative the system actually is. Preoccupied with the constitution and debates about the sharing of power between the
federal government and the provinces, Canada's political
leaders have all but ignored an even more important aspect
of our democracy: how the people who run Canada are
elected. From time to time there are commissions which
bring some modest improvements in the electoral system,
but, to a very large extent, our system of democracy is seriously flawed because it does not faithfully reflect the wishes
of the people.

The longer I have been involved in the public life of Canada and the more I have had the opportunity to observe how the back rooms of our federal parties operate, the more I am convinced that our political system is not only far less democratic than it should be, but that it is also much less democratic than the vast majority of Canadians suspect, cynical as they may now be. Thus, the place to start in changing Canada for the better is by improving and democratizing its political system. Without this, many of the other changes that are necessary will never happen. In what follows, I focus mainly on the federal political system, but the majority of my comments apply equally well to the current inadequacies of the provincial political process.

First, there is the way our elections do not accurately reflect the will of the people. Federally, our system might be a bit better if there were only two parties; it certainly does not work properly when there are three or more, because among other reasons, a minority of voters can and frequently do elect a majority government.

The inadequacies of our single-ballot, put-your-X-here system are reflected at both the federal and provincial levels, even when there are only two parties in the race. For example, in 1970 the Parti Québécois received 23.5 per cent of the votes yet won only seven of the 110 seats in the Quebec National Assembly. In 1973 it captured 30.8 per cent of the vote yet won only six seats! In 1979 the Conservatives formed the federal government with 22 more seats than the Liberals, even though the Tories had 4 per cent less popular vote in the election. In the 1980 federal election, the Liberals received 44 per cent of the popular vote but formed a majority government with 52 per cent of the seats. In 1984 the Mulroney Conservatives received just under 50 per cent of the popular vote but took almost 75 per cent of the seats in the Commons. And in New Brunswick, in the October 1987 provincial election, the Liberals won every single one of the 58 seats, with 61 per cent of the popular vote.

But it was Brian Mulroney's majority victory in the 1988 federal election (in which his Conservatives won 57 per cent of the seats with 43 per cent of the vote) that started people talking again about election reform. Had the popular vote been reflected in the number of seats won, the Tories would have captured only 127 seats, instead of 169, and the Liberals and NDP would have won 94 and 60 seats respectively — enough to form a minority government or coalition in the 295-seat House of Commons. (The Conservative candidate was chosen by a majority of votes in only 29 per cent of the constituencies.) Similarly, in Ontario's last provincial election, Bob Rae won 37.6 per cent of the vote but took 57 per cent of the seats. This has even the Conservatives talking election reform.

The old-fashioned "first-past-the-post," single-ballot, single-member majority system is archaic, unfair, and unrepresentative when there are more than two political parties. Only a few countries use our current voting system. Of the 160 members of the United Nations, only three other countries (the U.S., the U.K., and New Zealand) are tied to the system we use. Many countries use systems that have preferential votes, or single transferrable votes, or party lists, or proportional representation. Some use a mixed system that has members elected from constituencies and also members elected from lists that are offered by the parties. Each voter votes twice: for his or her own member and for his or her preference on the national list.

Various forms of proportional representation (in which the number of seats won much more closely reflects the number of votes) are very common. Many countries have opted for preferential voting. With this system, when there are more than two candidates on the ballot, voters mark their ballots 1, 2, 3, etc., in order of their preference. If no candidate wins a majority on the first count, the second choices are tallied and, if necessary, the third and fourth choices, until one of the candidates has a majority. (This is the system employed in most party leadership conventions.) In France and several South American countries, in many elections, if no candidate receives a majority, a run-off vote is held between the top two candidates. This is more time-consuming, cumbersome, and expensive, but it is more dramatic than preferential voting. It also provides voters with a second either-or opportunity to make a choice.

The pervasive role and control of money in Canada's political system is not understood by more than a very small percentage of Canadians. I am constantly amazed at how uninformed even many political journalists are on this subject; even people who are dedicated perennial party workers and political junkies do not adequately understand the role of big dollars in the political process. Much more so than most suspect, big money calls the shots in both the Conservative and Liberal parties.

The bagmen, who are often relatively unknown, are much more in control of party policy than are the delegates to any policy conventions. This is frequently one of the most important reasons why Canada's tax system is so skewed in favour of the wealthy and the large corporations, and it is the principal reason why we so often end up with government policies which the majority of Canadians oppose. Among the most amazing aspects of this process are the members of Parliament, cabinet ministers, prime ministers, and party executives who say they do not know where the money comes from. Show me a politician who claims not to know where his or her financing comes from, and I'll show you a blind, deaf, and dumb mythological creature. As well, those who believe that parties and politicians disclose all of their funding no doubt also believe that the GST was intended to be "revenue neutral."

Who are the major funders of the only two political parties that have governed Canada for the past 124 years? They have been and are the banks, the trust companies, the investment companies, the insurance companies, the large accounting firms, law firms of all sizes, the large natural resource companies, and the railways. In short, big business. (Or, to a lesser extent, medium-size business and professional firms that are looking to be added to the list for government contracts.) Of the top ten contributors to the Conservatives in 1988, five were banks. Of the top five contributors to the Liberal party, all five were banks! The five banks gave the Liberals and Conservatives some $892,500 — an average of almost $90,000 from each. Of course, they didn't consult each other; it was surely just coincidence that the donations of all five big banks were in the $80,000 to $90,000 range.

While the amounts that corporations contribute to political parties, candidates, leadership contestants, and other direct or indirect political activities are in themselves, when taken together, very substantial sums, the actual amounts of the donations, though important to the recipients, are often small potatoes to the corporations when compared with their advertising, public relations, and promotion budgets. At least as important (and often more important) for them, in gaining access to the decision-making process, is "the Desmarais effect." Paul Desmarais, CEO of the wealthy Power Corporation conglomerate, owns among other things the Montreal newspaper *La Presse* and controls Great-West Life Assurance and the Investors Group, which have combined assets of more than $20 billion.

The role of wealthy behind-the-scenes political influence is a common theme in Canadian history. But few Canadians today have any understanding of just how powerful and influential Paul Desmarais is. The head of Power Corporation has, among his most prominent friends, Brian Mulroney, Pierre Trudeau, and Robert Bourassa. Southam News, in February 1990, reported:

A Chrétien fund-raiser, who refused to be named [says]: "Desmarais will contribute to us. He'll probably contribute to Martin. He's contributing to Bourassa and Mulroney. And he'll have a lot left over."

> During the last federal election Power gave the Conservatives
> $72,145, the Liberals $76,202 and the NDP $5,000. Desmarais,
> his wife Jacqueline and his two sons also chipped in $5,000 each
> to the Tory war chest. . . .
> A prominent Montreal Conservative, who spoke on condition
> that he not be named, says that Desmarais is one of "a small
> number of Canadians that have enormous political clout." That
> power, the party insider says, comes not so much from cam-
> paign donations as from the extreme concentration of corporate
> ownership in Canada.
> "It's a hell of a small elite and these guys have tentacles in all
> the political parties. This country is so small and economic
> power is so concentrated it is simply unavoidable."

Two things are wrong with the Southam quotation. First, it
actually underestimates just how powerful Paul Desmarais has
been and is today in Ottawa. Secondly, it is nonsense to suggest that "it is simply unavoidable." The Tory source probably
thought that Tammany Hall and Watergate were unavoidable.
An undemocratic system yields undemocratic results, with
right wingers like Paul Desmarais wielding enormous power,
not only because of their vast holdings and not only because
of their political donations, but principally because their corporations also become havens for the boys from the capitals.
Among those who formerly worked for Power Corporation or
who now work for Desmarais are Paul Martin, Jr., Bryce
Mackasey, Jean Chrétien's campaign manager John Rae
(Power Corporation executive vice-president), and Pierre
Trudeau's former principal secretary, Senator Michael Pitfield.
The former premier of Ontario, John Robarts, sat on the
board of directors with Jean-Luc Pepin. And former Ontario
premier Bill Davis is on the board now, along with John Black
Aird, Charles Bronfman, former Royal Bank head Rowland
Frazee, and Arden Haynes, chairman and CEO of Imperial Oil.
    It is impossible to know the exact amount spent by big
business shortly before and during the 1988 federal election.

For example, we shall never know how much American Express spent in Canada, but it was likely a large sum. When one considers the spending of the Canadian Alliance for Trade and Job Opportunities, the Business Council on National Issues, the Canadian Chamber of Commerce and affiliates, the Canadian Manufacturers' Association, and other business organizations, plus the millions of dollars spent by individual corporations, by Ottawa, and by the governments of the Conservative provinces and British Columbia, the total probably amounts to more than $40 million.

Aside from their third-party political activities in the 1988 federal election, corporations contributed some $8.5 million to the federal Conservatives, representing some 65 per cent of the party's disclosed funding. However, disclosed funding is much less than actual funding. If all pre-election spending and free goods, free services, and borrowed personnel were to be counted properly, the total would probably be much closer to $25 million and the corporate share closer to 90 per cent.

During 1988, the pro-free-trade supporters outspent the anti-free-trade supporters by at least a twenty-to-one margin. Most of this time, in fact for almost all of the period leading up to the election, the public opinion polls showed that many more Canadians opposed the Free Trade Agreement than supported it. Clearly, big money bought the election. And the Mulroney government chipped in, with taxpayers' money, in a shameless manner. According to *Maclean's* (21 November 1988), quoting an unnamed Conservative source in Ottawa, "The Conservatives poured more than $23 million into promotional campaigns extolling the benefits of free trade. 'It was like Hitler at Stalingrad. It did not matter that the polls were saying that support was fading for free trade. The attitude was: we will just pump more money into it.'"

Arthur Drache, the respected Ottawa tax specialist, considers that Revenue Canada's decision to allow corporations to write off their pro-free-trade expenditures is "grossly unfair to the taxpayers of Canada." But it is much more than that. It is grossly unfair to democracy. In fact, it has nothing to do with the way democracy is supposed to function.

Big business loved what it managed to achieve in 1988 — pulling out the election for its Tory friends who seemed destined for defeat. But it was hardly an act of political altruism. The corporate elite were acting in their own self-interest. And just wait and see what happens in the next federal election if there seems to be a chance of a more democratic government taking office: the corporate spending will make 1988's look like petty cash. Besides, thanks to Revenue Canada, it's you, the Canadian public, who will be paying for the corporations' political activities, regardless of whether these are inside or outside the formal political process.

The enormous amounts spent during the last Liberal leadership convention are hardly a reflection of the way democracies ought to function. Both Jean Chrétien and Paul Martin, Jr., supposedly spent some $2.5 million dollars, but the actual spending was probably much higher. Party regulations did not require full disclosure.

One principle of an effective democratic system must be full and total disclosure of all political donations, without exception, and similar disclosure of the source of all funds spent by public-interest groups, lobby groups, politically oriented think tanks and the like, whether it's the Council of Canadians, the C. D. Howe Institute, or the National Citizens' Coalition.

It is fascinating to look at the disclosed contributions to the 1990 Liberal leadership campaigns of Jean Chrétien, Paul Martin, Jr., and Sheila Copps. There were a great many anonymous numbered companies among the contributors. Also well represented were big law firms, accounting firms, construction companies, drug companies, conglomerates, consulting firms, oil companies, resource companies, trust companies, brokers, insurance companies, real estate firms, and breweries, together with other corporations that tend to do a great deal of business with the federal government. Foreign-controlled companies were also prominent contributors.

I was a member of the Liberal party from 1968 to 1973, and during that time each cabinet minister had an A list, a B list, and a C list, based on financial contributions to the party. Government legal work, as well as work for contractors, engineers, architects, accountants, and so on, was parcelled out largely on the basis of who had put up how much. Many political meetings were devoted to discussions only about patronage. Anyone who thinks the system has changed since 1973 is naive. The funding of political parties, pork barrel, and patronage are inextricably linked.

The election laws adopted by the Parti Québécois in Quebec in 1977 prohibited donations from companies, associations, and unions, and from non-residents of Quebec. All individual contributions are limited and are subject to strict disclosure of source and amount. (From 1908 to 1930, Canadian election laws prohibited corporations from making contributions to political parties or to candidates.) Jean-Marc Hamel, Canada's retired chief electoral officer, says that our federal system will not be valid if third-party advertisers are allowed to continue to spend as they wish. Since the 1974 Election Expenses Act, federal candidates have had spending-limit restrictions and some form of mandatory reporting, but interest groups have no such restrictions.

In the United States, the delegates to the Democrat and Republican conventions overwhelmingly represent the well-to-do. Although things are not nearly so bad in Canada, delegates to both Liberal and Conservative conventions clearly are heavily representative of the top 20 per cent of income brackets. In the U.S., the average cost of a race for a seat in the House of Representatives is some $270,000; for the U.S. Senate it is $2 million. Winning senators average some $3 million in campaign spending. This compares with the average cost of $30,000 for a House of Commons election campaign.

Big money certainly controls the American political system: the wealthy are firmly in charge. The politicians are closely tied to big money through corporations and through well-financed lobby groups. (The absurd American gun laws are an example of how corrupt the system is.) At the same time, voter registration laws and political apathy play a role. Ronald Reagan managed his one-sided landslide 1980 election as president of the United States with the grand total of 27 per cent support from eligible American voters.

As modern technology has taken the place of old-style people-intensive politics, money has become more important than people. By means of television and by using targeted mailings and computers, well-financed parties and organizations can have a major and deciding influence in an election even if they do not have enough popular support to lure campaign workers. In the modern world of U.S.-style campaigns, money counts; individuals, much less so. Unfortunately, our political parties have been moving more and more to the U.S. type of packaging, advertising, and negative campaign techniques.

The NDP does much better than either the Liberals or Conservatives in attracting financial support from individuals. In 1988, 118,390 individuals donated to the NDP, more than the other two parties put together (30,624 for the Liberals; 54,900 for the Tories). In total, in the 1988 federal election, less than 204,000 individuals contributed to the parties or the candidates (just over 1 per cent of voting-age Canadians).

The Lortie Royal Commission, which will report shortly after this book is published, has been charged with making suggestions for the long-overdue revision of Canada's election laws. Unfortunately, the commission has no mandate to recommend "fundamental changes to Canada's system of direct election by simple majority on a single ballot," since such changes do "not fall within the ambit of its mandate."

Many Canadians are in favour of a system of proportional representation (PR), but not many Conservatives are. With PR, the centre-left would dominate the House of Commons. If PR had been in place in the last federal election, the Free

Trade Agreement would never have happened. With PR, the power of the big corporations would be substantially diminished. PR would produce governments far more representative of the Canadian electorate. But with Brian Mulroney and big business in charge, the chances of Canada getting proportional representation are about the same as the chances of the BCNI coming out in favour of limits on third-party election spending.

Numerous reforms are necessary in election spending. As noted above, the present system heavily favours big money. Most Canadians cannot afford to buy four-page newspaper supplements during an election when the party of their choice seems to be in trouble and in need of help. We need much tighter limits on election spending. There should also be far more mandatory free time available on radio and television, and all parties should have access to it on a fair proportional basis, which should be determined by results from the previous federal election and the current national public opinion polls. Third-party intervention should be allowed, but it should be publicly accountable and should be restricted in the same ways that political parties and candidates are restricted.

Another area in need of reform is our disclosure rules, which are totally inadequate. Corporations and parties constantly conspire to find their way around the law through the provision of goods and services, through people on corporation payrolls, and through detoured financial contributions. Obviously, trade union contributions to the NDP would have to be treated in the same way as corporate contributions to the Conservative, Liberal, and Reform parties.

This said, the more I have learned about how the political system in Canada works — and fails to work — the more convinced I am that political donations should be limited to individuals: no corporate donations, no union donations, no donations from organizations of any kind. And there should be a limit of $500 for each donation. This would mean a drastic reduction of election spending; campaigns would have to be labour-intensive, and people would count instead of big money. The political pros would hate it, of course, and so would corporations and unions. The National Citizens' Coalition would go berserk. But it would be much, much more democratic.

The recall system that the Reform party is suggesting for members of Parliament makes little sense. An infinitely better suggestion is to have federal elections on a set date every three years instead of every five. In the modern, increasingly complex world, five years is far too long a mandate. Three years would give those elected ample time to disclose their abilities and policies. And with shorter mandates, the type of public anger that arose during Pierre Trudeau's last reign and Brian Mulroney's current political fiasco could be channelled into the democratic system, rather than causing the sense of frustration and helplessness that has been felt for so long throughout the country. You can be sure, though, that virtually every elected and backroom politician will tell you that more frequent elections are not a good idea. But the reverse is true. In the modern world, especially in a country like Canada where voter turnout is high,[1] the voters should be given the opportunity far more often to reject or endorse the federal government. Three years is a long enough mandate.

On important national issues, a referendum should be held at the same time as a federal election. Many other countries do this when issues are very contentious or when an important departure that would change the direction of the country is proposed. (While the terms tend to be used loosely, traditionally a referendum is held when a government seeks the views of the people. The results may or may not be binding on the government. By contrast, a plebiscite usually implies that the government in power is asking the people for endorsement of a policy already adopted.) Where a significant percentage of the electorate petition — and it should be truly significant, so that single-issue groups are unable to tie up the process of government — the government should be required to give Canadians an opportunity to express their opinion via direct vote. The same tough rules that govern a reformed election system should apply for all referenda and plebiscites.

Election laws should be changed to correct the persistent imbalances in the number of voters in federal ridings across Canada. No one expects that each constituency should contain exactly the same number of voters, but our present system is unfair. For example, in the federal by-elections held on 10 December 1990, there were 129,479 eligible voters in York North but only 49,156 eligible voters in Beauséjour in New Brunswick (where Jean Chrétien was elected to the House of Commons). An independent commission should set and revise federal constituency boundaries.

Non-Canadians should not be allowed to intervene either directly or indirectly in the political process in Canada, whether they live in Canada or not. The intervention, both financial and otherwise, by foreign transnational corporations in Canada's 1988 federal election should have been an issue of great public debate. That it was not is another comment on the failure of the media and our opposition politicians to bring the matter to the attention of Canadians. Canada is not yet a banana republic, even though our government and our election laws are rapidly leading us in that direction.

During election campaigns, we should have at least four national television debates between party leaders (two in each official language). This decision should not be up to the prime minister. Nationally televised leader debates should be a formal part of all federal elections; they represent the only opportunity the voters have, during the campaign, to see the leaders in important debate about key issues. And once they are elected in our new democracy, wouldn't it be about time that members of Parliament were required to pledge allegiance to Canada instead of to Her Majesty Queen Elizabeth II?

Isn't it also time that we allowed more free votes in the House of Commons? The rules should be changed so that on many or even most votes, the government would continue in office even if it lost a vote in the House. This loosening of party discipline is already a common feature of many other democracies. Members of Parliament should be given far greater opportunity to express their own concerns and those of their constituents. (In terms of the operation of the House of Commons, the Mulroney government is going in exactly the wrong direction, curtailing debate instead of extending it, reducing the number of days the Commons sits, reducing the time allowed for speeches, making it easier for the government to invoke closure, curtailing witnesses appearing before Commons committees, and in general eroding democracy rather than reinforcing it.) It would be another step towards better democracy if the present system of political patronage in the appointment of returning officers was abolished. A non-partisan public agency should make such appointments and administer all aspects of federal elections. The present definitions of election expenses and campaign expenses are inadequate and outdated, and the new agency should make their clarification a priority.

Unfortunately, Canada, in recent years, has moved much closer to the formalized U.S. lobby system. We have always had lobbying in one form or another — all governments do — but lobbying in Canada has become a big business. Former cabinet ministers, chiefs of staff, senior personnel from the Prime Minister's Office . . . even the current chief financial officer for the Liberal Party of Canada are "public affairs consultants" producing "strategic consulting capacity" about how government works, how the players interrelate, and about the political context within which decisions are made. One senior non-Conservative Canadian businessman recently told me that it is virtually impossible to get any government business without going through a well-connected Ottawa lobby group. I suspect that Canadians would be disgusted if they really understood how the lobbying system in Ottawa works.

Finally, by far the most important thing we could do to make Canada a better country, if we only had the time, would be to teach Canadians how to get involved in politics. The political system and how it works should be a mandatory Grade 10 high school course, and all new immigrants should be given a solid course on Canadian democracy. Unfortunately, as things are, only a tiny percentage of Canadians belong to any of the political parties, and a much smaller number are actually active in politics; and, as we have seen, only 1 per cent of Canadians made donations to political parties in the last federal election.

The Spicer Report — the Citizens' Forum on Canada's Future — has shown that Canadians feel that they are not being governed the way they want or in a manner that properly reflects their values: "To the extent that reforms can be made which would [restore their faith in the political process] participants' demands for direct participation in decision-making would be less." The reforms are long overdue and are fundamental to any hope for the survival of Canada. But our chances of getting these reforms from Brian Mulroney lie somewhere between slim and nonexistent.

34

The Mulroney Agenda

The Dismemberment of Canada

I am not interested in a Canada that would be just a splash on the map, with a six-letter word scrawled across it. The only Canada I want to preserve is a Canada that can do something for its own people, for the hungry two-thirds of the world, for the survival of the planet; not a phantom that can only watch helplessly as we all tumble down a steep place to destruction.

EUGENE FORSEY, *Toronto Star, 24 February 1991*

Dr. Forsey . . . was passionately committed to Canada, but not just any Canada. He would not countenance so stripping Parliament of its power that Canada would be reduced from a nation to a mere economic and defence association of relatively insignificant states. He might have employed different words, but he would have endorsed the proposition that there is more to being a Canadian than being a resident of a particular province or territory.

CLYDE WELLS, *Eugene Forsey Memorial Lecture, Ottawa, 8 June 1991*

Brian Mulroney's constitutional strategy and his election strategy for 1992-93 will be to do again what he has always done so effectively in the past — give things away. As we have seen, even before the formal negotiations for the Free Trade Agreement began, the prime minister made a number of key concessions: in drug legislation, softwood lumber, investment, culture, energy, and various other areas. Then, in the actual agreement, he gave away things that no government with an ounce of integrity would have countenanced. Brian Mulroney's concept of defending the nation is to hand things over to whoever wants them, whether this means the Americans, big business, or the provinces.

Next in line come Quebec and the other provinces. In Mulroney's desperate bid to get re-elected, the campaign strategy will be simple: grant to Quebec most of what it wants and give the same thing to the other provinces, too. Most of the provincial premiers will be delighted. One can just see them gathered around the prime minister on national television, the great statesmen toasting "the rebirth of Confederation" in front of the cameras. The grins will be a mile wide. And there will be plenty of rationalizations. After all, Canada is an overcentralized country. Far too many decisions have been made in Ottawa — much too far away from the people. Already, the Allaire Report, the Belanger-Campeau Report, the Group of 22, and the likes of Don Getty, Bill Vander Zalm, and the BCNI have explained to us why a much more decentralized Canada would be a first-class idea. And it would, after all, help us to keep Quebec in Confederation and keep Canada united.

Or would it? As an example, let us compare government spending in Canada and Europe. In terms of all levels of spending (including federal, provincial, municipal and hospital), here are comparisons for 1988:

All Government Spending Compared with GDP

Canada	44.4%
OECD Europe	47.9%
European Economic Community	48.1%

By 1989, the figure for Canada had dropped to 44.3 per cent. In fact, total government spending in Canada in 1989, compared with GDP, was some 3 per cent lower than it was in 1983. So once again, contrary to what we are so often told, Canadian government spending is actually quite a bit lower than that in most developed countries.

But what about the problem of overcentralization? One of the great Canadian myths, and the favourite fable of the western premiers and the Reform party, is that Canada is an overcentralized country — that the federal government has far too much control over the lives of Canadians and that Ottawa is fully in command, like it or not. It is not only the premiers who love to tell this tale. This is also a favourite chorus of big business.

Provincial politicians fight and win many elections on the back of Ottawa, sometimes with good reason, sometimes not, and the editorial pages of western newspapers frequently echo the refrain of overcentralization and the need for the provinces to be given more powers. But once again, the reality is very different from the myth. In a recently released OECD study for 1988, of the twenty-three OECD countries, Canada stood twentieth in terms of central government tax revenues as a percentage of all tax revenues collected by government. Twentieth out of twenty-three! So if Canada is overcentralized, just what countries is it being compared with? The following chart needs little elaboration:

Central Government Tax Revenue as a Percentage of Total Tax Revenue, 1988

New Zealand	94.5%
Ireland	83.5%
Australia	80.0%
Turkey	74.8%
United Kingdom	69.8%
Portugal	67.6%
Denmark	67.1%
Greece	65.8%
Italy	64.3%

Luxembourg	62.7%
Finland	61.8%
Belgium	61.3%
Sweden	56.6%
Netherlands	54.0%
Spain	52.6%
Norway	52.4%
Austria	51.3%
France	47.0%
Japan	45.1%
Canada	42.1%
United States	39.4%
Germany	31.0%
Switzerland	30.1%
Average of federal countries	45.6%
Average of unitary countries	62.9%

In fact, federal spending represents only a small percentage of all spending in the Canadian economy, well below the average for federal countries. In 1960, Ottawa spent more than the provinces and municipalities combined. Today, the provinces and local governments far outspend Ottawa.[1] In contrast, in the United States, the federal government spends about nine dollars for every six dollars state and local governments combined spend.

Chart 52 looks at the top tax rates of the central governments of the G7 nations and Austria. As can be seen, Ottawa's rate is the lowest. In the latest years for which reliable comparative figures are available, only three OECD countries had lower top central government tax rates than Canada's 29 per cent. The OECD average was 36 per cent. By 1990, only Switzerland (the world's most decentralized nation) and Finland had lower central government tax rates than Canada.

Chart 53 shows the central government share of tax revenues in twenty-two OECD countries. Here too Canada is

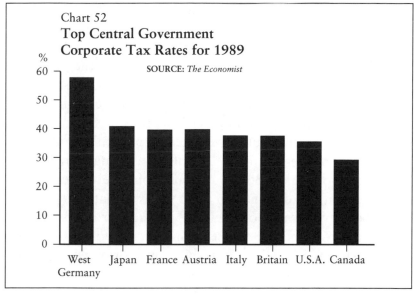

Chart 52
**Top Central Government
Corporate Tax Rates for 1989**
SOURCE: *The Economist*

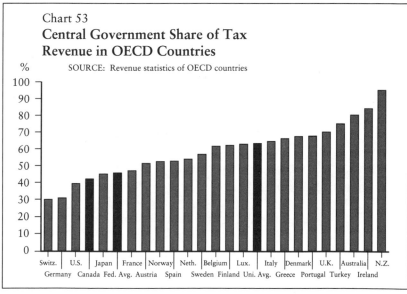

Chart 53
**Central Government Share of Tax
Revenue in OECD Countries**
SOURCE: Revenue statistics of OECD countries

below average even for federal countries, and of course it is
very much lower than the average for unitary states. So
again the question must be asked: Canada is overcentralized
compared with where?

When American state governors come to Canada and see the powers that our provincial premiers already have, in terms of education, social programs, health care, natural resources, and taxation, they can't believe that the provinces have so much jurisdiction compared with the U.S. states. Of all the world's federal nations, with the exception of tiny Switzerland, Canada has long been the most decentralized.

Yet there are still a number of people, particularly in southern parts of western Canada and also, amazingly enough, in Quebec, who think, "Boy, we should join the United States. We have so much domination from Ottawa that we would be much better off as part of the U.S." If that ever happened, the vast amount of power that the provinces would then lose would come as a huge shock to those uninformed people who say we don't have the ability to control our own future. Joining the United States would give Alberta and British Columbia, for example, about the same power in the union as an Arizona or a New Mexico — and that is not very much.

But hasn't Ottawa's share of the spending pie been increasing, as so much of what we read and hear seems to imply? Wrong again. Federal government revenues as a percentage of GDP are just about where they were two decades ago: in 1969-70 they amounted to 17.3 per cent of GDP; twenty years later they were 17.5 per cent.[2] Economist Arthur Donner has made the following comparisons of federal spending in Canada and the United States:

Federal Spending as a Percentage of GDP

	1960	1970	1980	1985	1989
Canada	6.18	5.11	4.52	4.93	4.60
United States	10.60	9.65	7.62	8.84	7.70

Federal Spending as a Percentage of Total Government Spending on Goods and Services

	1960	1970	1980	1985	1989
Canada	45.92	27.58	23.46	24.47	22.40
United States	53.55	43.52	39.23	43.25	38.90

So if you want to join the United States, you had better be prepared to give up a great many local, provincial, and regional powers to Washington.[3]

The premise that the governments closest to the people are inherently those in the best position to provide services and to determine policy is popular but flawed. How would you like to have Don Getty completely in control of energy policy or Robert Bourassa totally in command of environmental policies? And would you like to have had Bill Vander Zalm in charge of all foreign investment regulations or John Buchanan in charge of patronage and political financing reform?

Senator Heath Macquarrie has commented on the "closer to the people" theory (*Globe and Mail*, 11 May 1991):

> Perhaps the strongest supports for the centrifugal forces are well-meaning but illogical views about provincial and local governments. It is often said that because they are "closer to the people" their institutions exude a degree of freedom and sensitivity the "remote" central government could not attain. In the United States, if they had waited for the initiative of the state and local governments, what would have happened to the civil-rights campaign? . . . It's not going too far to say that if the federal politicians and the federal courts had not taken the lead, blacks might still be segregated. Nor need we confine our argument to the Great Republic. It was Quebec, not Ottawa, that imposed the Padlock Act in 1937. . . . Nor should we forget that the provincial government of Alberta imposed grievously repressive laws that were disallowed by the federal government.

It is important to understand, as so many wise commentators apparently do not, that even without obtaining more powers, the provinces will be far outspending the federal government by the end of this decade. In many important ways, we have already transferred to the provinces levers of power well beyond what other federal nations would even consider. But now, with federal cuts to transfer payments, there comes a growing chorus demanding more powers for the provinces. Now, with the increased nationalism in Quebec (another direct heritage of the wisdom of roll-the-dice Mulroney), the way out is clear: placate Quebec, and placate the other provinces too. Brian, our hero, will come to the rescue with a full plate of new powers and the rich spending-power gravy to go with them.

Allaire will be happy. Don Getty and Jim Horsman will be happy. Mazankowski will be happy. Even Lucien Bouchard and Jacques Parizeau will be happy (though they won't say so). But what of the country? What will we be left with? The new Northern Balkans? The Baltic States of North America? Will there be ten or twelve feuding fiefdoms, each eager to emulate the prime minister and give away as much as possible, as quickly as possible, to the transnational corporations? The new taxation powers of the provinces will inevitably accelerate the competition between them. It will be a question of who can attract Mitsubishi or Procter & Gamble most quickly. Even bigger tax credits will be offered, and huge incentives will be piled on top of existing incentives. Canada will become a tax forest, with clear-cut logging of all the good things that we Canadians have developed together over generations.

Federal transfer payments are meant to help raise the standard of living in the poorer provinces. This Canadian sharing is as basic and as fundamental a difference between Canada and the United States as our health-care system is. But in Brian Mulroney's or Preston Manning's new Canada, one of the first results will be a patchwork country with lower levels of services in all "have-not" provinces. Poorer regions will no longer be able to provide adequate health care and other vital social programs. Transfer payments will become a thing of the past, regardless of any temporary agreements to the contrary. The ties that have bound the nation will be severed, and Canada will be dismantled. The national government will become an insignificant force in Canadian society.

The federal government's strategy is clear. The 1991 budget was a road map to the future. The strategy is to offload deficits, responsibilities, and powers to the provinces. The same powers that Quebec demands will be given to all provinces, and so will more taxing authority; and funds for health, education, and culture will no longer come from Ottawa. The provinces will be in control.

The process of transferring more power to the provinces has in fact been underway since Brian Mulroney became prime minister, for the federal government's role has been gradually diminished in many key areas. But when the new tax system changes are announced, the irreversible balkanization of Canada will be formalized, and the permanent fragmentation of Canada will be a fact instead of just a fear. Parochial provincial potentates will be in charge of the remnants. There will be no country at all, nothing to hold the parts together, and there will be diminishing common goals and values. The formal Americanization of the principalities will then proceed.

Why would Quebec want to remain part of a dismembered, truncated, emasculated remnant of a country? Why would western Canada? There would be no national standards. There would be no national pride. There would soon be no nation. We know that Canada is often a difficult country to govern. We know this is because of the size of our country and the large distances involved, and because of our two official languages and various other complications. But Canada is also difficult to govern because it is already very decentralized. If the Mulroney government, after already abandoning so much authority under the FTA, succeeds in abandoning a long list of important national powers that are currently held by Ottawa, then that would really be the end of Canada.

The answers to Canada's problems do not lie in giving the provinces even more powers than they already have and weakening the federal government so much that it becomes impotent. A far better solution would be to start off by reforming our democracy so that the people of Canada can better and more effectively express their goals and aspirations in a truly democratic country — a country which the vast majority of Canadians love and want to preserve.

35

From East-West to North-South

The Reality of the American Dream

> Canada and the U.S. will soon be . . . demonstrating to all
> humanity that there are indeed no limits to what people
> can accomplish when they are free to follow their dreams.
> We're making that dream a reality. It is the American
> dream.   RONALD REAGAN, *Toronto Star*, November 1987

> Canada's captains of competitiveness are advocating
> changes that would transform the country as dramatically
> as anything envisioned by Quebec's separatist zealots.
> Continental north-south trade flows would supersede
> cross-Canada trade. . . . Canada's costly, cumbersome
> three-tier government would be rationalized — perhaps
> replaced by a streamlined system delivering whatever pub-
> lic services would remain through the regional level, close
> to consumers. Federal transfer payments would be cur-
> tailed, as income redistribution would no longer be appro-
> priate government policy. Official bilingualism, marketing
> boards and regulatory agencies — all hindrances to com-
> petitiveness — would be phased out.
>   GLOBE AND MAIL, *25 April 1991*

W HO ARE THESE CANADIAN "CAPTAINS OF COM-
petitiveness" that the *Globe and Mail* compares with Quebec
separatists? Who is it that would like to get rid of regulatory

agencies, transfer payments, and bilingualism, and who wants to have north-south supersede east-west, with reduced public services "benchmarked against those in the United States"? Surely we are talking about those ultra-right-wing reactionaries who are always with us but to whom nobody pays much attention. Unfortunately, this is not the case. As part of "the growing chorus clamouring for change," our national newspaper lists BCNI president Thomas d'Aquino, along with the Conference Board of Canada, the C. D. Howe Institute, and the head of Alcan Aluminium — by now, a somewhat familiar list.

We Canadians deliberately designed our nation in defiance of market forces. But we did much more than that; we built a much-admired country and achieved great social and economic progress, despite the difficulties of huge distances and cultural and regional diversities. For generations, we have believed that our elected national government should evolve programs promoting compassion, equality, and redistribution, and (until recently) we have tended to respect the country's public institutions and to believe in government intervention when necessary.

Many of the continentalist right appear to have a very different vision of Canada: no national environmental standards, no national educational policies, no national social assistance policies, and no minimum standards across the country — because there will be no one in charge. In this new (and temporary) Canada, there will be checkerboard programs and policies: no common energy policies, no common social policies, no policies relating to foreign ownership or corporate concentration, no thoughts of cushioning regional disparities, and no national science and technology policies. In fact, there will be no nation. Thomas Courchene, director of the School of Policy Studies at Queen's University, put it this way: "The point that is terribly important . . . is how do we integrate north-south, when the entire Canadian transfer system, generous as it is, runs east-west? At some time the two are going to clash and the victim of that is going to be the transfer system."[1] Of course.

As the east-west links deteriorate in transportation and communications, and the federal government's presence is drastically weakened by both the FTA and the Mulroney fiscal and monetary policies, north-south will become increasingly important, and the Canadian regions will become hinterlands to the U.S. hinterlands. Did the government of Brian Mulroney not understand the implications for east-west and for harmonization to U.S. standards as a result of the FTA? Here are the words of Donald Campbell who, as an assistant deputy minister in the Department of External Affairs, helped guide the negotiations: "Regions of Canada may be influenced by gradually stronger North-South economic orientation as they become part of the North American as much as the Canadian economic region." Well, yes, of course, the government did understand the implications.

What will happen to east-west transportation when new rail lines, along with already proposed new highways and new U.S. regional trucking facilities, link U.S. railways and U.S. ports with Canadian commodity producers, especially if those producers are American to begin with? What will happen to regional communities? For example, had there been a Free Trade Agreement in place a couple of generations ago, where would Winnipeg be today? Where would Calgary be? W.H. Loewen, chairman of Comcheq Services Ltd., puts it well: "Instead of being midway between Toronto and Vancouver, Winnipeg would be north of Bismarck. . . . [With the FTA] there would be a steady decline of services available to us, or an increase in the cost of those services. This would undoubtedly result in the significant decline of our economy."

With an increasing emphasis on north-south, and less and less on east-west, what will happen to our east-west transportation systems — to our rail lines, to the Trans-Canada Highway? If Cargill decides to ship Canadian grain down the Mississippi, what will happen to Prince Rupert and

Churchill? If our banks and other corporations decide to use U.S. telecommunication facilities, what happens to cross-Canada communications? As we continue to connect up the country with more and more cable packages from civilized places like Detroit while strangling the CBC, what happens to Canadian culture? And what happens to our sense of ourselves and to our self-respect? Or will we simply learn to love the latest news of murder and violence from Motor City? Thanks to the Mulroney government, we already have the privilege of reaping the abundant dividends from U.S.-style deregulation in trucking and in airlines and railways. Have you noticed the cheaper fares, the better schedules, the improved service? No, neither have I. And just wait until Brian Mulroney brings us "open skies."

In selling the Free Trade Agreement to Canadians, big business constantly pointed to the European Community as a model for Canada. But there are enormous differences between what is happening in Europe and the Canada-U.S. Free Trade Agreement. Setting aside the obvious cultural and language differences, in Europe no one country so dominates in population and GDP as the United States does in relation to Canada. Also, large corporations run the Canadian and U.S. economies to a far greater extent than they do in Europe.

In Europe it was clearly stated that "in the course of the construction of the single European Market, social aspects should be given the same importance as economic aspects." Following the Treaty of Rome, there were various agreements dealing with such things as regional assistance, the protection and improvement of the environment, the protection of health, the prudent use of natural resources, dialogue between management and labour, the improvement of working conditions, actions to protect the health and safety of workers, matters relating to unemployment, education, job training, poverty, social support, industrial relations, and so on. In short, they were compassionate social policies. Carla Hills and Mexican President Salinas would choke on a list like that. Social policies were completely absent from the FTA. The inevitable result will be that Canada is pulled down to U.S. standards. And then comes Mexico.

Somehow, the Group of 22, among others, seems to think that out of all of this, regional transfer payments can continue. Why? Why would Ontario want Nova Scotia to have more money so that the people and government of Nova Scotia could spend more buying goods and services from Boston? Why would Albertans want to subsidize Manitobans buying more in Minneapolis? For that matter, why would anyone want to help pay for a National Capital Commission? Or even a national capital? Economist Bruce Wilkinson has few doubts about the inevitable consequences:

> Whether the end result is a political union, or whether the relationship stops somewhat short of that, it is evident that more and more Canada will not be able to take legislative steps affecting economic or social policies or conditions without getting the approval of U.S. authorities and/or ensuring that big business is satisfied that there is sufficient harmonization of policies that their ability to move resources and goods between the two countries is unimpeded. Canada will become increasingly a mere satellite of the greater American entity. (Unpublished paper, 1990)

But, after all, our standard of living and self-determination are not everything. Surely we will still have sports, for example. No doubt Bruce McNall and Rocket Ismail will want to keep the Canadian Football League in business. And no doubt Canadians in Saskatoon and Halifax will thrill at the prospect of Milwaukee, Atlanta, Dallas, Houston, San Francisco, and San Diego being in line for new National Hockey League franchises.

36

Do We Want to Become Americans?

Do We Have a Choice?

> *We would like to think we're about to get the best of both worlds — Canadian stability and a more caring society, as well as U.S. markets — but what if instead we get their crime rate, their health programs and gun laws, and they get our markets, or what's left of them?*
> MARGARET ATWOOD, *Ottawa Citizen, 19 December 1987*

> *Within a mile of the Renaissance Centre, Detroit's landmark skyscraper, stand hundreds of handsome red brick houses . . . abandoned by their owners. Most have their windows boarded up or smashed. They have been stripped of their plumbing and other fittings. A few still house squatters: the poverty-stricken as well as drunks, whores, crack addicts and other riff-raff. The stench of urine in the hallways can be overpowering.* ECONOMIST, *19 May 1990*

> *There's a viciousness out there on the street with people with weapons. They don't care if they live or die, it seems, or if you live or die.* WARREN WOODFORK, *New Orleans police superintendent, Toronto Star, 7 April 1991*

W E HAVE ALREADY LOOKED AT SOME OF THE most important differences between Canada and the United States. But since the objective of the Mulroney government and of big business in Canada is to harmonize Canadian policies and standards with those of the U.S., perhaps we should briefly look a bit closer at where we are apparently headed if the Americanizers of Canada get their way.

While no one would deny that Canadians and Americans are similar in many important ways, we also know that we are not the same. Aside from the fact that we don't bankrupt the sick in Canada or ask them for credit cards before we let them into hospitals, there are numerous striking differences. The United States is a wonderful country to live in if you are white and wealthy, if you can send your kids to private schools, if you live in a high-income well-policed neighbourhood or compound, and if the city or town you live in isn't going bankrupt.[1] But although the United States is the world's most affluent and powerful nation, it is also a nation that has millions of impoverished families and hungry and homeless people who, on any comparative basis, receive far less aid than the citizens of any other developed nation.

There is no other developed country in the world that has remotely the same combined degree of violence, crime, homelessness, and poorly educated people. Stanley Meisler, writing in the *Los Angeles Times,* puts it this way: "You can hear the moments of boredom tick away whenever you tell Americans that no other industrialized democracy has the same dispiriting problems as the United States — not the crime, not the guns, not the homeless, not the unschooled. . . . Americans seem oblivious to the problems of poverty, education, unemployment, racism and inequality that spawn crime." A Baltimore social-work professor elaborates: "People have become somewhat jaded. . . . What seems to have happened here is that we have steeled people against the fact that murder is now part of our daily life."

The "right to bear arms" in the United States has become a grotesque pollution of the idea of freedom. U.S. gun laws, even with the latest "tightening-up" legislation, are in themselves a crime against humanity. The number of murders make the statistics from all other nations seem marginal by comparison. Homicide rates, violent crime rates, sexual assault rates, robbery rates, and crime rates in general are totally out of control when measured against those of Canada or any other country. In the U.S., there are some 150 million rifles in circulation and almost half that number of handguns. Uzi submachine guns and AK 47s proliferate. One in five Americans say they have been threatened with a gun. On average, five or six people are murdered every day in New York City, and almost 9000 Americans were killed by handguns alone in 1989. The chances of being killed by a gun are six times higher in Seattle than in Vancouver. The murder rate per 100,000 population in the U.S. is five times that of Western Europe. Similarly, it was five times that of Canada in 1990.

In 1990, in all of Canada, a nation of some 27 million people, there were 637 homicides (including murder, manslaughter, and infanticide). By comparison, the city of New York alone had 2245 homicides, and Los Angeles had 991. Houston, with a population of 1.63 million, had 617 murders; Dallas, with a population of just over a million, had 447 murders; Chicago, at some 2.8 million, had 849 murders; and Philadelphia, with 1.6 million residents, had 522 murders. In 1989, Canada's two major metropolitan centres, Toronto and Montreal, had a combined total of 157 murders. The same year, New York City had 1905 murders and Los Angeles 888 (see Chart 54).

In an average year, more people are killed with handguns in and around Miami, Florida, than in all of Western Europe. Six out of ten Americans say they have been a victim of a major crime, and one in seven either carries a gun or has one in the car. In 1987 there were three Canadian police officers killed in line of duty; in the U.S. the figure was 73. In 1990 two Canadian police officers were killed on duty; in the U.S. the figure jumped to 130.

The nation's capital, Washington, D.C., is also the murder capital of the United States. In 1989 there were 439 murders

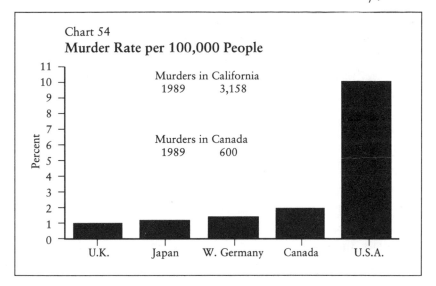

Chart 54
Murder Rate per 100,000 People

Murders in California
1989   3,158

Murders in Canada
1989   600

Percent axis: 0–11

Categories: U.K.   Japan   W. Germany   Canada   U.S.A.

in the tiny District of Columbia. In 1987 *Time* magazine reported that a black infant born within five miles of the White House is more likely to die in the first year of life than an infant born in a Third World country such as Trinidad. The infant mortality rate in Harlem, New York City, is three times the Canadian rate.

Three million crimes a year occur on U.S. school grounds. Many inner-city American children begin carrying handguns when they are ten or eleven years old. Gang wars involving cocaine, crack, and marijuana dealers are common, and frequently the gangs use the semi-automatic weapons they own. Obviously, the massive drug problems in the United States are directly related to the high crime rate. The U.S. has about 5 per cent of the world's population but consumes over 50 per cent of the world's cocaine. The crack epidemic seems beyond all control.

Thousands of homeless children in major U.S. cities do not attend school. Although more than 7 million U.S. children do not have health insurance, both Ronald Reagan and George Bush have cut back social benefits. On any given night, more than 100,000 American children are homeless. Since Ronald

Reagan's first election, over half a million poor Americans are no longer eligible for Medicaid assistance. Millions of handicapped children now receive inferior assistance.

As we have seen, American social programs are a pale shadow of those in Canada or those of other OECD nations. In the first half of 1991, only 42 per cent of the unemployed in the United States were covered by any unemployment insurance programs, and unemployment benefits for those who did receive assistance were about half of those received in Canada. Maternity leave in the U.S. is considerably shorter, and sickness benefits are inferior. Overall, only about one-half of the poor families in the U.S. receive assistance, and that help is generally inadequate. As well, safety and health regulations are much weaker than those in Canada.

As Allan Fotheringham has reported, "Because of the Reagan budget cuts in the social safety net, thousands of borderline cases in mental homes have been released to become street people in Manhattan, sleeping on the heating grates that exude steam alongside the curbs where the white stretch limos sit." In 1988, when President Ronald Reagan was asked about the homeless who slept on steam grates near the White House, he suggested that they were largely people who were there by choice.

Far more Americans are behind bars, as a percentage of the population, than in any other country: some 426 per 100,000 residents. This compares with 333 per 100,000 in South Africa and 268 per 100,000 in the Soviet Union. Furthermore, the American prison population is currently rising at an annual rate of 13 per cent.

Americans visiting Canada for the first time are often amazed at how safe and clean Canadian cities are and how much superior public services are. The first question many visiting Americans ask the hotel clerk is, "Is it safe to walk on the streets at night?" And when they check out, they frequently say, "I didn't know there were cities like this in North America."

While on average Canadians have a much stronger humanitarian idealism than Americans and are much more compassionate as a people, they do not have a compulsion to spread their ideology throughout the entire world. The United States, as Robertson Davies has pointed out, simply assumes that its political and moral views are superior to those of others. "My country, right or wrong" is a common attitude. As Peter Newman puts it, "Americans are obsessed with their self-imposed burden of saving the world for democracy." (Yet on a list of eighteen leading countries providing assistance to developing nations, as a percentage of GNP the United States was eighteenth. By contrast, Canada was eighth.)

If Americans are too patriotic and too nationalistic, Canadians on the whole are not patriotic or nationalistic enough. Americans are evangelical in their political beliefs, while Canadians are more laid back about trying to influence others, even though their voting record in national elections is consistently much higher — usually some 50 per cent higher — than that of Americans.

While the great American universities are superb, and while the wealthy and upper middle class in the United States receive excellent medical treatment, a great many U.S. post-secondary institutions are vastly inferior to most Canadian ones. Canada has a better all-round equal-access-to-education system, and its costs are more reasonable: tuition fees to the better U.S. universities are often ten to fifteen times those of top Canadian universities.

It has become a cliché to compare the two countries' constitutions, but there is some merit in mentioning yet once more that Canada's constitution is designed to promote "peace, order and good government" — the emphasis is on the collective good. The U.S. constitution, the Declaration of Independence, emphasize "Life, liberty and the pursuit of happiness" — the rights of the individual are emphasized rather than the collective good (i.e., the state).

Canadians, much more so than Americans, believe in the benefits of a mixed economy and the active participation of government in the affairs of the nation. In a phrase, Canadians are more social-democratic than Americans. In Europe such a statement would be regarded as an attribute, but in Canada it is the main reason why the Mulroney government and the BCNI would like us to harmonize with American policies and American standards.

God knows, Canadians are far from perfect. The previous pages list scores of areas where we need to improve, as well as some areas where we deserve to hang our heads in shame, most notably in our treatment of the aboriginal people.[2] Our quarrelsome preoccupation with the constitution is looked upon with despair and disdain by people both inside and outside Canada. Yet as I started off by saying, the combined standard of living and quality of life we have had, until very recently, has been unsurpassed. Year after year in poll after poll, Canadians, by an overwhelming majority, have said that they believe Canada is superior to the United States, in social security for the disadvantaged, in our health-care system, in racial tolerance, in the promotion of world peace, in the crime rate, in the educational opportunities, and in the overall quality of life. In the latter category, invariably for every Canadian who prefers the United States, at least seven or eight opt for Canada. All of this is not even remotely a smug superiority; it is just a simple recognition of basic differences and diverging values. Some 85 per cent of Canadians are against joining the United States while only 11 per cent are in favour; 74 per cent would not like to live in the U.S., and 58 per cent would not even send their children to university or college there.

Is all of this anti-American? Yes it is, if the millions of Americans who criticize the U.S. may also be termed anti-American. Is it un-American? Absolutely. By definition, Canadians are un-American. The founding of this country largely originated from a desire to form a separate nation on the northern part of North America. While most Canadians say "Vive la différence," the Mulroney government and most of Canada's business elite are now pushing us rapidly down the one-way road to economic, social, cultural, and political integration.[3]

Do we have a choice? Yes we do, but only if we act very quickly.

37

Our Greatest Asset

Remembrances of Things Past?

> *We may have to give some ground on political indepen-*
> *dence — or how we set social policies. I recognize many*
> *Canadians are nervous.* DONALD MACDONALD, *chairman,*
> Royal Commission on the Economic Union and
> Development Prospects for Canada, August 1985

> *This agreement can never be justified. By giving up*
> *sovereignty and jurisdiction over vital areas of our econo-*
> *my, we have reduced our status as a nation to that of an*
> *American colony. . . . If an American president had ever*
> *thought of giving up one-hundredth of the political juris-*
> *diction that we are throwing on the table, he would have*
> *been impeached instantly.* ERIC KIERANS, *House of Commons*
> Committee on External Affairs and International Trade, 3 December 1987

THE GREATEST ASSET THE PEOPLE OF CANADA HAVE
is not their oil or their ample reserves of natural gas, not the
magnificent freshwater rivers and lakes, not the lush fields of
grain, not the abundant mineral resources and forests, not
even the enormous space and natural beauty they have inherited. No, the greatest asset Canadians can possibly have is
the ability to control their own future. We have now lost that
ability, and unless something happens very soon, we will
have lost it forever.

264

Since the signing of the Free Trade Agreement, Canada has been led steadfastly towards the point of no return. There are now in place legal constraints, severe restrictions, and huge obstacles preventing any future elected governments from carrying out the will of the people. As long as the Free Trade Agreement is in place, it binds the hands of the democratic process in iron shackles. In American ownership and control of our country, in energy, culture, social programs, fiscal and monetary powers, public ownership, resource policies, and in dozens of other areas, the elected representatives of the people of Canada are now unable to act in the best interests of their constituents.

As every day goes by, as more and more factories close forever, as more production in Canada is "rationalized," as more and more of Canada is bought up by non-Canadians, and as more Canadian standards and policies are harmonized to those in the United States, the process becomes more irreversible. The integration and harmonization become accepted fact. The vulnerability grows to the point where future independence is inconceivable. Sadly, more than a few Canadians say it is already too late. Add them to the Americanizers of Canada — the Mulroney government and the BCNI — and the inertia becomes almost overwhelming.

Recently, the chancellor of a major Canadian university and the former leader of an important provincial political party agreed over dinner in my home that it was now too late: Canada had no choice but to join the U.S. The June 1991 issue of the *Economist* is direct and to the point: "Sooner or later, Canadians are going to become Americans. Too bad." Increasingly, young Canadians take the integration for granted. Increasingly, Canadians despair at the political vacuum they perceive.

Never before in my lifetime have I encountered a situation that so threatens the existence of our country. And never before have I felt so strongly that our nation and its people have been betrayed.

38

Quebec and the Constitution

The Two Turning Points for Sovereignty

Free trade with the United States will inevitably threaten Canada's political sovereignty. Canadians must be made aware of the dangers that lie ahead if Prime Minister Brian Mulroney leads us into an all-out free trade agreement with the Americans.   ROBERT BOURASSA, *Toronto Star, 1 February 1986*

How could you seriously say that Canadian sovereignty is at stake?   ROBERT BOURASSA, *Toronto Star, October 1987*

On the political level, (the FTA is) a very encouraging development and, as a separatist . . . obviously I hope it succeeds.   JACQUES PARIZEAU, *PQ leader, Le Devoir, February 1988*

The spearhead of the invasion of English into Quebec does not come from English Canada, but from American television.   NORTHROP FRYE, *speech to the SSHRC, fall 1990*

DID YOU NOTE THE SIMILARITY BETWEEN BRIAN Mulroney's remarkable about-face on the issue of free trade (completely changing his position between 1983 and 1985) and the equally remarkable flip-flop of his good friend Robert Bourassa, the Quebec premier, between 1986 and 1987? In 1986, free trade was dangerous because it could lead to political integration with the United States. A year later:

"How could you seriously say that Canadian sovereignty is at stake?" Apparently, the voters are expected to have short memories (and unfortunately they often do have). Certainly, the media in Quebec had a severe case of amnesia; they hardly noticed Mr. Bourassa's conversion.

There is no inconsistency, though, in the position of Quebec nationalists. Free trade would be a wonderful catalyst to allow Quebec to turn its back on Canada.[1] Only two provinces gave Brian Mulroney a majority in the 1988 federal election, the energy-exporting provinces of Alberta and Quebec. In the case of Alberta, the combination of strong support from the Getty government and the resource industries carried the vote. In Quebec, Robert Bourassa was the head cheer leader, and all Quebec separatists enthusiastically joined in.

Former Liberal cabinet minister Raymond Garneau had doubts: "Canadians who live in Quebec, and who have fought for Canadian unity, are wondering whether they have fought only to see the Conservatives put forward an economic policy whereby the regions of Canada shall see their future as being almost exclusively in the south." But Bourassa, like many converts, became a free trade zealot. Many people now firmly believe that the Quebec premier agreed to support Brian Mulroney's free trade initiative in exchange for Mulroney's support for Quebec's constitutional demands.

There can be little question that the Free Trade Agreement has been a big boost for Quebec separatists. The passage of the agreement was an important turning point for the sovereignty movement. But it was the combination of both the FTA and the bitter climate created by the Meech Lake fiasco that boosted Quebec separatism to new strengths. In short, the current constitutional crisis and the potential break-up of Canada is largely the creation of Brian Mulroney.

In December 1985, the Parti Québécois was devastated in the Quebec provincial election, winning only 24 seats. Subsequently, few people either inside or outside Quebec were interested in concentrating yet once again on constitutional discussions. But within four years, the Mulroney government somehow managed to present the people of Canada with an unpopular take-it-or-leave-it, no-changes-accepted proposal, along with repeated warnings that if the new proposal was not accepted, the nation would face an unprecedented crisis. A country, which in terms of national unity was doing very nicely indeed, was almost overnight deemed to be a terrible constitutional failure requiring urgent reform, with a quick self-imposed deadline.

In 1987, when René Lévesque died, few people in Quebec were talking of sovereignty; as recently as November 1989, some 70 per cent of Quebeckers said that they were Canadians committed to making Canada work. Another poll showed that for every one Quebecker who wanted Quebec to be a separate country, there were two who would rather live in the Province of Quebec. Only 20 per cent felt that the failure of Meech Lake would cause Quebec to separate. And in a fascinating insight, 65 per cent felt that a recognition of Quebec as a distinct society need not give Quebec any special status, while 62 per cent wanted the Charter of Rights to take precedence over the "distinct society" provisions. Two-thirds supported bilingualism in Quebec. Clearly, as is so often the case, the people were well ahead of the politicians and were also far more tolerant and more open to compromise.

The results of these and other public-opinion polls totally contradict the Lévesque, Bourassa, and Parizeau position that Quebec was "repudiated" by the 1982 patriation of the constitution, a position Brian Mulroney supported. Despite this, a June 1982 Gallup poll showed that 49 per cent of the people in Quebec thought the new constitution was "a good thing" and only 16 per cent said that it was not. Two years later, 64 per cent of Quebeckers said Canada would remain united, and only 18 per cent thought it would break up. Moreover, by June 1986, some three out of every four Canadians said they supported official bilingualism. Then Brian Mulroney went to work and presented

Canadians with an unchangeable Meech Lake Accord, which, in the words of pollster Angus Reid, was clearly "to be only the beginning, not the end of the constitutional reform process."

How is it possible that in such a very short period of time, Canada and Quebec went from an excellent spirit of optimism, cooperation, and good will to the prospect of the breakup of our nation? The rejection of Meech Lake was a rejection of the method and of the man as well as of the actual contents of the agreement. Many Canadians feared an apparently open-ended definition of "distinct society." "Distinct" was far too vague. What powers went with the definition? No one seemed certain. The public certainly wasn't.

Quebec's demands to be recognized as a distinct society would not normally prove troublesome. Of course Quebec *is* a distinct society, with its French language and French culture, with its own code of civil law, and with many other distinct attributes. But who can deny that Newfoundland is also distinct? So is the Yukon. And so is British Columbia. The most serious problems arose when both Brian Mulroney and Robert Bourassa told Canadians that they must accept the Meech Lake agreement unchanged and when it became apparent that there would be no clear definition of the meaning of "distinct society." The problem worsened when it became clear that for the Government of Quebec, a "distinct society" meant special status, with additional powers.

Clearly, the deception, the intransigence, the backroom negotiations and ploys, the take-it-or-leave-it proposal put to the people of Canada, the perception that Brian Mulroney and Robert Bourassa had cooked up a secret, self-serving deal, and general distrust of the entire process were all key factors in the rejection of Meech Lake. The public mood soured. Soon it became bitter.

For Canadians outside Quebec, the perception grew that Quebec's demands were unreasonable and would likely be interminable. In Quebec, the perception grew that the rest of

Canada was hostile and that Quebec was being rejected. The entire process and the results became highly symbolic and the positions of the adversaries wildly distorted. The political leaders in Quebec and the Quebec media told Quebeckers, in no uncertain terms, that they were being humiliated. And all the while, Brian Mulroney was telling all Canadians, in both official languages, that if Meech Lake was rejected, there would be a serious crisis in the land. By repeating this, he guaranteed a crisis.

A good leader, a caring prime minister, would have calmed the waters. He or she would have explained much more forcefully that they were all trying very hard to make a deal — and that if they were not successful, there would be opportunities in the future to go back to the drawing board and try once again. Patience, mutual respect, and good will would be the key. Brian Mulroney could hardly be expected to explain that the failure of Meech Lake was very largely due to his own unpopularity, his deceptive tactics, and his lack of ability. But he could have made it much clearer that the torpedoing of the agreement was *not* a rejection of Quebec. Instead, a petulant, frustrated, angry prime minister fed the flames of Quebec separatism and later enraged all Canadians by proudly admitting, in his famous "roll-the-dice" interview, that he had intentionally delayed calling the premiers together until close to the last minute.

What can we say about a prime minister who not only failed to adequately repudiate the idea that Quebec was "humiliated," but whose representatives actually supported the idea that the people of Quebec were being rejected? While many Canadians believed they were endorsing a strong Canada in their opposition to Meech Lake, Brian Mulroney allowed that endorsement to be translated into a hostile rejection of Quebec. With the Quebec media very strongly nationalistic, and with the two Quebec provincial political parties taking similar positions, it was up to the prime minister of Canada to counter the false impressions spread by separatists. Not only did he fail to do so properly, but his weak performance encouraged the impression the separatists were fostering. Is it any wonder that Quebec nationalism reached record heights?

What the Meech Lake fiasco managed to accomplish was to create an "anti-English Canada" feeling in Quebec and an anti-Quebec feeling among thousands of people outside that province who had previously been sympathetic to the French community, to bilingualism, and to Quebec's special character. What Brian Mulroney's evasive, deceptive rolling of the dice managed to accomplish was, for the first time that I can remember, to create a feeling among a great many Canadians that they really didn't care if Quebec left Canada. And in the process, the sleaziness, the power plays, and manipulation turned Canadians off politicians and helped strengthen the Reform party, with its anti-Quebec stance.

Today, thanks to the prime minister, far more Quebeckers seriously consider sovereignty to be a desirable option, and the young in Quebec are much more fervently nationalist than ever before. The Government of Quebec has now set a deadline: either the rest of Canada presents Quebec with an acceptable constitutional offer, or the province will hold a referendum no later than 26 October 1992. Moreover, the Quebec government has made it clear that it will not feel bound by the results of any national referendum conducted by the federal government. Two commissioned reports to the Government of Quebec have provided a long list of federal or jointly shared powers which the appointed authors feel should now reside exclusively with the province. When the prime minister was confronted with the list of demands in the Allaire Report, he responded: "I don't see it as a threat."

The Bourassa government has stated that "there can be no constitutional reform if it does not include . . . the explicit recognition of Quebec as a distinct society." As well, Robert Bourassa has repeatedly reiterated that he would not agree to the "distinct society" clause being qualified by the Canadian Charter of Rights and Freedoms. Yet most Canadians want the Charter to be protected and effective in any new constitutional package; the people of Canada have clearly shown that they want a country that guarantees equality of rights, available to all, regardless of who they are or where they live. At the same time, most Canadians were repelled by Quebec's Bill-178, which banned the use of English on exterior commercial signs. Almost overnight, opinion turned against overrides to the Charter. Minorities across Canada became concerned about the possible suppression of their rights. And Mulroney? Brian Mulroney eventually made hesitant, half-hearted, feeble comments critical of Mr. Bourassa's sign law, and left it at that. The result was that even more Canadians turned against the prime minister and against the concept of a distinct society and special status for Quebec.

By the spring of 1991, polls showed that over three-quarters of Canadians were opposed to giving Quebec special status in the form of extra powers that were not available to other provinces. At the same time, more than three in five people in Quebec approved of special powers for their province.

How would Quebec fare if it decided to leave Canada? The argument that the province can now go it alone because of the great financial and economic progress it has achieved during the past twenty years is strange, to say the least. The financial and economic progress has been achieved as a province of Canada, not as an independent state. Currently, half of those polled in Quebec believe that their standard of living would decline if Quebec were to separate.

I fail to understand why more people in the Liberal party, in the NDP, and in the trade union movement and other national organizations are not much stronger in their outright condemnation of separatism. Why are they not more articulate *in Quebec* about the dangers to the people of Quebec if the province's leaders are allowed to fracture the nation? The fear of offending the Québécois has been taken to the ridiculous extreme that far too many Canadians are now afraid to speak out strongly for national unity. Since the people of Quebec are constantly being told about the abundant good fortune and freedom that awaits them if they choose sovereignty — and how few problems such a choice would create, and how easy those problems would be to resolve — why is there such reticence to explain the real perils that certainly would come with what would inevitably be a traumatic and painful severing? Anyone who underestimates the potential problems of separation for the people of Quebec is doing the population of that province a great disservice. The economic and social penalties, the animosity, the complex legal problems, will all be enormous. Historian Michael Bliss has suggested that a "better metaphor is amputation, a brutal severing of Canada, done without an anaesthetic. It would be terribly painful and it would be bloody."

Both Robert Bourassa and, to a greater extent, Jacques Parizeau have misled the people of Quebec about the consequences of separation. Although Bourassa has clearly been backtracking lately, both he and Parizeau have made separation seem like a viable option, whose results would be acceptable in light of the supposed freedom of self-determination that would be gained. And both have painted a rosy portrait of future monetary and other cooperation with the rest of Canada. They are far too optimistic.

Financing Quebec's $100 billion share of the national debt would be a much greater burden than the people of the province are being told. It would be impossible for Quebec to share a common currency with Canada and have any significant say in monetary policy. Moreover, if Quebec separated, Canada would likely be highly sympathetic and willing to assist the aboriginal people in northern Quebec with their own claims of sovereignty. Quebec would be caught in a bind. After all, how could it legitimately deny the northern native people the same rights of separation that it had itself demanded? And who would then control Quebec's hydropower?

Quebec would have to negotiate new trade agreements with both Canada and the United States — and inevitably

Washington would then jump all over Quebec in demanding concessions relating to cultural industries, agriculture, automobile production and parts, the financial sector, subsidies, public participation in private industry, and so on. Many rights and freedoms that Quebec now takes for granted would disappear or would be severely constrained. Hydro-Québec and government procurement policies would constantly come under the U.S. trade representative's microscope; so would the activities of the *Caisse de dépôt*. Soon, Quebec's much-treasured financial institutions would begin to fall into U.S. ownership. Inevitably, Hydro-Québec would be told that it could no longer provide electricity in the province at lower rates than it charged for export. Much in Quebec would have to change. Quebec's freedom would be sharply curtailed — not expanded.

The picture commonly painted in Quebec that a parting of the ways, the break-up of a country, need not produce acrimony, bitterness, and strife is not only misleadingly optimistic, but it also fails to recognize the problems, complications, and inevitable serious disagreements that would result. As the Spicer Report makes clear, the majority of Canadians want Quebec to remain within Confederation, but not at any price. If the province insists on leaving, most non-Quebeckers want the break to be "clean, complete and final." Few people in Quebec understand this. Few people in Quebec understand the conflict that would arise over assets and liabilities, geography, economic and trade matters, the environment, and other vital areas.

The greatest danger to the future of Quebec, and to the future of the French language and French culture in Quebec, comes not from federalism but from the United States. The French language and culture are flourishing in Quebec and have been for many years. French literature, the theatre, and music are stronger now than ever before. But a Quebec turned away from Canada to face the United States, a Quebec that would then automatically be forced to use more English, would be infinitely more vulnerable to the influences of the greatest culture-exporting nation in the world. One can imagine, for example, the bargaining power that Quebec's minister of culture would have with the U.S. State Department and Jack Valenti when the subject of film distribution and television content regulations came up for discussion, as they would on the heels of Quebec separation.

Perhaps the greatest irony of all is that in an independent Quebec the people would, without question, have to use English much more than they do now. The commercial intercourse between Quebec and Canada, and between Quebec and the United States, would be conducted in English. Inevitably, the entire school system would have to produce students fluent in English. Moreover, one can also imagine the response Quebec's trade minister would receive from Carla Hills when the U.S. trade representative was informed that all goods shipped into Quebec from the U.S. would require bilingual labels, bilingual instruction booklets, and bilingual point-of-sale advertising material.

Quebec already has considerably more power than the vast majority of subnational governments around the world, and the standard of living of its people is already much higher than that in the vast majority of nations in the world. It already has enormous powers over resources, social programs, education, culture, language, immigration, energy, housing policy, and many other areas, powers that are the envy of any American state politician. It also has its own civil legal code, and it is the recipient of considerable net direct financial benefits from the federal government.

In simple terms of language and culture, are 6 million French-speaking Quebeckers more likely to thrive in an officially bilingual Canada of 27 million people or as a separate island in a sea of 270 million English-speaking North Americans?

For twenty-two of the last twenty-three years, the prime minister of Canada has come from Quebec. Since 1968, the influence of French Canadians in the federal government, in

Parliament, and in the federal civil service has grown steadily, while French business leadership has been thriving in Quebec and is of growing influence in other parts of Canada. At the turn of the century, French was the mother tongue of over 80 per cent of the people in Quebec. Today, the figure is virtually identical.

In the past, when required, prime ministers have appealed to the people of Quebec, and to the people of other provinces, over the heads of the provincial governments. But Brian Mulroney courted and greatly depended on both Quebec nationalists and Robert Bourassa in his election campaigns. The prime minister brought ardent Quebec nationalists into his caucus and into senior positions in his cabinet.

A prime minister of courage and integrity, a prime minister who really cared about the people in Quebec, would clearly and forcefully explain to them that they are already masters of their own destiny to a remarkable degree, compared with almost all other peoples around the world. That prime minister would campaign day and night in Quebec, explaining how important it is that Quebec stay in Confederation and how the vast majority of non-Quebeckers very much want Quebec to stay. But the prime minister would also have to explain, very forcefully, that it is impossible to meet all of Quebec's constitutional demands, since the result of doing so would leave a badly weakened nation, or perhaps no nation at all.

Throughout all of the current made-in-Ottawa crisis, it is interesting to see that the polls show that almost twice as many Quebeckers now approve of the way Pierre Trudeau, the advocate of strong central government, handled his job as prime minister compared with Brian Mulroney. Also worth reflecting upon is the result of the April 1991 Globe/CBC poll which asked Quebeckers whether "Canada is the best country in the world to live in"; 83 per cent of the people in Quebec agreed or strongly agreed. As noted earlier (and as we shall see again shortly), the people are often way ahead of their political leaders.

The Allaire Report and other strongly nationalistic suggestions coming from Quebec sovereigntists would destroy the federal government's ability to act in the interests of Canadians. Yet, obviously, a total rejection cannot be the rest of Canada's answer to Quebec. If there are two fundamental characteristics of the Canadian identity, they are compassion and compromise. I have already dealt extensively with the former. Clearly, it is compromise that is in order now.

Down through the years, Canadians have been masters of compromise. In the past, we have been wonderfully resilient, and we can be resilient once again. While most Canadians are primarily concerned about their jobs, their standard of living, and their quality of life, our politicians have become constitutional hypochondriacs, obsessed with a debate that most Canadians rank far down in their list of priorities. It would be marvellous if the first ministers spent even half as much time debating the unfair tax system, excessive corporate concentration, and the Americanization of Canada as they do the division of rights between federal and provincial politicians. But the constitution is on the agenda for Canada, like it or not. So let us return to what Quebec was requesting in advance of the aborted Meech Lake Accord.

Today, many Canadians support and many reject some or all of the original five demands:

- a Quebec veto on constitutional amendments affecting the province;
- a formal say in appointments to the Supreme Court (this was intentionally left vague);
- a limitation of the federal government's spending in areas of provincial jurisdiction;
- a voice in immigration policy;
- the recognition of Quebec's status as a distinct society.

It was the fifth demand that caused most, but not all, of the problems. The Spicer Report summed it up nicely: "We can say that — providing the word 'distinct' does not mean 'superior' or 'superiorly entitled' — the expression 'distinct society' as a description of Quebec seemed acceptable to some forum participants. With a little probing, quite a few agreed that if 'distinct' really meant 'different but broadly equal,' they could, in effect, echo, '*Vive la différence!*'"

The vagueness of the definition of "a distinct society" has caused great apprehension across Canada. As well, the repeated statements of both Bourassa and the minister of intergovernmental relations, Gil Rémillard, that Meech Lake represented minimum demands and that Quebec would use the "distinct society" clause to seek substantial new powers in the future, in a broad range of jurisdictions, has caused concern to more and more Canadians. Rightly or wrongly, a growing number of Canadians outside Quebec began not to trust Bourassa and to look on him as a man who would not stand up for Canada if the public-opinion polls and the Quebec business community supported sovereignty.

In view of all that has happened in Canada during the past two or three years, special status for Quebec — giving it new powers that are not available to other provinces — must now be out of the question. There are two reasons for this. First, the overwhelming majority of Canadians are opposed to the idea. Second, if Quebec gets special status, what will become of federal institutions? Historian Ramsay Cook quotes a Lévesque government 1980 document:

> Special status for Quebec would place Quebec members of Parliament in Ottawa in an absurd and untenable position. How could they vote on federal laws that would apply to all Canada except Quebec? How could they impose on Canadians taxes that Quebeckers would not pay? And how could the prime ministers come from Quebec, where many federal programs would not apply? The entire operation of responsible government would be paralysed.

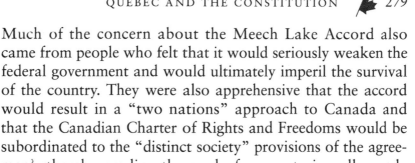

Much of the concern about the Meech Lake Accord also came from people who felt that it would seriously weaken the federal government and would ultimately imperil the survival of the country. They were also apprehensive that the accord would result in a "two nations" approach to Canada and that the Canadian Charter of Rights and Freedoms would be subordinated to the "distinct society" provisions of the agreement, thereby eroding the goal of guaranteeing all people across Canada the same fundamental rights and freedoms. The erosion of federal spending powers was seen as endangering new national initiatives. The provision for greater provincial control of appointments to the Supreme Court caused concern about the provinces becoming stronger still, and Ottawa weaker. As well, there were many Canadians who feared that the Senate would become exclusively a creature of the provinces, and that allowing every province a veto over future constitutional changes was a recipe for a made-in-concrete constitution that could never be changed.

So how do we now find our way out of the morass created by our inept leaders? Here are some fundamentals for a new Canadian constitution:

First, nothing should weaken the federal government's economic powers. If anything, they should be strengthened.

Second, any constitutional changes should be tied directly to the removal of interprovincial barriers.

Third, official bilingualism should be reaffirmed, but much more emphasis should be placed on teaching children both official languages.

Fourth, the Canadian Charter of Rights and Freedoms should be supreme, except in matters relating to language.

Fifth, to help protect against the dangers of the erosion of the French language and culture in Quebec, that province should be allowed domain over cultural and language policies within the province. English-speaking Canada would have to agree not to challenge the legitimacy of Quebec language laws.

Consequently, six, all provinces must be given the right to control language and cultural policies within their borders, to the extent to which they may choose to do so.

Seventh, the federal government should retain control of and strengthen such national cultural institutions as the CBC, the National Film Board, Telefilm Canada, the Canada Council, and the National Gallery of Canada.

Eighth, only persons willing to pledge allegiance to a strong, united Canada should be allowed to sit in the House of Commons, and a formal statement of allegiance to Canada should be included in the constitution.

Ninth, each province should be allowed the option of having the same immigration powers that the Province of Quebec now has. However, nothing should be done to inhibit any resident of any province in Canada from moving to another province at any time, or to restrict already guaranteed Canadian mobility rights in any way.[2]

Tenth, the federal government should be obliged to consult with each province from which it chose to appoint a Supreme Court justice. Nevertheless, the actual selection would remain the prerogative of the federal government.

While Quebec and perhaps some other provinces would inevitably adopt restrictive language policies, there is good reason to believe that enlightened public opinion would win out eventually. As recently as early 1990, four out of five Canadians agreed that both English and French should have official status in Canada, and three out of four hoped that their children would be bilingual. In the Globe and Mail/CBC News poll published in April 1991, 92 per cent of French-speaking Canadians and 61 per cent of English-speaking Canadians thought that the federal government should provide services in both English and French across the country. Only 36 per cent of English-speaking Canadians disagreed. And a large majority felt that the two official languages should be maintained. Finally, three out of four Quebeckers and three out of five Canadians outside Quebec reject the idea of "French only" in Quebec and "English only" in the rest of Canada. Once again, the people of Canada seem much wiser than many of their political leaders and infinitely wiser than the people in the Prime Minister's Office.

Canada should be proud of its bilingualism, not defensive. Yes, there are bigots who stomp on the *fleur-de-lis* and bigots who burn the maple leaf, but every single public-opinion poll shows that they are a small minority. Why should we be intimidated by them? Why should we let such a small minority try to change the generally tolerant nature of our society? After all, most Canadians continue to support the concept of official bilingualism. Moreover, curtailing official bilingualism would inevitably have exactly the opposite effect of what was desired. It would be certain to please Jacques Parizeau no end and to please every separatist in the Province of Quebec, not to mention racists in other parts of the country.

Bilingualism should be viewed not as a divisive force in the country but as a means of keeping the country together. That the Prime Minister's Office has even been considering the idea of abandoning it in order to pander to separatists and racists in Quebec, and in the rest of Canada, is an indication of the short-sighted expediency of people prepared to sacrifice the principle of two official languages in a desperate, confused bid to stay in power. (Incidentally, the entire annual cross-Canada costs of bilingualism could easily be paid for by a one-third of 1 per cent drop in Canadian interest rates and the resultant savings on the cost of financing the federal debt.)

Contrary to the wishes of Quebec's political leadership, a June 1991 poll showed that four out of five Quebeckers want the Canadian Charter of Rights and Freedoms to have precedence over other legislation. Robert Bourassa is out of step with the people of his province. A strong prime minister would have no hesitation pointing this out in Quebec.

The Government of Ontario is now advocating an expansion of the Charter of Rights and Freedoms to guarantee every Canadian access to basic health, social, and other services. The expanded Charter could establish national standards so that residents in all provinces would be guaranteed basic levels of services. Since the existing Charter helps define individual rights, and since the expanded Charter would help define collective rights, an excellent balance would be achieved which might help end the interminable federal-provincial battles and the obsession with constitutional struggles over power sharing.

Of course, Mr. Bourassa would be against the proposal and therefore so would Mr. Mulroney and the federal government. But the idea is a good one that would be popular with Canadians in all regions. More and more, it becomes increasingly clear that we need new and far better political leaders if we are to achieve a resolution of these problems.

One thing is certain. In any constitutional reform on the horizon, we shall have to have an elected Senate. The West, or much of it, wants a triple-E Senate: elected, effective, and equal. But it will have to settle for elected and more effective. Quebec and Ontario would never agree to a Senate with equal representation from all provinces (any more than the West, Ontario, and the Atlantic provinces would agree to Quebec getting everything on its wish list). The merits of a provincially equal Senate can be argued, as they have been, back and forth and upside-down and over; but it won't happen. It's just not on. Quebec will have to make concessions, and so will the West.

However, the long struggle for Senate reform has been most worthwhile. If our election laws could be changed so that elections were conducted more democratically, as described earlier, and if the new senators were charged with representing all of Canada and not just their provinces or regions, and if they were given clarified powers to allow for delay of legislation, plus powers to scrutinize appointments, and to monitor and dismantle interprovincial barriers, and if the number of senators from the Atlantic provinces, Quebec, Ontario, and the rest of Canada were equal from the four regions (perhaps 100 senators, 25 from each "region"), then it would be a major improvement over our present unpopular system. As the Group of 22 suggests, the Senate should also "oversee the development and enforcement of national standards in appropriate areas of provincial activity."

Since veto power for only Quebec is unacceptable to the rest of Canada, and since veto power for each province would certainly shackle future constitutional change, the obvious solution is regional vetoes: for the Atlantic provinces, for Quebec, for Ontario, and for the West.

By all means, let us spell out that Quebec is a distinct society in the preamble to the constitution, but at the same time let us clarify that this distinction does not accord Quebec any new special status or the ability to demand new powers that are not available to other provinces. But we shall have to go further than this, although many of us would prefer not to. Quebec will have to have jurisdiction over its language and culture — and this means that a similar option must be extended to all provinces. Official federal government bilingualism in government services would remain the law of the land, but each province would have the option of establishing its own provincial rules and regulations relating to language use. Obviously, this is far from the ideal solution, but thanks to Brian Mulroney, it may now be a necessary compromise, for the time being, at least. While Ottawa would maintain and, one hopes, strengthen the vitally important trans-Canada cultural institutions mentioned previously, the provinces would have the choice of opting out of other federal cultural programs and of being reimbursed accordingly, providing they pledged to spend the funds on similar specifically defined cultural programs. Once again, this is hardly an ideal proposal, and in fact it is one whose ramifications distress me. But it seems a compromise that may have to be made.

Something else should be added to the new constitution. In the words of Al Johnson: "a ringing affirmation of Canadian nationhood and shared values." It is long past the time when we Canadians need be timid about our past and about our accomplishments and all that we have achieved together.

Had Brian Mulroney not made such a mess of national unity, the growing feeling across Canada that all Canadians should be treated alike, regardless of race, religion, language, or place of residence, would almost certainly have much more strength today in Quebec. I am confident that if we can get by the current crisis without destroying the nation in the process, all Canadians will agree to the basic presumption of guaranteed equality.

If only Robert Bourassa had been a man with greater character and less bending-with-the-polls political expediency, what a hero he could have become! Alas, it is not to be. He and his friend the prime minister seem determined to dismantle the country.

Both the federal government and Bourassa have been strongly opposed to constituent assemblies. But, once again, they are out of step with those they are supposed to represent. A strong majority in both Quebec and the rest of Canada support the concept of a constituent assembly. Such an assembly, properly constituted and democratically elected, could be very popular and, one hopes, innovative. But obviously, a great deal of thought would have to go into the composition of the assembly, the election process, and its mandate.

No constitutional changes should be made without the approval of the people of Canada. For some reason, those who endorsed Meech Lake were not fazed by the fact that 53 per cent of Canadians opposed the agreement while only 35 per cent supported it.

Most Canadians, including most Quebeckers, are in favour of a national referendum to approve or reject any new constitutional agreement (by almost a three-to-one margin outside Quebec, and by 57 per cent to 35 per cent in Quebec). It is true that referenda in the past have sometimes polarized voters along linguistic lines, but Canada did not break apart as a result. As stated previously, in a democracy the people should be given the opportunity to express their opinion before any crucial changes are made that alter the structure or direction of the nation in a profound way. The combination of a truly democratic constituent assembly and a referendum would appeal strongly to most Canadians. Perhaps a referendum could be considered binding if it received majority support in the Atlantic provinces, in Quebec, in Ontario, and in western Canada plus the Territories — that is, in four regions of Canada (if one might be permitted to include the Territories as part of one of the regions; or they could be divided into the four regions).

In 1984 and again in 1988, Brian Mulroney made a marriage of political convenience with Quebec separatists. This unprincipled political expediency is one of the most important reasons why Canada is now in danger of disintegrating. Why should we now trust this man to change our constitution in the best interests of Canada? What has he done in his seven years in office to inspire trust? Why should we allow a man who is despised by most Canadians to continue to bargain away our future?

In March 1991 an Angus Reid/Southam News poll showed that 78 per cent of Canadians outside Quebec do not trust Brian Mulroney to represent Canada's interests in new constitutional negotiations. More and more, Canadians are wondering if it wouldn't be better to delay important constitutional decisions until someone they do trust is the leader of the nation. As historian Michael Bliss has pointed out (in a notion supported by many other Canadian historians), "If we have learned anything from the constitutional wars of the 1980s, it should be that we do not have anything like the citizen consensus to support major change and large-scale constitutional engineering is fraught with unintended consequences and other perils."

Whatever we do, it would be much, much better to avoid rushing. We can hope for enlightened new leadership. We can embark on a well-thought-out constituent assembly and give it plenty of time to do a proper job. The worst possible thing we can do is march — or stampede — to imposed deadlines, whether they come from Quebec City or Ottawa.

All indications are that Canadians want a strong national government, not a weaker one; but Brian Mulroney is going in exactly the opposite direction. The prospects of another fiasco like that of Meech Lake are very real. With a referendum coming in Quebec within a year, that could clearly be disastrous. The same mistakes are being made all over again: secret proposals are being drafted in the Prime Minister's Office; Canadians are being presented with an early final deadline; behind-the-scenes deals are being made by a government and prime minister that have the support of only one in eight Canadians.

Canada in 1991 is a confused country. We have trade union leaders afraid to attack Quebec separatists, politicians terrified at the prospect of attacking Robert Bourassa or even Jacques Parizeau, while, at the same time, four out of five Quebeckers feel that Canada is the best country in the world to live in and 83 per cent agree with the proposal that "we should feel proud about the joint achievement of English and French in this country."

Probably the most important thing Canadians outside Quebec can do is to talk directly to the people in Quebec. We must explain, passionately and clearly, that we respect and admire them, that we want them to continue as part of Canada, and that we are confident that with new political leadership we can go on together to build a better, stronger country, with a better standard of living and an even better quality of life.

A strong Canada would be Quebec's best insurance for the preservation of the values it cherishes and for the ability of all French Canadians to maximize their freedom. However, as Canada's national programs are weakened, as more and more of the country becomes owned and controlled from abroad, as less and less commercial intercourse takes place east-west and more and more is north-south, and as the rest of Canada's culture becomes more and more the culture of the United States, why should the people of Quebec be proud of Canada?

All Canadians should be proud Canadians. Of course, it is often very hard for our aboriginal peoples to be proud of their country, given what we have done to them. It is also hard for people locked into oppressive poverty, with little or nothing to look forward to. For the people in Quebec, with their own strong language, their own vibrant culture, and their own proud heritage, being part of a nation that is selling itself off day by day, part of a nation that has badly mishandled its economy, and part of a nation that is rapidly moving towards harmonizing its standards and values with those in the United States . . . this is hardly something we can ask them to aspire to, admire, and respect.

Ironically, a stronger, more nationalistic Canada would inevitably help to diminish Quebec nationalism. A better-managed economy would do so, too. A government and prime minister that Canadians admired and respected would help as well. I doubt very much that we have a bad constitution. (In fact, it is a remarkably flexible document.) I do know that we are in an era of bad political leaders. The problem in Canada is less a question of francophones against anglophones, or anglophones and francophones against multiculturalism as it is a problem of inept politicians, who seem preoccupied with elevating disagreements into constitutional crises.

A careful examination of almost all the public-opinion polls shows a great deal of evidence that we could keep Canada together with the right leadership.[3] Perhaps it will take five or even ten years to sort the constitutional problems out properly, but the logic of Confederation is there for all parts of Canada. What we must avoid, at all costs, is to let our current poor leadership destroy our country.

39

Last Chance for Canada

The Politics of a Disappearing Country

> *Many Canadians are bothered by the enormous amount of American investment in Canada. . . . When I was Minister of Industry, Trade and Commerce, I was even considered soft on the issue of foreign ownership because I felt positively about it.*   JEAN CHRÉTIEN, *Straight from the Heart, 1985*

> *My dad . . . lived to be ninety-three. . . . He would . . . have been pleased when my daughter, France, became a lawyer and married André Desmarais, the son of Paul Desmarais, the chairman of Power Corporation. It owns Consolidated-Bathurst, the paper company for which my father had worked all his life. He used to say, "I never thought I'd see the day when a French Canadian would own that mill."*
> JEAN CHRÉTIEN, *Straight from the Heart, 1985*

> *I did represent the seller. . . . Why should I work for free?*
> MAURICE SAUVÉ, *husband of Governor General Jeanne Sauvé,*
> *regarding his share of a $26 million finder's fee for the sale of*
> *Consolidated-Bathurst to Stone Container of Chicago*

THE NEXT FEDERAL ELECTION IS THE VERY LAST chance for Canada. If the Conservatives are re-elected, with Brian Mulroney or with a new leader, then Canada is finished once and for all time. If the Conservatives form the next government with the participation, formal or otherwise, of the Reform party or the Bloc Québécois, or both, then Canada will be finished even more quickly. While the Bloc and the Reform party have different objectives, they share the same strong desire that the federal government's powers be substantially weakened, and of course the Bloc would like them to be of no concern to the people of a sovereign Quebec.

The next federal election will probably be held within eighteen to twenty-four months, most likely in the late spring or early summer of 1993. It is not impossible to see a scenario whereby the Conservatives, the Bloc, and the Reform party win enough seats (say, 50 each) to form a majority government in the 295-seat House of Commons.

The Canadian public is angry, frustrated, disillusioned, cynical, and desperate for change, and it is easy for many people to like the ultra-conservative and seemingly honest Preston Manning, with his populist U.S.-style policies for reforming the political decision-making process. Above all, he is new, and he seems genuine and straightforward. After seven years of "sacred-trust" Mulroney, that is an enormous advantage.

Canadians are fed up with corruption, patronage, and pork barrel, with lying politicians, and with the ethics or ineptitude of the likes of Bill Vander Zalm, John Buchanan, and so many other current or recently departed political leaders. A measure of how low our politicians have sunk in public esteem is the fact that someone who simply appears honest, such as Manning, should be so popular in spite of advocating policies that would surely lead not only to a fractured Canada but to a disjointed remnant that would likely prove untenable geographically, politically, and economically. Certainly, whatever balkanized regional entities were left would be a far cry from the Canada that most Canadians, from every province and every region, say is the best country in the world. Rather than "a new Canada," Mr. Manning would leave no Canada.

Preston Manning may be very honest, and some of his ideas relating to populist democratization may be appealing in view of the last few awful years we have all had to endure, but the Reform party's agenda, its attitude to Quebec, its policies of decentralization, its opposition to regional programs, its antipathy to any industrial strategies, its support for the Mulroney Free Trade Agreement, and its attack on Canada's social programs — all sold as reform — are giant neoconservative steps backwards. If you like the Conservative government of Brian Mulroney and what it has done for the economy and for national unity, you will love Preston Manning and the Reform party.

The Reform party would never address the basic structural changes that are necessary if Canada is to survive: the abrogation of the Free Trade Agreement, the end to increasing foreign ownership and control, the strong laws necessary to curtail corporate concentration, a truly progressive tax system, and other policies that I discussed earlier. Rather than a new Canada, Manning represents the old far-right Conservative and Social Credit agenda, along with the politics of divorce. Make no mistake about it, Reform *wants* a Canada without Quebec, and it wants our national medicare system to be turned over to the provinces to control.

In all of this, there is a truly sad element that is rarely considered. There are many thousands of dedicated, solid Canadians who are attracted to the Reform party because it seems to represent something good and something new, and because they care about their country and are desperate for a solution to its problems. While it is true that the party attracts western separatists and racial bigots, as well as religious fundamentalists and others who brook no compromise with their rigid beliefs, at the same time, thousands of caring, patriotic Canadians have turned to the Reform party because they are fed up with the existing parties and with politicians that are unprincipled or corrupt or inept or deceptive. The success of the Reform party stems not so much from the charisma of Preston Manning, or from the party's platform, as it does from wide-spread conservative disappointment in (and dislike of) Brian Mulroney and the fact that the Liberals and the NDP have failed to come up with populist new policies and communicate them to the people of Canada.

The Reform party could hold the balance of power after the next election, or it might perhaps enter a formal coalition, unless the Liberals and NDP sharply and quickly improve their performance. The dream of Canada would then certainly be over. Peter Newman comes close to the mark:

> The Reform party's New Canada without Quebec is no Canada at all. Yet a Canada without Quebec is where [Preston] Manning's policies clearly lead. . . . As architect of the Reform party's determination to capture a majority of the seats in the House of Commons by rejecting Quebec's aspirations, Manning has launched himself on a risky political venture. Should he succeed, Quebec would have no choice but to separate. That would leave Ontario with 99 seats — predominant in the new Canada he advocates. He would then have to face the anger of his western followers (with a maximum of 86 seats) who started the Reform movement, only to find that it helped consolidate Ontario as the country's power centre. (*Maclean*'s, 24 June 1991)

Peter Newman is close to the mark but not quite right on, because British Columbia and Alberta would never accept a new Canada in which Ontario was so dominant. The Gordon Gibsons and Jim Grays of British Columbia and Alberta would likely soon begin to talk of a separate western Canada or of Alberta and B.C. leaving on their own.

With superb timing and excellent communications and organizational skills, the Reform party has stepped in to fill an enormous political vacuum. And it has a potential partner or two:

> There is an adage that politics makes strange bedfellows, but the Bloc Québécois and the Reform Party? The Bloc's leader, Lucien

Bouchard, is a big fan of Reform chief Preston Manning and says he can see the day when his pro-sovereignty group of Quebec MPs will forge strategic alliances with the Reform Party in the House of Commons after the next federal election. (*Globe and Mail*, 1 May 1991)

The other partner would be Brian Mulroney's Conservative successor.

The quotations at the beginning of this chapter tell a great deal about the future of the Liberal party. When Jean Chrétien was minister of finance (1977-80), he was both conservative and continentalist. He was indeed "considered soft on the issue of foreign ownership." It is ironic that in his autobiography he makes a point about how proud his father was that a French Canadian owned the mill he worked in. Four years later, Jean Chrétien's daughter's father-in-law sold Consolidated-Bathurst to a union-busting Chicago company for $2.6 billion. As Paul Desmarais said, the price was right. Jean Chrétien was a member of the board of directors when "Connie B" was sold. And, yes, long-time Liberal Maurice Sauvé, the former cabinet minister who was husband of the governor general, collected a handsome fee as part of the sale. Could anything be more symbolic about what is wrong with Canada?

With Jean Chrétien as leader of the Liberal party, the chances of the Liberals taking a strong position against increasing foreign ownership are somewhere between slim and none. A Liberal party influenced by Chrétien, Paul Martin, Jr., and Roy MacLaren will never do anything about corporate concentration in Canada. In fact, the last two seem to want even more of it, judging by their articles and speeches. The Liberal party of Jean Chrétien, of party president Don Johnston, and of Martin and MacLaren would never abrogate the Free Trade Agreement. Jean Chrétien seems blind to much of the heavy damage the agreement has caused Canada, though he does understand the potential problems of the energy provisions. His reluctant, evasive claims that he will renegotiate the trade agreement are never backed with an explanation of exactly what he would do if the Americans refused to renegotiate or made even further demands. The Liberal party of bagman Senator Leo Kolber and the above will never change the Canadian tax system to make it more progressive, to make large corporations pay their fair share of taxes and make foreign corporations pay their proper share. And the Liberal party will not abolish the GST. Given Chrétien's performance as finance minister, there seems little hope that a Liberal government led by him would do anything other than follow the same harmful high interest rate policies and high dollar policies of the Mulroney government.

One indication of what is wrong with the Liberal party of today can be neatly summed up in a long conversation I had with a very senior Liberal last year. Although I have not been a member of the party since 1973, I am frequently asked to speak at Liberal functions (just as I am asked to speak at NDP functions). In 1990, I was the keynote speaker to the Liberal party's first leadership forum, held in Toronto. The speech, a strong plea for progressive reform in the party, was interrupted with applause from beginning to end. The senior Liberal later asked me what specific policies the party would need to adopt to regain power in the next federal election, and I spelled out a number of basic populist policies and principles similar to those outlined in this book. He was most interested and enthusiastic. I then said, "You know, each and every one of the policies I've mentioned will be anathema to the business community from whom you are now trying to raise the money to wipe out your deficit, and to whom you'll be turning for the millions of dollars you're going to need to finance the next election." There was a lengthy pause and a frown. His answer was clear: "No way." There is no way that a Liberal party dependent on big business for big dollars is going to adopt the kind of policies that are necessary to save Canada, even though these policies would be popular with the people of Canada. The Liberals can have a hundred thinkers' conferences and policy debates, but it will be the bagmen and the people around Chrétien who will call the shots in the end.

Aside from their policies on Quebec, does anyone, anywhere (including Ottawa) know what the Liberal party of Jean Chrétien stands for? For far too many Liberals, particularly those around Chrétien, all that matters is regaining power. Principles and policies are way down the list; money for the party is at the top — money from big business. The corporate power elite in Toronto and Montreal, the banks, Paul Desmarais, the trust and insurance companies, the oil companies, and the rest of the big political funders will come rushing to the Liberals (and many to the Reform party, too), if the Tories look as if they are going down the tube. The Liberal government of Jean Chrétien may well be every bit as much a creature of the BCNI as Brian Mulroney's Conservatives are today. Unless . . .

There is a powerful left-right struggle going on in the party today. The right, led by Paul Martin, Jr., is winning. The left, led by Lloyd Axworthy and Herb Gray, is losing. There is a chance, though I think only a modest chance, that enough new young Liberal MPs who care about an independent Canada and who have a social conscience might be elected to tip the balance in the caucus and put pressure on Jean Chrétien. A chance.

Chrétien is not doctrinaire. By temperament and experience, despite his entertaining populist image, he is cautious and conservative. A strong progressive caucus could be far more influential with Jean Chrétien than with a dominant Pierre Trudeau. This scenario is one frequently mentioned to me these days by concerned Liberals on the left of the Grit caucus. But it takes a "leap of faith," and we have already had one too many of those. Chrétien has a deep and genuine love of Canada, but he is too tied to big business and to the

Canadian establishment and is too conservative to make the profound changes that will save our country.

The NDP is the only Canadian political party pledged to abrogate the Free Trade Agreement. It is the party most likely to legislate against growing corporate concentration. It has a better understanding of the need for genuine tax reform than the other political parties in Canada. And its position on social programs, along with that of its predecessor the CCF, has been instrumental in helping to push former federal Liberal governments into implementing comprehensive and compassionate social programs for all Canadians. But, based on all the evidence we have to date, the NDP will not form the next government of Canada. I doubt very much if many members of the NDP would disagree with this statement.

Even with the potential of provincial election victories in Saskatchewan and British Columbia, the bad luck of an unexpected win by an ill-prepared provincial NDP party in Ontario has hurt the federal party badly. The bitter, distorted campaign by the right-wing press against Bob Rae has been damaging. Audrey McLaughlin is an extraordinary person, one of the finest and most capable people I know. But the federal NDP, despite the poor performance of the Conservatives and Liberals, seems to be missing the boat, just as it did so disastrously in the free trade election of 1988. With a virtual monopoly on so many key public issues, the federal party seems lethargic, lacking in inspiration, and totally unable to explain to Canadians why it offers a unique choice that would benefit the nation.

The biggest failure of the NDP is its inability to evolve alternative economic policy. Where is its substitute industrial policy to replace the Free Trade Agreement? Why do the vast majority of Canadians have no idea whatsoever of what the NDP's position on tax reform is? Why has the NDP been so silent about the damage being done to Canada by foreign ownership? Where is its economic agenda for Canada? Many things will happen between now and the next federal election, and much will change. But unless the NDP changes, the best it can possibly hope for is to hold the balance of power in a Chrétien minority government.

Many concerned Canadians hoped that the Liberals and NDP would put the country ahead of party in the 1988 federal election and somehow join together to fight the common enemy. Those of us who believed that a Mulroney majority and free trade could prove fatal to the country were deeply worried that there would be a split vote which would allow another Conservative victory. Our pleas fell on deaf ears. Even worse, the NDP decided to focus on attacking the credibility of John Turner and the Liberal party, and gave a pitifully poor campaign performance on the vital issue of free trade. Meanwhile, the Liberal party establishment's close ties to whatever elements of the business community had not abandoned it because of Turner's stand against the trade agreement, plus a long-standing arrogance and a deep dislike of the NDP, made any real high-level dialogue impossible.

Just 148 seats were required to form a majority government. The Mulroney Conservatives, with 43 per cent of the 13,175,599 valid votes, won 169 seats. Brian was free to proceed with his plan to change Canada beyond recognition.

Hindsight is always easy. Winning an election after the results are in is a mug's game. But what can be learned from 1988 that can be applied to 1993, the last chance for Canada?

First, no matter how logical it might seem and no matter how deeply many people feel about the viability of such a strategy, the chances of the Liberals and NDP cooperating in a federal election are remote, at best. The two federal parties care more about their own fate than about the disappearance of our country. Audrey McLaughlin, Dave Barrett, Lloyd Axworthy, and a few others might consider the possibility, but the trade unions would be stridently opposed, and the hierarchy of the Liberal party would never even consider discussing the idea.

If there was only one centre-left party in Canada, it would win the next federal election with a strong majority, just as it would have won the last election. A single centre-left party would much more closely reflect the mix of free enterprise and social democracy that is representative of the Canadian electorate. A single party in power with a solid majority would be strong enough to make the tough turnaround decisions that are going to be necessary to save Canada. But it is not going to happen. Nor are the Liberals and NDP likely to agree to cooperate in any way in the next federal election. Even though the nation is disintegrating, the party comes first.

Where does this leave the country? Some believe that perhaps the Conservatives and Reform party will split enough votes to allow more Liberals and members of the NDP to be elected. The pessimistic view is that the Tories, Reform, and Bloc will join together to shatter the nation once and for all. One thing you can be sure of — big business will be there with many millions of dollars from both sides of the border.

What to do? Are we Canadians simply going to sit back apathetically and just let events unfold, hoping that somehow things will turn out well? Probably. In other countries, people would be marching in the streets demanding the resignation of the leaders who have betrayed the nation. Behind-the-scenes discussions would be taking place in full recognition of the dramatic urgency of the situation. Pressure would be brought to bear to force parties to unite or to offer only one candidate in certain ridings. In other countries, there would be rage and anger at the sellout of the nation. People would be prepared to put forward their lives for their country. The passion would become the power that would ignite the population. But in Canada? In Canada the Liberal and NDP leadership look on with confused awe as an ultra-conservative prairie populist steps into an enormous political vacuum, preaching the rhetoric of William Aberhart and Fraser Institute "reform."

What to do? There are only two possibilities. One is a well-organized strategic voting campaign. It would take an enormous amount of work and lots of money, and even though the Liberals and NDP would not cooperate, it could work. Done well, it should work.

In the last federal election, the results from London-Middlesex in Ontario looked like this:

Progressive Conservative	18,534
Liberal	18,526
NDP	11,103

If only nine people who voted NDP had voted instead for the Liberal candidate, one less Tory MP would have been elected. In Rosedale, in Toronto, the results were:

Progressive Conservative	22,704
Liberal	22,624
NDP	8,266

In this case, 81 NDP votes going to the Liberal candidate would have defeated another Conservative. In Regina-Wascana the results were:

Progressive Conservative	15,339
NDP	14,829
Liberal	14,804

Here, despite almost 30,000 votes against the Mulroney government, the Conservatives still won a seat in the House of Commons with just over 15,000 votes. If 511 Liberal votes had switched to the NDP, an excellent NDP member of Parliament would have been elected. The results in Cariboo-Chilcotin in British Columbia were similar:

Progressive Conservative	11,525
NDP	11,256
Liberal	7,886

So if only 270 people who voted Liberal had voted for the NDP, another Mulroney Conservative would have been defeated.

The Conservatives won 169 seats in 1988. Had they won twenty-two fewer seats, they would not have had a majority. In twenty-two constituencies, from South Shore, Nova Scotia, to Vancouver Centre in British Columbia, only 19,039 votes (some 0.145 per cent of the valid votes cast) would have denied Brian Mulroney a majority.

As I said before, hindsight is easy. Targeting ridings prior to an election would take an enormous amount of hard work and money for advance polling. It would take a well-organized group to handle the polling and canvass candidates, and then to work hard for the Liberal or NDP candidate most likely to be elected. A maximum of only forty constituencies need be selected, based on the results of the last election and on extensive interviews with the candidates and advance polling. Many Liberals and NDP members would be angered by a campaign organized at steering voters away from their candidates in certain constituencies; but of course the opposite would be equally true: candidates who received support would be delighted. There are many concerned Canadians who advocated a strategic-voting campaign in the last election. There are also many who think it is essential in 1993 if Canada is to survive. Yet, at this writing, nobody is doing a thing about it. In a disappearing country, it is Preston and politics as usual.

There is one other alternative: a new political party, a United Canada party, a party of *real* reform. If the Liberals pursue a right-wing agenda that is only slightly less continentalist than Mulroney's (and I believe that is a real possibility) and if the NDP continues to be mired in the low to middle 20 per cent range in public-opinion polls, then perhaps it is time to start afresh. Every political pro in sight and everyone in the backrooms will say that it can't be done. Every single member of the press gallery will scoff at the idea and talk of split votes and the shortage of time before the next election.

But unless the two established parties soon turn things around in an important way, a new party may be the best idea of all.

Most Canadians are not far to the right in their political beliefs. Most are relatively tolerant and compassionate. Most want a tax system based on the ability to pay. And most want Canadians to control their own country and their own future. As well, most Canadians are fed up. They are tired of broken promises, tired of poor government. They are desperately hoping for new ideas and new leadership. A new political party of progressive reform, a party that is dedicated to a strong, proud, independent and united Canada, could do extremely well in the next election. If the party promised true democratic reform, open government, and policies which would allow Canadians to control their own economic, social, and cultural future, if the party promised to abrogate the trade agreement and limit foreign ownership and corporate concentration, and if it promised to make certain that Canadian savings were available to Canadians, then it would be very popular.

If a campaign of strategic voting is launched and is successful, or if a new party holds the balance of power in a divided House of Commons, or if a Liberal and NDP coalition forms the next government, there should be two top priorities: first, the abrogation of the Free Trade Agreement; second, the introduction of democratic reforms, including proportional representation. With proportional representation, Canada would be much safer from the conservative Americanizers of the country and the tentacles of the BCNI; with proportional representation, Canadians would be in control of their own destiny.

Keith Spicer said, "There is a fury in the land against the prime minister." That fury must be channelled into progressive political action.

Conclusion

IT WAS NOT UNTIL I WAS IN MY LATE TWENTIES AND EARLY thirties that I began to have the opportunity to travel extensively across Canada. The more I saw of the incredible beauty of our country and the more I got to know exceptional men and women from different regions, the more I began to understand just how fortunate we Canadians are. And like so many other Canadians, I realized this even more when I travelled abroad.

For the past thirty years, a year has rarely gone by when I have not travelled the country from coast to coast and often visited the northern coast as well. All this travel has taught me an important thing: that we can have enormous confidence in the abilities and perceptions of the Canadian people. Over the years, I have developed abundant faith in and respect for their convictions and good sense. The wonderful people I have had the opportunity of meeting, from Victoria to St. John's and from Tuktoyaktuk to Windsor — the hardworking men and women in small and medium-sized businesses, the devoted trade union members, the hundreds of farmers, the many thousands of dedicated teachers, professional people, nurses, clerks, and students, and the brilliant artists and writers — all have left me with a great admiration and affection for the people of Canada.

We Canadians come from many different backgrounds with different ethnic origins, religions, philosophies, and political persuasions. Nevertheless, most of us have one thing in common, even though we rarely say it. Most of us love Canada. Most of us believe we are extraordinarily fortunate to live here. And most of us are totally confident that we have the ability and the potential to create an even better country in the future.

What we need now is a new shared vision of Canada, of the kind that has been pathetically absent in recent years in far too many of our political and corporate leaders. We need a new vision of a free, democratic, and independent Canada, a Canada where we are able to maximize our abilities to determine our own future. In a rapidly changing world, there can be few things more important than the freedom of citizens and society to adapt to change. The foremost betrayal of Canada is that our current leadership has been destroying our freedom. No other nation in the world would have abandoned the right to self-determination the way Canada has done since Brian Mulroney became prime minister.

The Canada we created before Mulroney set out to change it so profoundly was far from perfect. But it was in many ways a truly heroic accomplishment. We created a nation of relative fairness, relative tolerance, a nation of compromise, sharing, and compassion, with a strong sense of social justice. Canada has been a comparatively peaceful, comparatively non-violent nation — no melting pot, but a healthy mixture of cultures, a non-aggressive nation containing relatively well-educated people who enjoyed a very high standard of living in a land of enormous space, abundant resources, and spectacular beauty.

The institutions we developed, though we still haven't realized it, were in many cases compromises that were well ahead of their time, compromises of the kind nations and regions around the world are today striving for. We managed to develop a fair balance between public and private that worked well, and a balance of community rights and the rights of individuals. We mixed a potentially strong (but normally flexible) central government with powerful provincial rights, and an open attitude towards other nations with some protection of our own best interests. Had we done poorly in the past, perhaps the disintegration and disappearance of our country might now be less of a tragedy. But given all that we Canadians have accomplished, given all that we have created, we must not accept the betrayal of our country without profound anger and without a dedicated renewed struggle to save our nation.

Canadians are not against trade; they are not in favour of massive new protectionism, and they are not interested in a closed society. On the contrary, Canada, as we have seen, has always been one of the most open countries in the world. But then Mulroney and big business proceeded to plunge us into an immense and radical departure from our history, into the so-called "leap of faith." However, from the beginning, big business fully understood that with a Free Trade Agreement, new investment would be heading straight south. The banks understood. The transnationals understood.

Those who have betrayed Canada now say that the hundreds of thousands of lost jobs and the hundreds of thousands of new unemployed were not caused by the trade agreement, they were caused by the recession. That is like saying that drunkenness is caused by falling down. The high interest rates and high dollar, and the outflow of investment and the hemorrhaging of profits and service payments out of Canada, are all intrinsically intertwined with the agreement. Yes, the recession will end, but the human and economic debris will be with us for as long as we can see into the future.

The single most important overall impact of the Free Trade Agreement is already clear — a big decline in the standard of living of Canadians. And the future will be much worse. The less obvious result is as certain as the fact that you are now reading these words — the destruction and disappearance of our country. Ultimately, the blame for what has happened rests not with big business, even though its agenda means the destruction of the country. Ultimately, the responsibility lies with the inadequacies of our political system and of our current political leaders.

If there is one fundamental question this book raises, it is this: Who should be in charge of society — the community or big corporations? If there is one fundamental policy area we need to act upon, it is the need to reform our democracy and our political institutions so that the citizens, not the corporations, are in charge. It is strange that the badly needed reform of our democracy has taken such a back seat to our seemingly constant preoccupation with the constitution. But one of the main reasons we have had to dwell so much on the constitution, instead of on the economy and the well-being of our citizens, is in fact our less-than-democratic political system and what it produces.

The Americanizers of Canada, who fooled so many Canadians with their slick, expensive media campaign extolling the virtues of the Free Trade Agreement, had a clever slogan: "The *status quo* won't do." They were right — and even more so in 1991 than in 1988. The sellout of Canada won't do. Nor will the destruction of our social programs, the squandering of our energy resources, the melding of our country into the United States. The mentality that says we have no responsibility to future generations of Canadians — that it's fine to sell off the ownership and control of our industry, our businesses, our resources, and our land to foreign corporations — simply won't do.

Three out of five Canadians now want Brian Mulroney to resign. He should go. Three out of four say he and his government are mishandling the Canadian economy. They are right. Seven in ten say Mulroney government policies lengthened and deepened the recession, and three in five Canadians oppose a trilateral trade deal with Mexico. All for good reason. But this terrible prime minister is still with us, and Canada is plunging relentlessly towards the precipice. With increasing harmonization, rationalization, integration, and with more and more American ownership and control of our country, we will soon be at a point of no return. With Mulroney's constitutional agenda on top of the Americanization of Canada, there will soon be very little left for Canadians to stand on guard for.

The betrayal of Canada is a modern national tragedy. Equally tragic is the fact that much of the fury in the land — the rage and the anger — is being cleverly channelled into support for another ultra-right-wing continentalist political party — and that the Liberals and NDP are allowing this to happen.

I want Canada to be a country where people who want to work can find jobs, a country where future generations won't have to debate whether or not there is such a thing as the Canadian identity. Perhaps most of all, I want Canada to be a nation where the vast majority of Canadians can translate their love for their country into real democratic power.

A Canada that has regained control of its own agenda, a more prosperous and democratic Canada, can then go out more confidently into the world community and play a greater role as a proud peace-making nation, willing to share its knowledge, expertise, and wealth. There are so many great things we can do as masters in our own house, but very little we can do as frightened tenants who have nothing left with which to pay the rent.

Canada is worth fighting for. Are we going to watch, with a quiet whimper, as it is destroyed? Or are we going to be able to tell our children and grandchildren that we found the courage and strength to defeat those who tried to betray our country?

Fly the flag! Sing the anthem! Stand proud! Above all, go to work now to save Canada. If you don't do so very soon, it will be too late.

Notes

CHAPTER 1
THE FREE TRADE AGREEMENT
A Real Beauty for You

1. The term "continentalist," as it is commonly used in Canada, refers to people who urge closer integration between Canada and the United States, ranging from closer economic cooperation to full economic integration, and going all the way to political union. Few Canadians support the latter option, and a recent poll shows that only 4 per cent support economic union. However, big business in Canada (especially the BCNI, our right-wing think tanks, our powerful major banks, and some of our business press) have increasingly become strong supporters of continentalism in recent years.

CHAPTER 2
THE FATAL FLAW
Stupidity or Conspiracy?

1. The Softwood Lumber Products Export Charge Act went into effect on 7 January 1987. Softwood lumber exports from Canada to the U.S. (billions of board feet) for the two years prior to the FTA and the first two years of the FTA were as follows: 1987, 14.448; 1988, 13.792; 1989, 13.639; 1990, 11.963. The Canadian share of the U.S. softwood lumber market dropped from 33 percent in 1987 to 26.7 per cent in 1990. A

report in the *Financial Post* (15 Feb. 1991) suggests that "up to 50,000 jobs are threatened" in the industry.

2. The participants in the current Uruguay Round of GATT negotiations include 97 full members, 29 provisional members, and 12 observer nations.

3. Canada's merchandise trade surplus with the U.S.:

	($ million)
1970	1,007
1971	1,340
1972	1,607
1973	1,430
1974	1,148
1975	-999
1976	690
1977	1,748
1978	2,967
1979	603
1980	1,632
1981	3,323
1982	11,025
1983	13,667
1984	18,923
1985	20,386
1986	16,899
1987	17,620
1988	14,213
1989	12,618
1990	17,390

4. Throughout the almost four-year-long free trade debate, the Canadian people were repeatedly assured by our leading pro-free-trade economists that the value of the Canadian dollar would be "a guaranteed safety valve" if Canada ever got into trouble as a result of the agreement. The "safety valve" is broken. As this is being written, the value of the Canadian dollar is more than 87 U.S. cents.

5. Article 2106 of the Canada–U.S. Free Trade Agreement stipulates: "This Agreement shall remain in force unless terminated by either party upon six-month notice to the other party."

CHAPTER 3
EMPLOYMENT AND UNEMPLOYMENT
The Devastating Impact of the FTA on Jobs in Canada

1. Readers should not be misled by enthusiastic reports of increasing GDP. While they are welcome signs of some recovery, they are based on comparisons with the depressed economic activity in 1990.
2. An April-May 1991 Angus Reid poll put the Conservative party in its traditional bastion of western Canada at only 9 per cent, its poorest-ever showing since public opinion polling began in Canada in 1941. Across Canada, the federal Tories have been well below 20 per cent of the decided vote for a year and a half. Some recent polls put the Mulroney government in fourth place, behind the Reform party, with only 15 to 16 per cent support.

CHAPTER 4
THE DEINDUSTRIALIZATION OF CANADA
On the Road to a Warehouse Economy

1. Economic Council of Canada, *Venturing Forth* (Ottawa: Supply and Services Canada), vol. 8, no. 4.

CHAPTER 5
THE BOTTOM LINE
The Performance of Canada's Economy

1. Among the forecasters was Simon Reisman, who said: "Before this thing has worked its way through, Canadians will earn on average, in real terms, at least twenty-five per cent more than they do today as a result of this agreement" (*Toronto Star*, October 1987).

CHAPTER 6
HEADING SOUTH
What the "Trade" Deal Was Really All About

1. Mississippi has industrial wages as low as $3.85 an hour, with one week of unpaid holidays per year. On average, in the southeast United States, the manufacturing wage is some 30 per cent lower than in Ontario.

   The Fair Labor Standards Act in the U.S. establishes minimum wage, overtime pay, and other labour standards affecting some 75 million workers. The FLSA does not require vacation, holiday, severance, or sick pay; meal or rest periods, holidays off, or vacations; premium pay for weekend or holiday work; pay raises or fringe benefits; a discharge notice, reason for discharge, or immediate payment of final wages to terminated employees; or any limits on the number of hours of work for persons sixteen years of age and over.

2. The Council of Canadians, our national organization committed to preserving and strengthening Canadian sovereignty, now has over 21,000 members from across Canada. The first meeting of the COC was held in Edmonton on 11 January 1985; the second was in Toronto on 7 February 1985, and the founding national convention was held in Ottawa, in October 1985.

   The COC was instrumental in founding the Pro-Canada Network (now the Action Canada Network) at the third annual COC convention, in Ottawa in 1987. The Action Canada Network includes many national organizations representing teachers, students, labour, nurses, churches, senior citizens, environmentalists, anti-poverty groups, aboriginal groups, farmers, and others — a total of forty national organizations and ten provincial coalitions, representing over 10 million Canadians. Both the COC and the ACN are led by charismatic and articulate leaders: Maude Barlow, chairperson of the COC since 1988; and Tony Clarke, chairperson of the PCN and later the ACN, since May 1988.

   The address of the Council of Canadians is Suite 1006, 251 Laurier Avenue West, Ottawa, Ontario K1P 5J6.

CHAPTER 7
PROFITS AND PROPHETS
Adam Smith Gone Haywire

1. Douglas Peters, senior vice-president of the Toronto-Dominion Bank, was
quoted in the *Financial Times* (3 June 1991) as saying: "Profit as a percentage of gross domestic product, is as low as it was in 1931" during
the Great Depression. Forecasters predict a further drop in profits in
1991 of some 30 per cent.

CHAPTER 10
FORGETTING ABOUT THE MORTGAGE PAYMENTS
The Real Bottom Line of Trade

1. Statistics Canada has long wanted to add the retained earnings of foreign corporations in Canada to the current account balance, but the federal government has consistently refused to allow it to do so, even though
the balance of payments manual of the International Monetary Fund indicates that retained earnings should be included. Many other countries
(e.g., the United States, Germany, Sweden, Australia, New Zealand,
Denmark, Switzerland, and Finland) have concluded that it is necessary to
add the retained earnings of foreign corporations in their country, and also
their own retained earnings abroad, in order to provide a more accurate
reflection of the true current account position.

For the most recent year for which reliable figures are available,
1986, if retained earnings had been included, Canada's current
account deficit would have been $16.634 billion instead of $10.155
billion, a significant difference. If figures had been available for 1990,
the discrepancy would have been greater still.

CHAPTER 11

OPEN FOR BUSINESS AND UP FOR SALE

Foreign Ownership, Foreign Investment, and Foreign Control

1. Canada's Net International Investment Position

	($ billion)
1945	−4.1
1950	−4.3
1955	−8.3
1960	−16.2
1965	−21.9
1970	−30.0
1975	−49.7
1976	−60.7
1977	−68.1
1978	−87.6
1979	−99.4
1980	−106.3
1981	−130.3
1982	−130.8
1983	−136.6
1984	−150.6
1985	−172.5
1986	−193.7
1987	−209.2
1988	−218.9
1989	−235.1
1990	−259.2

Source: Statistics Canada, *Canada's International Investment Position 1988-90* (Ottawa: Supply and Services Canada, 1991), cat. no. 67-202 : 42-43.

CHAPTER 12

INVESTMENT CANADA

The Ultimate Hypocrisy

1. The term "foreign direct investment" refers to investment intended to own or control a business. It does not include shares or bonds pur-

chased simply for return on investment with no intention of acquiring
ownership or control.

The Book Value of Foreign Direct Investment in Canada
($ billion)

1945	2.7
1950	4.0
1955	7.7
1960	12.9
1965	17.4
1970	26.4
1975	37.4
1976	40.3
1977	43.7
1978	48.3
1979	54.3
1980	61.7
1981	66.6
1982	68.9
1983	77.4
1984	83.4
1985	87.2
1986	92.4
1987	101.5
1988	110.1
1989	118.5
1990	126.6

Source: Statistics Canada, *Canada's International Investment Position 1988-90*
(Ottawa: Supply and Services Canada, 1991), cat. no. 67-202.

2. The number of Canadian companies taken over by non-residents in
recent years is dismaying. Below are listed just a few of the firms that
became foreign-owned and foreign-controlled. They cover the entire
Canadian economy — from high-tech industries to resources, from
agriculture to manufacturing, and from mining to funeral parlours.
Remember, as you go through this list, that most of the money used to

acquire these companies came from Canada, not from foreign countries: AES Data; Alberni Engineering & Shipyard Co.; The Banff Park Lodge; The Bank of British Columbia; B.C. Forest Products Ltd.; B.C. Hydro's rail freight division; Bowring Department Stores; Bow Valley Industries; Cadillac Fairview Corp. Ltd.; Canada Packers Inc.; The Cascade Hotel; Cintech Computer Technology; CMQ; thirteen Coast hotels, and five hotel properties in Whistler; Columbia Computer Services; Commonwealth Hospitality Ltd.; Connaught BioSciences Inc.; Consumers' Gas Limited; Consolidated-Bathurst; The Continental Bank of Canada; Coorsh Specialty Meats & Salads; R. L. Crain Inc.; Crown Forest Industries; Dataline; The Delta Bow Valley Inn; Dome Petroleum; Dominion Textile Bedding Unit; Executive Consultants Ltd.; the Expo '86 site; Factory Carpets; Facelle Company Ltd.; Federal Pioneer Ltd.; First Memorial Funeral Services; Foster Advertising; Four Seasons Hotels in Edmonton and Ottawa; The Harrison Hotsprings Hotel; Hayhurst Advertising Ltd.; Hiram Walker, Gooderham & Worts; The Inns of Banff Park; The Keg restaurants; Lake Ontario Cement; Leigh Instruments Ltd.; Lumonics Inc.; Maclaren Advertising; Maple Leaf Mills; Massey Combines Corp.; McLean, McCarthy Securities; Medis Health & Pharmaceutical Services; Mr. Lube; Mitel Corporation; The Nancy Greene Lodge; Oakwood Petroleum; O'Doul's Hotel in Vancouver; Public Affairs International; eight major pulp and paper mills across Canada; The Radium Hot Springs Resort; Rimrock Inn in Banff; Ronalds Reynolds & Company Ltd.; I. P. Sharp; Sulpetro Limited; Star Oil and Gas Ltd.; Terochem Laboratories; Toronto Argonauts; United Canso Oil & Gas; Wampole Inc.; Westburne International Industries; West Kootenay Power and Light; The White Swan division of E. B. Eddy; Wilkinson Company Ltd; The Windsor Arms Hotel; G. H. Wood & Company; 23 Woodward's food stores; Xicon Technologies; Zanthe Information. In addition, there are five Simpsons and two Bay department stores now under foreign ownership and control, as well as numerous office buildings in Calgary, Edmonton, Halifax, Ottawa, Toronto, Vancouver, Victoria, and many other Canadian cities.

The two largest private translation companies in Quebec have been taken over by a U.S. computer company from Salt Lake. Their CEO said he didn't think it was important that he speak French. More than 70 per cent of advertising agency billings in Canada are now made by U.S.–controlled companies, and foreign corporations control over 50 per cent of British Columbia's forest industry.

3. Investment Canada has increasingly been regarded as a joke, even in Ottawa. To counter its poor image, there has been pressure for the agency to reject at least one foreign takeover so as to present the image of an institution "on guard" for Canada. That it failed to reject the 1989 takeover of Connaught BioSciences, the pioneering and profitable firm whose roots go back to Nobel Prize winners Banting and Best, is an indication of just how hypocritical the whole "screening" process is. As Peter C. Newman so aptly put it, "If the Connaught sellout is approved, Investment Canada's director should be impeached and his joke agency disbanded" (*Maclean's*, October 1989). As this is being written, there is renewed pressure for the agency to appear to "do something" in relation to the outrageous demands for a billion dollars in Canadian government assistance to allow a French and Italian government-owned aircraft consortium to take over de Havilland. That Investment Canada and the Mulroney government have even entertained such a ludicrous proposal is an indication of just how servile they have become.

CHAPTER 13
FREE TRADE AND AMERICAN OWNERSHIP OF CANADA
The Impossible Combination

1. **Business Service Payments from Canada to the U.S.**

	($ million)
1961	324
1962	350
1963	341
1964	370
1965	389
1966	463
1967	597

1968	643
1969	854
1970	896
1971	1,016
1972	1,107
1973	1,219
1974	1,474
1975	1,652
1976	1,938
1977	2,076
1978	2,355
1979	2,689
1980	3,143
1981	4,006
1982	4,109
1983	4,301
1984	4,968
1985	5,440
1986	6,667
1987	6,533
1988	7,030
1989	7,350
1990	7,562

Source: Statistics Canada Catalogue 67-001.

2. It is amusing to note that the issue of transfer pricing is now making headlines in the U.S. In July 1990, a U.S. congressional committee was warned: "It is well established that, through intercompany pricing, multinational corporations can significantly affect the amount of taxes they pay or don't pay. . . . More than half of the 36 foreign-owned subsidiaries in the U.S. investigated by the subcommittee paid little or no Federal income tax. . . . In cases reviewed, the foreign subsidiary in the U.S. paid too high a price for goods it purchased from its overseas parent. This resulted in a lower level of taxable profit in the U.S. . . . The companies investigated used various methods to shift income from the U.S. through excessive freight, insurance, interest, and other fees or

charges." As of February 1990, cases in appeals and litigation amounted to some $20 billion, but this was thought to be only "the tip of the
iceberg."

3. Lorraine Eden, "Free Trade, Tax Reform and Transfer Pricing,"
   Canadian Tax Journal, Jan./Feb. 1991, pp.90-112.

   "Double dipping" is a method of taking interest payment deductions twice, in two different countries, using a tax haven as a channel
   for the transfer of funds. "The Dutch treat" involves the transfer of
   funds to holding companies in the Netherlands Antilles and offers an
   effective reduction of withholding taxes from 15 per cent to 5 per cent.
   "Butterflies" is a tax loophole that provides a method of stripping
   assets out of Canada and repatriating income back to the United
   States, avoiding taxes in Canada. "The rhythm method" is a way of
   timing both dividend remittances and deductions to take advantage of
   varying tax rates in Canada and the United States (see Alan M.
   Rugman and Lorraine Eden, *Multinationals and Transfer Pricing*, New
   York: St. Martin's Press, 1985, pp158-61).

4. While there has been much recent discussion of growing Japanese
   direct investment in Canada (which has more than doubled since Brian
   Mulroney became prime minister), it still represents less than 4 per
   cent of foreign direct investment in Canada, compared to 64 per cent
   for U.S. direct investment here.

CHAPTER 14

THE BIGGEST MYTH OF ALL
Foreign Investment and Jobs for Canadians

1. The following are extracts from a confidential federal government
   report leaked to the author in early 1988:

   > Canadian companies in this industry are small, multi-product,
   > short production run operations which mainly mix and pack-
   > age ingredients imported from parent firms. The U.S. fully-
   > automated industry is fifteen times bigger and, according to
   > the Department of Regional Industrial Expansion, "In most
   > cases, the capacity of U.S. plants is so great that a ten per cent

increase to a production run in order to satisfy Canadian demand would not be difficult. . . . The majority of branch plants in Canada are not permitted by their U.S. parent to export into the U.S. market and compete with them there." Among the long list of "not free-to-export" companies are: Avon, Revlon, Gillette, Mennen, Noxema, Max Factor, Jergens and Lever Bros.

The U.S. appliance industry currently is operating at well below capacity and could easily increase production by ten per cent, which would be sufficient to satisfy the Canadian market. As well, it is highly unlikely that small Canadian-owned producers would be able to compete in Canada with the influx of imports from the U.S. multinationals. This industry could be totally wiped out with a loss of 9,000 jobs.

2. The following table shows unemployment rates for all twenty-four OECD countries combined, compared to Canada's unemployment rate.

	Total OECD	*Canada*
1970	3.1%	5.6%
1971	3.5%	6.1%
1972	3.5%	6.2%
1973	3.2%	5.5%
1974	3.5%	5.3%
1975	5.1%	6.9%
1976	5.2%	7.1%
1977	5.2%	8.1%
1978	5.1%	8.3%
1979	5.2%	7.4%
1980	5.9%	7.5%
1981	6.7%	7.5%
1982	8.0%	11.0%
1983	8.6%	11.8%
1984	8.1%	11.2%
1985	8.0%	10.5%
1986	7.9%	9.5%
1987	7.4%	8.8%

1988	6.9%	7.8%
1989	6.4%	7.5%
1990	6.2%	8.1%
1991	6.7%*	10.0%†
1992	6.9%*	9.8%†

*OECD projections
† Dept. of Finance projections

3. A resident of Winnipeg who recently analysed the 1990 edition of the *Financial Post 500*, found that for every million dollars in sales in Canada, Canadian-controlled corporations provided 70 per cent more jobs in this country than U.S. corporations did. Employment in Canada by giant U.S. transnationals such as General Motors, Ford, Chrysler and IBM, to name but a few, is a fraction of worldwide employment based on sales comparisons.

4. **Jobs per $million in Sales, 1987**

	U.S.	Canada
General Motors	6.1	3.5
Ford	5.0	2.7
Chrysler	3.7	1.9
IBM	5.8	3.9
Burroughs	8.6	6.0
Digital Equipment	9.6	5.0
Motorola	11.9	8.2
Caterpillar	5.7	2.0
John Deere	7.1	2.1
Black & Decker	9.3	6.5
General Mills	8.0	6.0
Ralston Purina	8.6	3.3
H. J. Heinz	8.2	5.9
Campbell Soup	8.1	6.2
Quaker Oats	5.9	3.9
Allied Chemical	11.3	7.4
American Cyanamid	7.2	5.6
Monsanto	6.0	2.8

In all of the following industries, many more jobs were created per million dollars in sales in the U.S. than in Canada: motor vehicles and parts, office equipment and computers, pharmaceuticals, soaps and cosmetics, rubber, plastic products, electronics, and industrial and farm equipment (Source: Business Council for Fair Trade). Note that these figures are for 1987. The disparity since the FTA will be much greater.

5. Nick Hall, spokesman for General Motors of Canada Ltd., makes no bones about who the boss is: "We've got to come up with a business case and let our masters in the U.S. know . . . we've eliminated any roadblocks and that we have a case for that [Oshawa No. 2] plant" (*Financial Post*, 19 June 1991).

6. *Financial Post*, 6 February 1991.

CHAPTER 15
THE PETROLEUM INDUSTRY
How Americans Put the Oil and Gas in the Ground

1. The Petroleum Monitoring Agency report for 1990 shows that foreign-controlled petroleum companies control almost 60 per cent of the oil and natural gas industry in Canada and made 57 per cent of the industry's $2.4 billion in profits.

CHAPTER 18
CANADA'S HIGH INTEREST RATE POLICIES
The Competitive Kiss of Death

1. It is fascinating to examine the question of the Bank of Canada's and the Mulroney government's high interest rate policies based on the premise that they are necessary to battle inflation. If high interest rates are intended to dampen (soak?) demand and curtail inflation, and since these high interest rates have been successful to the extent that they and the FTA helped create our recent long and deep recession, then how is it that, at the supposed end of the recession, inflation is some 50 per cent

higher than it was when the recession started? Obviously, high interest rates and government policies such as the GST boost inflation.

2. The differentials between Canadian and foreign interest rates vary, but most comparisons are between Canadian and U.S. rates. Recent differences in these rates have been historically unprecedented both in spread and as measured in terms of real interest rates (inflation removed). In 1990, U.S. short-term rates averaged 4.7 per cent, Canadian 10.9 per cent. In recent years, Canada's interest rates have been the highest in the industrialized world. In 1989 the average real interest rates for the ten leading industrial nations (Canada not included) was 4.7 per cent. For Canada it was 7.7 per cent. Recently, while many Canadian corporations were paying interest rates of close to 17 per cent, large Japanese firms were paying 5 per cent. Canadian taxpayers, courtesy of their federal government's borrowing abroad, have paid interest rate premiums 50 per cent higher than Americans and more than 100 per cent higher than Germans and Japanese.

Real Short-term Interest Rates

	1988	1989	1990
United Kingdom	3.6	7.1	9.1
Canada	5.0	8.3	10.9
United States	4.8	5.5	4.7
Germany	2.7	4.6	5.1
Japan	3.6	2.9	5.1

Source: Department of Finance, March 1991

It is interesting to note the mirror-image effect relating to unemployment, going back to the early 1980s. As our interest rate spread increased, our unemployment rates also increased.

CHAPTER 19
PRODUCTIVITY AND COMPETITIVENESS
The Blind Man with a Hundred Telescopes

1. Of the eleven largest economies, Canada was number eleven in productivity growth from 1983 to 1989. From 1981 to 1989, the average

annual growth of output per hour in manufacturing in Canada was only 1.7 per cent compared to 3.9 per cent for all the G7 nations combined.

From 1946 to 1973, Canada's productivity growth in terms of labour output per hour in the business sector was at an annual average rate of 4.1 per cent. From 1973 to 1990, it dropped all the way down to 1.4 per cent. In the broader measurement of combined productivity factors, the decline for the same periods was from 2.3 per cent to 0.9 per cent. Michael Wilson has estimated that productivity in Canada would increase by only an average of 1.1 per cent annually from 1989 to 1994.

Business Sector Productivity 1979–1988
Average percentage change at annual rate

	Labour productivity	Capital productivity
United States	0.8	–0.4
Japan	3.2	–1.7
Germany	1.6	–1.1
France	2.6	–0.5
Italy	1.6	–0.6
United Kingdom	2.4	0.4
Canada	1.5	–2.0
OECD	1.6	–0.8

Source: OECD

Labour productivity is defined as real value-added per employed person. Capital productivity is real value-added per real capital investment.

2. There has been a constant refrain that wage increases in Canada have been too generous, but recent OECD figures show that from 1977 to 1990 the increases in hourly earnings in manufacturing in Canada were actually below the OECD average and were well below the EEC average. Of the twenty leading OECD countries, ten had higher labour costs than Canada, including benefits, in 1990. In manufacturing, labour represents less than 15 per cent of the average selling price. In terms of productivity, some of the most important factors are spending on capital equipment, the development of new processes and proce-

dures, energy costs, the ability to utilize new technology, and a well-educated and well-trained labour force. Countries like Germany and Japan not only have high comparative productivity, but they also manage to provide excellent real wage and benefit increases.

In Canada, real worker earnings actually decreased by 3.4 per cent during the 1980s, while real productivity increased by over 15 per cent.

3. From 1979 to 1988, investment in new machinery and equipment in Ontario was close to 30 per cent lower per worker than similar investment in the United States.

4. Spending on worker training in Canada is about half of that per worker compared to the U.S. and only a small fraction of that in Germany and Japan. Ottawa's training expenditures as a percentage of GDP dropped from 0.27 per cent in 1976-77 to 0.16 per cent in 1988-89.

5. Canadian bankers boldly tell their shareholders that, within a decade, they expect to do half their business in the United States. Meanwhile, Canadian entrepreneurs are unable to find financing for their businesses (*Globe and Mail*, 30 April 1991).

6. Doug Peters is one of the leading critics of the Bank of Canada's high interest rate policies. Here are some brief extracts from his presentation to the Standing Committee on Finance of the House of Commons, 26 March 1991:

> Canadian consumers and businesses pay interest rates three to four percentage points higher than do their major competitors to the south. . . . These are the direct result of government policies, and . . . adversely affect Canada's competitiveness in world markets. These [interest rates] ensured both that the Canadian economy would go into recession and that the recession would be long and severe. In addition . . . the exchange value of the Canadian dollar had risen in successive years from a low of 70 to 72 United States cents in 1986 to a peak of over 88 United States cents in 1990. That is a rise in percentage terms of almost 25 per cent. Thus, Canadian businesses not only had to face higher interest costs, but they were also getting almost 25 per cent less for the goods and services they exported in Canadian dollar terms. If they were competing with imports from the United States, they faced imports

that cost 20 per cent less. Under such circumstances, how could Canadian firms compete? The answer was, of course, that they could not. . . . Beginning in 1986, Canada seemed to pursue an exchange rate policy that sharply reduced its trade surplus, sharply increased its need to borrow abroad, and sharply reduced the competitiveness of both its export industries and those industries that compete with imported goods. This has been a disastrous policy. . . . The economic costs of this recession . . . will cost the Canadian economy at least $100 billion in lost production. If the Canadian economy had continued to grow even at a moderate rate in early 1990, by the end of 1992 the additional total production of goods and services would have been the equivalent of a new car in front of every family home in Canada or enough to reduce the national debt by one-quarter.

CHAPTER 20
RESEARCH AND DEVELOPMENT
Canada as a Trust Territory

1. **R & D Expenditures as a Percentage of GDP, 1990**

Japan	3.04
Germany	2.82
United States	2.79
Sweden	2.76
France	2.39
United Kingdom	2.20
Canada	1.36
Italy	1.28

Source: Statistics Canada

2. The Natural Sciences and Engineering Research Council calculates that from 1978 to 1987 inclusive, Canada's trade deficit in technology was an enormous $53 billion. Our high-tech goods as a percentage of exports are just over one-third of those of the United States, less than one-half those of Japan, and less than one-half of the combined exports of the newly industrialized countries; and they are well below

the average for the European Community exports. Canada is now facing increasing annual deficits in computers, fax machines, and a multitude of other technology-intensive products.

3. "Among all the major industrialized countries (except Italy) Canada spends less on research and development — about half, relative to GNP, that of the United States and Japan. Further, over the last 25 years, this share did not increase significantly in Canada, compared to a significant increase in Japan, Germany, France, Italy and the United States. In Canada, the R & D 'intensity' of private industry (R & D as a percentage of total output) is 0.7%, about one-third that of Germany, Japan, Switzerland, Sweden or South Korea. It is less than that of India (1.00%) and only slightly higher than Mexico (0.6%). Thus, below-average R & D is mainly a private sector phenomenon" (Sylvia Ostry, chairperson, Centre for International Studies, University of Toronto; speech, 9 May 1991).

4. In 1987, Canadian-owned business-machine companies spent 12.9 per cent of sales on R & D; foreign-owned business-machine companies in Canada spent 2.9 per cent. In drugs and medicines the comparison was similar, 10.7 per cent for Canadian-owned companies and only 2.6 per cent for foreign-owned firms. In scientific and professional equipment, the spread was even more pronounced: 11 per cent to 0.9 per cent. It is most interesting to note that large U.S. firms in Canada doing little R & D often run large deficits on services with their parent or affiliates in the U.S., while Canadian firms often have a surplus position in services trade.

5. Report of the Premier's Council, *Competing in the New Global Economy*, 1990.

CHAPTER 21
DEBT, DEFICITS, AND DECEPTION
Are We Really Bankrupting the Nation?

1.   **Federal Government Gross and Net Public Debts**

	Gross debt ($ million)	Net debt ($ million)
1979-80	113,170	76,684
1980-81	130,307	90,987
1981-82	146,763	106,528
1982-83	175,060	135,262
1983-84	212,241	167,985
1984-85	249,452	206,497
1985-86	285,139	241,080
1986-87	319,618	271,813
1987-88	351,229	300,014
1988-89	382,219	328,965
1989-90	408,483	357,961

2. Here are comparative figures for federal government debt charges as a percentage of GDP for the 1970s:

1970	2.1
1971	2.0
1972	2.1
1973	2.0
1974	1.9
1975	2.2
1976	2.3
1977	2.3
1978	2.7
1979	2.9

Source: Department of Finance, March 1991

3. It is interesting to compare the total debt charges of the federal government with the government's transfers to persons:

	Transfer to Persons ($ million)	Debt charges ($ million)
1980	16,470	9,897
1981	18,684	13,739
1982	24,380	16,675
1983	28,079	17,412
1984	29,699	20,897
1985	31,738	24,620
1986	33,191	26,107
1987	34,266	27,801
1988	36,180	31,882
1989	37,952	37,309

In 1980, Ottawa's debt charges were 60 per cent of transfers to persons; by 1989 they had increased to 98 per cent.

4. Here is Doug Peters again: "During the current fiscal year which ends March 31, the miscalculations by the Department of Finance of two percentage points in short-term interest rates may have caused an increase in the federal fiscal deficit of three and one-half billion dollars. If the Bank of Canada brought short-term interest rates in this country down to the level that they are in the United States — surely an appropriate action when we have been in a recession for six months longer than the United States — then the federal fiscal deficit would decline by about $7 billion. I can think of no other acceptable government expenditure cut that would come anywhere near equalling that magnitude" (Speech at annual meeting of the Rubber Association of Canada, 1 March 1991).

5. Average rates of interest on unmatured federal debt for the fiscal years ending March 31, were as follows:

	%
1940	3.40
1950	2.61
1960	3.98
1970	6.09
1975	7.24

1980	10.46
1981	11.70
1982	14.03
1983	11.14
1984	10.59
1985	11.31
1986	10.66
1987	9.34
1988	9.61
1989	10.50
1990	11.20
1991	11.30 est.

Source: Public Accounts of Canada

6. Many business writers who should know better, and others who rely on the business press, use numbers that tend to exaggerate the public debt and debt costs. Critics have been overstating the public debt and debt costs by ignoring government assets and return on government investments. The right-wing in Canada always uses figures from the left-hand column below, but a much fairer measurement would be the right-hand column.

Fiscal year ending March 31	Interest on public debt ($ million)	Return on investment ($ million)	Net interest on public debt ($ million)
1980	8,339.0	3,441.1	4,994.9
1981	10,500.6	4,130.6	6,370.0
1982	14,948.4	5,095.0	9,853.4
1983	16,756.0	5,016.5	11,739.5
1984	17,899.4	4,746.7	13,152.7
1985	22,211.8	5,201.7	17,010.1
1986	25,165.4	4,533.2	20,632.2
1987	26,395.4	4,626.8	21,768.6
1988	28,700.6	4,436.7	24,263.9
1989	32,834.0	5,900.5	26,933.5

Source: Public Accounts, Department of Finance, Canadian Tax Foundation

7. An excellent article on "The Growth of the Federal Debt," by H. Mimoto and P. Cross, is to be found in the June 1991 issue of the *Canadian Economic Observer*, the first-class monthly publication of Statistics Canada. Among its conclusions: "Broadly speaking, government program spending as a share of GDP did not rise significantly over the whole period from 1975. . . . During this period expenditures on social programs did not contribute significantly to the growth of government spending relative to GDP. . . . Social program spending has not increased relative to GDP over the last 16 years. . . . However, interest payments on the debt have soared from about 2% of GDP in the first half of the 1970s to 6% today. . . . Put another way, interest payments are equivalent to 32% of all revenues today, compared to 11% in 1974-75.

CHAPTER 22
DOWN TO THE LEVEL PLAYING FIELD
The Right-Wing Assault on Canada's Social Programs

1. Marshall (Mickey) Cohen is president and CEO of The Molson Companies Ltd. He is a director of the BCNI and the C. D. Howe Institute. In November of 1989, the *Toronto Star* referred to him as "Mr Corporate Canada." He is a member of several corporate boards, including the International Advisory Group of the American Insurance Group chaired by Henry Kissinger. Linda McQuaig, in her excellent book *Behind Closed Doors: How the Rich Won Control of Canada's Tax System* (Viking/Penguin, 1987), described Cohen as "the man who, probably more than any other individual, has shaped Canadian tax law over the past two decades." As Marc Lalonde's deputy minister of finance, Cohen was responsible for the notorious Scientific Research Tax Credit (SRTC) which the *Star* describes as "widely conceded to have been the worst tax measure in Canadian history." The SRTC ended up costing taxpayers some $3 billion. Under Michael Wilson, Cohen helped fashion the $500,000 capital gains gift for wealthy Canadians. He left government in 1985 to work for Paul Reichmann as president of Olympia & York. In 1988 he joined Molson.

2. Eric Kierans, to whom this book is dedicated, is an economist and a former cabinet minister in both Quebec and Ottawa. He was president of the Montreal and Canadian stock exchanges and is currently Fellow in Residence at the Institute for Research on Public Policy in Halifax. He has taught economics at both McGill and Dalhousie universities. One of the most important books published in Canada in many years was *Wrong End of the Rainbow: The Collapse of Free Enterprise in Canada*, co-authored with Walter Stewart (Toronto: Collins, 1988). It has not received the attention it deserves.

3. Combined federal, provincial, and local government social services expenditures as a percentage of total government gross expenditures:

	%
1975-76	21.30
1976-77	21.59
1977-78	21.38
1978-79	20.92
1979-80	20.42
1980-81	20.35
1981-82	19.43
1982-83	21.04
1983-84	21.79
1984-85	22.23
1985-86	20.76
1986-87	21.28
1987-88	21.18
1988-89	20.88
1989-90	21.10
1990-91	21.87

4. Federal government social services expenditures as a percentage of all federal government expenditures (including social security, Canada Pension Plan, Quebec Pension Plan, old-age security, unemployment insurance, worker's compensation, family allowances, veterans' benefits, and social welfare assistance):

	%
1974-75	31.30
1975-76	31.62
1976-77	31.48
1977-78	31.66
1978-79	30.92
1979-80	29.42
1980-81	28.86
1981-82	27.56
1982-83	30.17
1983-84	30.86
1984-85	28.86
1985-86	29.46
1986-87	29.95
1987-88	28.98
1988-89	28.81
1989-90	28.97
1990-91	30.65

5. Federal government expenditures on social programs as a percentage of GDP:

	%
1979-80	9.2
1980-81	9.3
1981-82	9.0
1982-83	10.6
1983-84	11.1
1984-85	10.9
1985-86	10.3
1986-87	10.2
1987-88	10.1
1988-89	9.2
1989-90	9.2
1990-91	9.5

Source: *Canadian Economic Observer*, June 1991

6. Public debt charges as a percentage of GDP:

	%
1974-75	2.1
1975-76	2.3
1976-77	2.4
1977-78	2.5
1978-79	2.9
1979-80	3.1
1980-81	3.4
1981-82	4.2
1982-83	4.5
1983-84	4.5
1984-85	5.0
1985-86	5.3
1986-87	5.3
1987-88	5.3
1988-89	5.5
1989-90	6.0
1990-91	6.1

Source: Department of Finance, *Quarterly Economic Review*, March 1991

7. Federal government major transfers to other levels of government as a percentage of GDP:

	%
1975-76	4.1
1976-77	4.3
1977-78	4.0
1978-79	4.0
1979-80	3.9
1980-81	3.7
1981-82	3.6
1982-83	3.7
1983-84	4.2
1984-85	4.1

1985-86	3.9
1986-87	3.8
1987-88	3.6
1988-89	3.6
1989-90	3.5
1990-91	3.5

Source: Department of Finance, March 1991

CHAPTER 24
MEDICARE
Taking It from People Who Really Need It

1. Federal, provincial, and local government health expenditures as a percentage of total government gross expenditure:

	%
1975-76	12.39
1976-77	12.61
1977-78	12.14
1978-79	12.10
1979-80	12.11
1980-81	11.96
1981-82	12.29
1982-83	12.06
1983-84	12.47
1984-85	12.04
1985-86	12.18
1986-87	13.04
1987-88	12.79
1988-89	13.13
1989-90	13.22
1990-91	13.03

2. Spending on Canada's health care system is strongly endorsed by Canadians. A May 1991 Angus Reid/Southam News poll indicated that most Canadians support increased funding for cancer research,

research into children's diseases, old-age homes, the purchase of high-tech medical equipment, and public-health education; 86 per cent of Canadians say they are pleased with Canada's medicare system; 81 per cent oppose privatizing hospitals; 91 per cent are confident they would receive competent medical care after an accident; and 88 per cent are opposed to cutting health-care costs as a means of deficit reduction. Contrast this with a recent Canadian Chamber of Commerce survey that showed strong support among businesses for private health-insurers, extra-billing, and user fees.

CHAPTER 25
CANADA'S UNJUST TAX SYSTEM
The Myth of "Tax Reform"

1. At the provincial level, in 1980, corporation income tax made up 4 per cent of all provincial tax revenue, and personal income tax 14.3 per cent. By 1989, the corporation share had dropped to 2.5 per cent, and personal tax had risen to 15.5 per cent.

2. In June 1990, I talked to two very senior former officials of the Department of Finance about the astonishingly low rates of tax paid by Canada's big wealthy banks. I told them that I could not possibly understand how our prosperous banks could get away with paying such tiny effective tax rates on billions of dollars in profits. The two officials (who lived thousands of kilometres apart) gave me virtually the same answers on the same day: "Mel, you have to understand the power of the banks in Ottawa." This is probably the most chilling analysis of one of the most fundamental things wrong with Canada that I have ever heard. It speaks volumes about the reforms that are necessary in our democratic system and about the quality of the parliamentarians who have run Canada in recent years.

3. Federal government tax receipts from corporations and government business enterprises compared to federal government transfer payments to business:

	Tax receipts ($ million)	Transfer payments to business ($ million)
1987	11,694	9,050
1988	11,682	7,713
1989	11,420	7,460
1990	9,864	6,234

Source: *Canadian Economic Observer*, June 1991

4. Federal corporate tax rates dropped from 46 per cent in January 1987 to 38 per cent in July 1991. But large corporations pay nowhere near these statutory or nominal tax rates. Corporation taxes as a percentage of profits have averaged well below such rates in recent years. Corporations also benefit from tax deferrals, whereby a significant portion of their tax expense is not paid until many years later, if ever.

At the same time, under Michael Wilson's "tax reform," individuals with incomes of $100,000 in Canada paid an effective average tax rate of only 23.1 per cent in 1987, and only 20.3 per cent in 1988. There are now only three federal marginal income tax brackets for individuals: 17 per cent, 26 per cent and 29 per cent. In 1990, a person who earned $565,510 would have exactly the same 29 per cent rate as someone who earned $56,551, even though the earnings were ten times higher.

CHAPTER 26
CORPORATE CONCENTRATION
Who Owns and Controls Canada?

1. In terms of distribution of income in Canada, contrary to the abundant rhetoric emanating from both Liberal and Conservative federal governments over the years, the lowest fifth of Canadians now receive almost exactly the same share (4.8 per cent) of total income that they received forty years ago. During the same period, the top fifth increased their share from some 42.8 per cent to 43.2 per cent.

CHAPTER 27
THE AMERICANIZATION OF CANADA
Gobbling Up the Neighbour

1. Recent comments by Maclean Hunter executives provide an insight into the motivations of the media giant: "Maclean Hunter is 'relatively indifferent to the outcome of any trade agreements with the United States.' This is because a significant portion of its publishing, printing and cable television business already is outside Canada, and this is the area in which it expects to see most of its future growth" (*Globe and Mail*, 3 May 1991). "The bulk of Maclean Hunter's future growth will, I am afraid, be outside of Canadian borders" (Donald Campbell, chairman, Maclean Hunter Ltd., 2 May 1991).

2. One fascinating survey revealed that 73 per cent of business had not read the actual agreement or studied its implications.

3. More than fifty corporations that we know of refused to disclose the amount of their contributions to the Canadian Alliance for Trade and Job Opportunities. Among these were foreign-controlled firms such as Cargill Ltd., AT & T Canada Inc., Bechtel Canada Inc., BP Canada Inc., Fletcher Challenge Ltd., General Motors of Canada, Lloyds Bank Canada, and 3M Canada Inc. The Canadian corporations that refused to disclose the amount of their contributions included the Bank of Montreal, the Bank of Nova Scotia, the Canadian Imperial Bank of Commerce, Dominion Securities, Falconbridge Ltd., Stelco Inc., and Trizec Corp. Some 99 per cent of the Alliance funds were from large corporations. Contributions from individuals amounted to less than one-fifth of 1 per cent of total contributions.

   Large foreign-controlled corporations were major contributors. For example: Amoco Canada Petroleum, $30,000; American Barrick Resources, $25,000; Dow Chemical Canada Inc., $23,000; Ford Motor Company of Canada, $68,750; General Electric Canada Inc., $28,750; General Foods Inc., $15,000; IBM Canada Ltd., $100,000; Imperial Oil Ltd., $200,000; Shell Canada Ltd., $250,000; and Texaco Canada Inc., $100,000.

   Among the major Canadian-controlled corporate contributions that were disclosed were: Alcan Aluminium Ltd., $250,000; Canadian

Pacific, $250,000; Inco Ltd., $100,000; Manufacturers Life, $110,000; Noranda, $200,000; Northern Telecom Ltd., $107,500; Olympia and York, $100,000; Royal Bank of Canada, $200,000; and Sun Life Assurance, $140,000

Of course, many of these same corporations contributed substantial sums directly to the Progressive Conservative party's 1988 election campaign and to individual Tory candidates. Foreign-controlled corporations such as Merrill Lynch Canada Inc., Nabisco Brands, and Lab Railway (Iron Ore Co.), contributed more than $100,000 each to help with Mulroney's re-election. A few of the many foreign-controlled contributors to the Conservative coffers include Imperial Oil, Weyerhaeuser, Fletcher Challenge, Texaco, Panavision, Du Pont, Dow Chemical, Amoco, General Electric, Avon, Safeway, Continental Can, Cargill, Suncor, Prudential-Bache, Boeing, Chevron and Hyundai.

4. In his new book, *President Reagan: The Role of a Lifetime*, the *Washington Post* White House correspondent Lou Cannon writes about the time when White House chief of staff James Baker gave Ronald Reagan a briefing book to study in preparation for the next day's world economic summit at Williamsburg. When Baker discovered the next morning that the commander-in-chief hadn't so much as looked at the papers, he asked him why. "Well, Jim," said the president, "The Sound of Music was on" (*Edmonton Journal*, April 1991).

5. In *Lament for a Nation*, Grant wrote: "No class in Canada more welcomed the American managers than the established wealthy of Montreal and Toronto. They lost nothing essential to the principal of their lives in losing their country."

CHAPTER 28
GLOBALIZATION
Walking All Over Governments

1. Real GDP per capita in terms of purchasing power parity, 1988:*

	(U.S. $)
United States	19,850
Canada	17,680
Switzerland	17,220
Iceland	16,820
Sweden	14,940
West Germany	14,620
Australia	14,530
Luxembourg	14,290
Finland	13,980
Norway	13,820
Japan	13,650
Denmark	13,610
France	13,590
United Kingdom	13,060
Belgium	13,010
Italy	13,000
Netherlands	12,680
Austria	12,350
New Zealand	11,310
Israel	10,860
Spain	8,250
Ireland	7,020
Greece	6,440
Portugal	5,980
OECD average	15,280
Industrial country average	14,350

Source: United Nations

* Note that this was before the FTA went into effect.

2. James Gillies writes: "More and more it is apparent that one does not have to be large to compete — one has to be smart. Small-scale plants with efficient technology are beginning to dominate manufacturing everywhere. Products designed to meet specific customer needs are in demand. Lean corporate headquarters and management structures are successful — the Behemoths are being beaten at every turn."

CHAPTER 29
LOUGHEED AND HEARST ARE HAPPY
And Pop Is Pleased Too!

1. Section 409 of the U.S. implementing legislation actually makes it much easier for U.S. corporations or trade organizations to call for American government protective action against Canadian imports. Now the U.S. trade representative must investigate complaints, even though no proof of injury accompanies the complaints, as was required previously.
2. It is interesting to look at a number of other economic indicators for the two years before the FTA, and for the first two years of the agreement:

Canada's Share of North American
Softwood Lumber Sales
1987	40.4%
1988	39.9%
1989	39.6%
1990	37.8%

Housing Starts in Canada
1987	245,986
1988	222,562
1989	215,382
1990	181,630

3. In the words of Wayne Easter, president of the National Farmers Union: "Supply management marketing boards are severely threatened

by the Free Trade Agreement which reduced tariffs on raw farm products and processed products from the United States. This will reduce
the available market for Canadian product, thereby shrinking the production base, lessening farm income, and likely forcing a reduction in
the number of family farms in Canada" (letter to the author, 30 July
1991).

4. New York State is now offering Canadian companies "special financing as low as 3%, loan deferrals for up to three years, investment tax
and wage tax credits and utility reductions."

5. Contrast Peter Lougheed's exuberance over the fact that Canadians
have lost the ability to set their own oil and natural gas prices and the
fact that we now have to share our resources with the Americans on a
mandatory basis, with the following extract from his Alliance's four-
page cross-Canada newspaper supplements during the 1988 federal
election campaign:

> Q. Don't we have to sell Americans our energy resources at the
> same prices as we pay here in Canada?
> A. Not so. The U.S. has gained no rights to Canada's resources . . . .

6. "Canada's dwindling reserves of light and medium crude oil — the pre-
ferred feedstocks for oil refineries — are shrinking faster than they
were a year ago and significantly faster than expected, the Canadian
Petroleum Association says" (*Financial Post*, 18 July 1991).

7. During the free trade debate, the pro-agreement forces attempted to
confuse Canadians by suggesting that Canada's energy obligations
under the FTA were no different than existing obligations relating to the
International Energy Agreement (IEA). The IEA, however, covers only
oil, not other forms of energy such as natural gas and hydropower, for
example; and it has no enforcement provisions and has never been
invoked. The FTA energy provisions are far more onerous and potentially dangerous than any commitments Canada has under the IEA.

CHAPTER 30
ON THE ROAD TO MEXICO
Free Trade Part Two: The Three Amigos

1. The *maquiladoras* factories are low-wage labour-intensive assembly plants and manufacturing operations in Mexico with special privileges allowing duty-free entry of their products into the United States.
2. According to the Ecumenical Coalition for Economic Justice, "the cost of employing a young woman to assemble products in a *maquiladora* fell from U.S. $1.53 an hour in 1982, to just sixty cents in 1990. Mexican labour costs employers less than one quarter of what they'd pay in Hong Kong, Taiwan or Singapore." Amnesty International calls Mexico a "human rights emergency."
3. An excellent place to begin would be to start substituting our substantial purchases of U.S. fruit and vegetables with fruit and vegetables grown in Mexico. Our total imports from Mexico would immediately double, and the cost to Canadians would be lower.

CHAPTER 31
INDUSTRIAL POLICY
Marching Blindfold into the Twenty-first Century

1. Anyone who thinks the United States does not have an industrial strategy is dreaming. The North American Free Trade Area is part of that strategy. So is the Defense Department and the Pentagon. U.S. industrial development is a product of the military-industrial complex that has for so long been in charge in the U.S. economy and, many would argue, in charge of the U.S. political system too.

CHAPTER 32
PRINCIPLES AND POLICIES
Alternatives and Solutions

1. Chart 51 is out of date. Australia, New Zealand, and Canada now have no wealth taxes. Note that even Japan's comparatively "high"

rate is only just over 1.1 per cent. Wealth taxes are deemed a fair method of taxation if there is thought to have been less-than-fair tax policies in place in previous years which failed to tax the well-to-do adequately compared to the rest of society.

2. Neil Brooks makes some interesting points in the March/April 1991 issue of the *Pro-Canadian Network Dossier*:

> Some of Canada's largest corporations and wealthiest families are real estate developers. This is not an accident — it is because, in part, they have received billions of dollars of government handouts through the tax system. Real estate developers can write off the cost of the buildings they build or purchase, even though these buildings will likely appreciate in value.
>
> Business spends hundreds of millions of dollars every year lobbying governments for special treatment. A special rule inserted in the Tax Act in the early 1960s allows these expenses to be deducted. The result of this tax rule is that the public is forced to subsidize the efforts of businesses to influence the political process, but not groups representing other points of view.
>
> Canadian multinationals receive billions of dollars of subsidies under the tax laws, often to the detriment of the Canadian economy. Many of these subsidies have the effect of encouraging them to locate their manufacturing operations overseas. Thus, Canadians lose jobs, plant closings devastate communities, and Canadian interests are undermined. For example, multinationals that borrow money in Canada to finance overseas operations, can deduct the interest expense from their profits earned in Canada, even though the income the borrowed money earns in the overseas operations will never be taxed here. Billions of dollars have been borrowed from Canadian financial institutions for this reason. Thus, not only does the subsidy encourage foreign investment by Canadian corporations and increase Canada's current account deficit, but it also keeps Canadian interest rates needlessly high.

In the above paragraph, Brooks points to one of the key tax changes that Canada must make. When Allan MacEachen was minister of finance, he regarded this as a serious problem requiring urgent change; but the proposed changes were caught up in the overwhelming resistance of the business community to the MacEachen budget.

3. Here is a comparison of net household savings as a percentage of disposable household income:

	United States	Canada
1980	7.3	13.6
1981	7.7	15.4
1982	7.0	18.2
1983	5.5	14.8
1984	6.3	15.0
1985	4.5	13.3
1986	4.3	10.7
1987	3.0	9.4
1988	4.3	10.0
1989	4.7	11.0
1990	4.6	10.9

Source: OECD *Economic Outlook*, July 1991

CHAPTER 33
THE MOST IMPORTANT PRINCIPLE OF ALL
Canada's Flawed Democracy

1. Voter turnout was 75 per cent in the Canadian federal election in 1988. This compares with some 50 per cent in the U.S. federal election the same year, and only 36 per cent in the U.S. congressional election in 1990.

CHAPTER 34
THE MULRONEY AGENDA
The Dismemberment of Canada

1. Government Expenditures in Canada, Excluding Grants,
as a Percentage of GDP

	Total federal, provincial, & hospital expenditures	*Federal expenditures*
1960	28.8	14.6
1965	28.7	12.4
1970	34.9	13.3
1972	36.6	14.3
1973	35.3	13.8
1974	36.7	14.8
1975	39.9	16.3
1976	38.9	15.3
1977	39.9	15.6
1978	40.1	15.8
1979	38.8	14.9
1980	40.3	15.6
1981	41.3	16.4
1982	46.3	18.8
1983	46.9	19.0
1984	46.5	19.5
1985	46.8	19.4
1986	46.1	18.6
1987	45.1	18.0
1988	44.0	17.5
1989	44.0	17.6

2. **Federal Government Budgetary Revenues
   as a Percentage of GDP**

1969–70	17.3
1970–71	16.8
1971–72	17.1
1972–73	17.7
1973–74	17.6
1974–75	19.2
1975–76	18.5
1976–77	17.4
1977–78	15.9
1978–79	15.3
1979–80	15.2
1980–81	15.8
1981–82	16.9
1982–83	16.2
1983–84	15.8
1984–85	16.0
1985–86	16.1
1986–87	17.0
1987–88	17.7
1988–89	17.2
1989–90	17.5

Source: *The National Finances*, Canadian Tax Foundation

3. As Geoffrey Stevens has asked, can anyone anywhere imagine President George Bush sitting down, for days on end, in front of national television, to debate the essence of the future of the United States with the fifty U.S. governors?

CHAPTER 35
FROM EAST-WEST TO NORTH-SOUTH
The Reality of the American Dream

1. On a lighter note, Thomas Courchene has come up with one of the better lines of the year. Hearing of the rumoured move of Hudson's Bay Company warehouses over the border to New York State, Courchene suggests a new book: *The History of Canada in Three Centuries — From Buffalo to Buffalo.*

CHAPTER 36
DO WE WANT TO BECOME AMERICANS?
Do We Have a Choice?

1. As this book was going to press, New York City was threatening to dismiss more than 20,000 employees and turn off street lights, close Central Park Zoo, and end drug treatment and prenatal care programs. The *Economist* in June 1991 reported: "Bridgeport, the largest town in Connecticut, filed for bankruptcy after even the elimination of street-sweeping failed to close its budget deficit. Chelsea in Massachusetts ran out of money to pay its employees. New York City and the state of New Jersey both sent out dismissal notices to thousands of their employees."

   While it is true that tax rates in the U.S. are lower than Canada's, in many U.S. communities and in entire states the public infrastructures are decaying rapidly — roads, bridges, prisons, hospitals, and other public facilities are badly in need of repair, restoration, or replacement. Some surprises are in store for Canadian companies moving to the U.S.: State taxes, of necessity, are on their way up.

2. The Assembly of First Nations said in Ottawa on 17 April 1990: "It's impossible to resolve the concerns of the indigenous people in Canada when most of the key decisions about our future are made in the United States."

3. In October 1989, the Canadian-American Committee, sponsored by our friends the C. D. Howe Institute in Canada and the National

Planning Association in the U.S., released a widely reported commissioned study (*Continental Divide: The Value and Institutions of the United States and Canada*), which said, among other things, that the Free Trade Agreement would still allow Canadians to maintain their distinct values. The American author of the study, sociologist Seymour Lipset, said at a press conference in Toronto that "the typical American attitude is that Canadians are Americans who don't live in the States for some reason." Some indication of the study's objectivity may be found in the author's comment that the Mulroney government is still in the traditional Canadian mold. While the bulk of the funding for this "study" remains secret, it is know the Canadian government contributed at least $10,000. So we have an American sociologist, paid by the Canadian government and by two right-wing continentalist big-business organizations, telling Canadians that they need have no fear for their values and identity as a result of the FTA, and that the Mulroney government is in the Canadian traditional mold. This in itself is not unexpected. In fact, it fits well with the pattern we have seen for the past few years. Unfortunately, what also fits well is that the press in Canada, with few exceptions, widely reported the study as the wise words of an expert on Canada, without for a moment questioning the motivation for the commissioning of the work, the source of the funds, or the validity of the conclusions.

CHAPTER 38
QUEBEC AND THE CONSTITUTION
The Two Turning Points for Sovereignty

1. Jacques Parizeau and I once spent a short while together in a bar after a conference in Peterborough. After a couple of drinks, I asked him how he intended to get the foreign capital he would need to help finance an independent Quebec. Without hesitation, he said he had already had preliminary talks with officials in Washington about selling off parts of northern Quebec to the Americans for their use as strategic military bases.

2. It must be mentioned here that Brian Mulroney's recent side deal with Robert Bourassa, granting Quebec special immigration powers that are not available to the other provinces, concerns many Canadians. If, since 1945, some 40 per cent of all immigrants to Quebec have left that province, it behooves Quebec to do more to make immigrants feel wanted and at home in Quebec society. Canadians do not like special side deals between Ottawa and the provinces. Once again, Brian Mulroney has made a serious mistake, and once again he has given powers away in advance that might have been part of a give-and-take constitutional package.

3. Most people in Quebec (by a two-to-one margin) and most people in the rest of Canada (by a five-to-three margin) support the concept of a group specially chosen to recommend changes to the constitution.

Index

Crispo, John, 14, 36
Crosbie, John
  on consumer savings, 43
  inept or secretive?, 14
  on investment, 29
  on unemployment insurance, 116
cross-border shopping, 44, 97, 188-89. *See also* retailers
Crow, John, 91, 93-94, 214, 215
Crown Forest Industries, 314n.2
culture
  federal rights, 280
  harmed by FTA, 189
  provincial rights, 279-80, 283
  U.S. plans, 197
Culver, David, 174, 176-77
currency, value of. *See* dollar value
current account
  deficit increasing, 49-52, 87
  inaccurate reports, 311n.1
  interest rates, 96
Custom Trim, 199

dairy industry, 188
d'Aquino, Thomas, 174, 176, 252
Dataline, 314n.2
Davies, Robertson, 261
Davis, Bill, 231
day care, 209, 222
decentralization, 242-45
de Havilland, 315n.3
deindustrialization, and trilateral agreement, 199
Delta Bow Valley Inn, 314n.2
democracy
  flaws in election spending, 229-35
  flaws in voting system, 227-29
Denmark, industrial policy, 204
Department of Finance
  on Canadian savings, 211
  on economy, 28, 45
  on FTA, 42, 45
  on GDP, 27
  inept or secretive?, 14
  on interest rates, 94
  on job creation, 17
  tax statistics, 147
  on unemployment, 18
Desmarais group of companies, 166

Desmarais, Paul, 166, 230-31, 288. *See also* Power Corporation
developing nations, Canadian aid *vs* U.S. aid, 261
disclosure rules, election spending, 236
"distinct society" clause, 269, 271-72, 277-79, 283
dividends, paid to U.S., 63-64, 67, 75
Dobson, Wendy, 13, 36
doctors, charge more in U.S., 130
dollar value
  increase devastating, 12-15
  natural level, 216
  reduction needed, 209
  as safety valve, 308n.4
Dome Petroleum, 314n.2
Dominion Securities, 336n.3
Dominion Textile Bedding Unit, 314n.2
Donner, Arthur, 91, 217, 246
double dipping, definition, 317n.3
Douglas, Tommy, 139
Dow Chemical, 336n.3, 337n.3
Drache, Arthur, 232
drug abuse, U.S., 259
drugs, generic, 11, 143
Du Pont, 175, 178, 337n.3
Dutch treat, definition, 317n.3

Easter, Wayne, 339-40n.3
east-west communications, 223, 253-54
east-west transportation, 253-54
E.B. Eddy, 166, 314n.2
Economic Council of Canada (ECC)
  campaigned for FTA, 174
  on foreign indebtedness, 86-87
  on high interest rates, 95
  on industry, 22
  on job creation, 17, 22
  on job training, 210
  predicts good economy, 28
economic integration
  result of FTA, 10-15, 171-79
  result of U.S. investment, 87-88
  result of U.S. ownership, 68-69
economic policies, alternatives, 214-16
economy. *See* gross domestic product (GDP)

Texaco Canada, 83, 163, 175,
336n.3, 337n.3
textiles industry, 188
Thatcher, Margaret, 181
Thibault, Laurent, 118
Third World. *See* developing nations
Thompson group of companies, 166
3M Canada, 175, 336n.3
Thurow, Lester, 101, 213
Todd, James, 125
Tokyo Round, GATT talks, 13
Toronto Argonauts, 314n.2
Toronto-Dominion Bank, 211. *See
also* Peters, Doug
Toronto Star, covered energy sellout,
190
trade
alternative policies, 212-13, 221
between parent companies and
branches, 33, 47
between Quebec and U.S., 273-75
compared with other countries, 221
diversification needed, 221-22
unfair U.S. practices, 220-21
trade balance
1970-90, 308n.3
combined with investment income,
87
declining, 12-13, 46-47
and jobs, 47-48
machinery and equipment, 224
trade disputes
continue, 188
settling, 12, 187
U.S. legislation, 187, 339n.1
trade policies
alternatives, 212-13, 221
should be toughened, 216
trade subsidies, 189-90
transfer payments. *See* federal-provincial transfer payments
transfer pricing, 66-67, 207, 316-
17n.2
transportation, east-west, 223, 253-
54
Trizec Corp., 166, 336n.3
trucking industry, 188
Trudeau, Pierre
centralist, 276
and Desmarais, 166, 230

public anger, 237
Turner, John, 296
Twaits, W.O., 174

underemployment, 19-20
unemployment. *See also* job losses
after FTA, 18-21
compared with other countries, 215,
318-19n.2
and foreign ownership, 73, 75
and trilateral agreement, 199
unemployment insurance, cutbacks,
21, 123
Union Carbide, 175
United Canada party, 299-300
United Canso Oil & Gas, 314n.2
United Kingdom. *See also* Great Britain
capital gains taxes, 208
social spending, 120
unemployment rate, 215
voting system, 228
United Nations, 209
United States
constitution, 261
corporate concentration, 161-62
crime, 257
education, 257, 261
foreign ownership policy, 88
health care, 125-35
homelessness, 257, 259-60
interest rates, 214
job training, 210
labour standards, 310n.1
poverty, 209, 257
prisons, 260
social spending, 120-21
taxes, 208
trade, 212, 221
unemployment, 215
violence, 257
voting system, 228
universality of health care, 139-40,
141-43
Uruguay Round, GATT talks,
308n.2
user fees, 139

Valpy, Michael, 171
Vander Zalm, Bill, 242, 289